General Editor's Introduction

Asbury Theological Seminary Series in World Christian Revitalization Movements

This volume is published in collaboration with the enter for the Study of World Christian Revitalization Movements, a cooperative initiative of Asbury Theological Seminary faculty. Building on the work of the previous Wesleyan/Holiness Studies Center at the Seminary, the Center provides a focus for research in the Wesleyan Holiness and other related Christian renewal movements, including Pietism and Pentecostal movements, which have had a world impact. The research seeks to develop analytical models of these movements, including their biblical and theological assessment. Using an interdisciplinary approach, the Center bridges relevant discourses in several areas in order to gain insights for effective Christian mission globally. It recognizes the need for conducting research that combines insights from the history of evangelical renewal and revival movements with anthropological and religious studies literature on revitalization movements. It also networks with similar or related research and study centers around the world, in addition to sponsoring its own research projects.

Mark Lewis' study of black gospel music within the context of Danish Methodism is a first rate specimen for the kind of cross cultural impact that revitalization movements are currently manifesting in world Christianity. His longtime service in with Danish Methodism, combined with his research skills and lucid writing style, make this a most welcome contribution to the ongoing research of the Center.

We are pleased to commend it to our readers.

    J. Steven O'Malley
    General Editor and Director
    The Center for the Study of World Christian Revitalization Movements
    Asbury Theological Seminary

Sub-Series Foreword

Intercultural Studies

The behavioral science approach to the study of revitalization movements has a long history that has developed several models. Anthropologists, among others, observed that people responded to colonialism and the expansion of the West in various ways including armed resistance, selective acceptance, and passive resistance. The problems of the colonial frontier led to a memorandum on acculturation written by Robert Redfield, Ralph Linton and Melville Herskovits in 1936. Elsewhere in the world, anthropologists observed "nativistic" or "cultural renewal" movements as well: cargo cults in Melanesia, messianic movements in South Africa, and political revolutions in Latin America. Anthony F. C. Wallace brought some order to this area of study with his 1956 article where he named the stages and subsumed the movements under the name of "revitalization movements." Harold Turner contributed the notion of New Religious Movements to focus on the indigenous responses to mission work seen on every continent. This can be seen as part of a larger development, from the 1960s on, to develop Social Movement Theory where people are seen as agents intentionally acting to renew and reform society by organizing others to resist or dethrone the powers that be. Such movements develop a culture and social organization that give meaning and impetus to action on behalf of the movement's aims.

In this book, Mark Lewis takes us inside the Gospel Music movement in Denmark that is, in some ways, successively revitalizing the church, society and Christianity itself. Lewis explores the "irony" of a music genre heavily embedded in its culture of origin, a lively expression of the suffering and hope of African-Americans, finding its way into an overly-contextualized stoic European culture such as the Danish church represents. What does it mean? In this age, different things to different people, but for some, it means being introduced all over again to Christian claims about God's salvific purposes in Jesus Christ and the empowering work of the Holy Spirit.

Michael A. Rynkiewich
Editor for the sub-series on Intercultural Studies

The Diffusion of Black Gospel Music in Postmodern Denmark

How Mission and Music are Combining to Affect Christian Renewal

Mark W. Lewis

The Asbury Theological Seminary Series in
World Christian Revitalization Movements in Intercultural Studies, No. 3

EMETH PRESS
www.emethpress.com

*The Diffusion of Black Gospel Music in Postmodern Denmark:
How Mission and Music are Combining to Affect Christian Renewal*

Copyright © 2010 Mark W. Lewis
Printed in the United States of America on acid-free paper

All rights reserved. No part of this book may be reproduced, or stored in a retrieval system or transmitted in any form or by any means, electronic, mechanical, photocopying, recording, scanning or otherwise, except as permitted by the 1976 United States Copyright Act, or with the prior written permission of Emeth Press. Requests for permission should be addressed to: Emeth Press, P. O. Box 23961, Lexington, KY 40523-3961. http://www.emethpress.com.

Library of Congress Cataloging-in-Publication Data

Lewis, Mark W.
 The diffusion of black gospel music in postmodern Denmark : how mission and music are combining to affect Christian renewal / Mark W. Lewis.
     p. cm. -- (Asbury Theological Seminary series in world Christian revitalization movements in intercultural studies ; No. 3)
 Includes bibliographical references and index.
 ISBN 978-1-60947-004-3 (alk. paper)
  1. Gospel music--Denmark--History and criticism. 2. Vocal music--Denmark--African-American influences. 3. Music--Social aspects--Denmark. 4. Music--Religious aspects--Denmark. I. Title.
 ML3187.L48 2010
 782.25'409489--dc22
                                     2010022507

(Photograph on front cover by Ole Birch. Used by persmission.)

Contents

	Acknowledgements	vii
	Introduction	1
1.	The Value of Diffused Gospel Music to Research and Reflection	7
2.	The Framework of Missiology in the Study of Black Gospel Music	21
3.	Gospel Music in Ethnohistorical Perspective	29
4.	The Diffusion and Adoption of Gospel Music in Denmark	47
5.	Meaning and Identity through Gospel Music Participation	77
6.	The Cultural Christian Heritage of Denmark and Implications for Religious Life and Faith	93
7.	The Impact of Global Currents and Imported Spiritualities	117
8.	Gospel Music's Power to Form Meaning through Emotional Experience and Sublimity	131
9.	The Application of Ritual Process in the Formation of Gospel Identity	153
10.	The Future of the Gospel Music Movement in Denmark and Beyond	165
	Bibliography	173
	Index	193

Acknowledgements

There are many people I would like to acknowledge with heartfelt gratitude for the roles they have played in this ongoing journey. Although most names are not mentioned in these pages, their support is appreciated and not forgotten. They serve as a testimony to the value of community and as a reminder that one person's recognition is indelibly linked to others who help to pave the way.

There are several persons that merit specific mention. First and foremost, I am eternally thankful for my wife and lifelong companion, Nina, and our children, Jacob, Rebekah, Thomas, and Hannah. They have all been willing captives in this process, and remind me by their very existence that Intercultural Studies is not just an academic discipline – it is, for us, a daily reality.

I am appreciative to the faculty, staff, and my colleagues at the ESJ School of World Mission and Evangelism at Asbury Theological Seminary for their helpfulness and collaboration over our years of association. I am especially grateful to Chuck Hunter, Mike Pasquarello, and Mike Rynkiewich for their wisdom, insight, and for, at times, rescuing me from "muddy waters." I am furthermore humbled by those who have deemed this study a worthy contribution to the Emeth Press series on revitalization.

I would also like to acknowledge the Methodist Church of Denmark for granting me two precious commodities: time and financial resources. My past and present congregations in Denmark have been very gracious to my family and me in light of my research interests, and their connection with gospel choirs has positioned me not only to reflect on the movement, but to do something else I also love – playing music.

I am indebted to the leaders and participants of the gospel music movement in Denmark and beyond. They are the true visionaries, and I can only hope that the analysis and reflections in the pages that follow do justice to what they have done all along – for the sake of the music, the participants, and ultimately for God's Kingdom. Special thanks to Peter Steinvig, who has inspired me a great deal through his leadership and friendship and to the late Etta Cameron, Denmark's "Queen of Gospel."

Finally, I dedicate this work to the memory of my mother, Eutha Godfrey. She was not around for the conclusion, but without her gentle and loving push, this venture may not have gotten started.

Mark W. Lewis
April 2010

Sing to the Lord a new song;
sing to the Lord, all the earth. (Psalm 96:1)

Introduction

During the past two decades, a secondary movement has been sweeping across Europe and Australia, and is now taking root in East Asian countries, such as Japan and China. The source of this phenomenon is African-American, or "Black" gospel music. Each year, new gospel choirs are formed in many countries, attracting professional, amateur, and neophyte singers and musicians of all ages, and generating interest that often moves from churches into mainstream culture, and vice versa.

A mere glance at some of the many Black gospel music websites begins to reveal the expanse of gospel music's global impact. In France – a Catholic yet secular country with no gospel music tradition – gospel choirs are, according to one report, "taking off," and concert venues featuring traditional Black gospel music are generally packed (Kline 2003). In Belgium, gospel music is demonstrating the ability to "whip an uptight crowd into a thigh-slapping, foot-tapping frenzy," appealing as much to grandparents as to grandchildren (Lubbock on Line 2005). In Lutheran state church contexts such as Germany and Scandinavia, workshops and festivals are attracting some of the biggest names in traditional and contemporary gospel music, while gospel choirs are becoming widely recognized for instilling "life" into churches reputed for their "lifelessness" (Gospel Flava 2005, 2005a, 2005b, and 2005c). In Ireland, "gospel groups are springing up all over [the country]; many of them are based in particular churches," while others are playing in "bars and other popular venues" (Burke 2005). In Poland – a country with "no African rhythm, but plenty of opera houses," as well as a reputedly "stoic" worship tradition – gospel choirs are providing a fertile ground for Christian evangelization and church planting, as Poles are becoming reintroduced to the Christian message through this medium (C. Lewis 2004). In Japan, gospel music is striking a chord in a culture renowned for concealing emotions in favor of what the Japanese call *ganbatte* (to fight), while the number of gospel workshops, concerts, and record sales are aptly described as "phenomenal" (Tokyo Journal 2000).[1] In Beijing, China, a new interest in "grafting" Western traditions onto their own, most notably the Christmas tradition, is accompanied by the sounds of gospel choirs shouting, "Glory! Glory!" in marketplaces beneath Buddhist pagodas and among a constant stream of shoppers and onlookers (Marquand 2002).

Although gospel music can be noted for its global appeal, it is likely that the gospel milieu in each country has a specific story to tell.[2] This is certainly the case regarding the spread of Black gospel music in Denmark. Since around 1990, an estimated two-hundred gospel choirs have formed throughout the entire country, and the rate of proliferation has only intensified in recent years (Gospel Factory 2005).[3] Catalyzing events, such as the Copenhagen Gospel Festival (CGF),[4] as well as the global marketing of Black gospel music have provided a springboard for the diffusion of gospel music across cultural boundaries – from the African-American ethnic and religious context to the world.

When one considers the legion of choir and festival participants, concert-goers, gospel worship service attendees, and aficionados who have become involved with gospel music on some level, it becomes apparent that a significant cultural trend is taking place. While churches, which otherwise are sparsely attended during worship services fill up when gospel music is on the agenda, larger events, such as gospel festivals, are reputed for packing concert halls with up to a couple thousand audience participants. This places gospel music among one of the more marketable and popular music genres in all of Denmark, and likely positions it as the most viable alternative to classical music among religio-musical expressions. In a country with a population of only five million residents, the number of people amassing around this African-American Christian music form is thought-provoking.

The story of gospel music's diffusion and adoption in Denmark is similar to what is taking place in many other countries. Each year in Denmark new gospel choirs are formed on a strictly volunteer basis, often in churches, but not always. All who are interested are invited to participate in weekly rehearsals as well as the concerts, worship services, festivals, and social events which are arranged for the members. One does not have to be a professing Christian to join a gospel choir, and in some cases, it is not necessary to be particularly talented as a singer, although the more ambitious choirs tend to require tryouts and have waiting lists. The primary emphasis is on the experience of singing the rhythmic sounds of Black gospel with texts that convey a biblical message in English,[5] but in a relatively non-technical language that is easily accessible to those who speak English as no better than a second language. The fact that gospel songs in Denmark, as well as most other European countries, are usually not translated into their indigenous languages but sung almost exclusively in English suggests something very significant about the whole process of diffusion and contextualization.[6]

The rapid proliferation of gospel choirs and the general popularity of gospel music among the Danes is intriguing given their reputation as a reserved people who are dispassionate about religious matters (Iversen 2006:8; Davie 2002:6).[7] It is noteworthy that contemporary scholars, such as sociologist of religion, Grace Davie, argue that Europeans are as religious as ever (2000:17). Philip Jenkins, chronicler of the shift of Christianity from the West to the global South (2002), likewise argues in the third book of his trilogy, *God's Continent* that the reports of Christianity's death in Europe are exaggerated (2007). This would imply Denmark as well. However, current expressions of this so-called interest in religion or "spirituality" are not elucidated by traditional standards of measurement, such as church attendance or even a classical belief in God, which one

Danish scholar has classified as "in crisis" (La Cour 2005:59). Even though close to eighty-five percent of all Danes are baptized members of the Danish National, or "Folk" Church,[8] there is no way to quantitatively determine whether or not Christianity has more than a cultural significance to the vast majority. Given that no more than two to three percent of the population is active regularly in terms of church worship attendance, the form of Christianity that does exist has been referred to as "churchless" (Harbsmeier 1995:74), and the passive members of the national church are categorized as "Cultural Christians" (Iversen 1999:6).[9] Against this background, the ability of gospel programs to draw people into churches in significant numbers strongly suggests the presence of missiological impulses.

Personal Involvement

My own involvement with Black gospel music and gospel choirs in Denmark has been a journey in itself. Not having been raised on Black gospel music, my relationship to it throughout much of my life can be described as a "distant appreciation." My introduction to Black gospel music, like many other whites, came by listening to mainstreamed contemporary gospel artists, such as Edwin Hawkins (of "O Happy Day" fame) and Andrae Crouch. Since I have played bass guitar and guitar in jazz, rock, and Christian settings for a number of years, I became well versed in related music genres from a performance standpoint. Yet my real appreciation and curiosity was not aroused until after I moved to Denmark in 1994, commencing an eight year stretch in cross-cultural ministry, mission administration, and teaching.

In October 1994, I took advantage of an opportunity to attend and participate in the Copenhagen Gospel Festival (CGF), not realizing at the time that I was about to step into "a different world." As a "transplant" Caucasian U.S. American pastor newly embarking on ministry in the Northern European county of Denmark, I found the sight of hundreds of predominantly white Europeans singing, swaying, clapping, and "praising" to the rhythmic sounds of African-American gospel music to be an odd juxtaposition. Though the guest artists of CGF were well-known catalysts in the American and British gospel music industry, the participants, by and large, had no tangible connection to the cultural dynamic from which the music originally emerged. After talking with a number of them, I discovered that neither was Christian faith regarded as a common denominator in the overall experience.

Subsequently, in 1996, I was appointed as a United Methodist minister to a suburban congregation in Copenhagen – a congregation that featured a fifty-five member gospel choir under the leadership of one of Denmark's most significant gospel music innovators, Peter Steinvig.[10] As chaplain to the choir, as well as bass singer and part-time bass guitarist, I had the opportunity to develop some insights into the appeal of gospel music, but I also saw the resistance to its usage in church settings by members who found the sound and style too "foreign," and too "boisterous." Occasionally, church members expressed concern that people who "do not have a relationship with Christ" were allowed to perform in worship settings. My years as pastor in Copenhagen were spent in part as a "bridge-builder" between the energetic choir and a sometimes less than receptive congregation.

Through subsequent involvement, including numerous conversations and informal interviews, I began to see that Black gospel music appeals to people regardless of their religious convictions, not to mention their ethnicity or cultural heritage. Even though the content of the songs is explicitly and uncompromisingly Christian, and though some choir members can be characterized as evangelical Christians, gospel choirs tend to create a non-imposing milieu where even "dyed-in-the-wool" atheists and New Age adherents feel comfortable participating. As an original member of a "gospel pilot group," our task, in part, was to harness the appeal of gospel music and choir participation, as well as to "educate" churches regarding the missionary potential inherent within the proliferation of gospel choirs.

After returning to full-time ministry following three years of study, I have been assigned to a Methodist pastorate on the Danish island of Bornholm. The congregation in the city of Rønne houses a forty-something member gospel choir, called *Noiz*, of which I have taken an active part as chaplain, singer, and guitarist since our arrival here. It is within this context that I now address the issues which are germane to this study – issues dealing with the diffusion and adoption of Black gospel music in a postmodern European country, and the movement's relevance to missiological reflection.

Notes

1. The assessment of gospel music's popularity in Japan is based on a December 2000 article found online in *Tokyo Journal* (www.tokyo.to/gospel/) as well as informal conversations with Japanese church officials at the Lausanne 2004 Conference in Pattaya, Thailand. Thanks to Dr. Eunice Irwin for drawing my attention to a 2002 article, "Some Soul to Keep," which also documents the impact of Black gospel music in Japan.

2. In stating that the gospel milieu in each country likely has its own story to tell, I am implying that the diffusion of gospel music is nuanced by the cultural conditions and major leaders in each context. This does not mean that there are no similarities and common trends cross-culturally.

3. The Gospel Factory is a website that contains quantitative data on the formation and existence of gospel choirs in Denmark. According to 2004 statistics, there were one-hundred twenty-three registered gospel choirs, which have changed to one-hundred three in 2006. This does not include unregistered choirs as well as those which have disbanded from around 1990 to the present. The precise tally of participants is not known, although calculations suggest that there are at present more than 5,000 regular choir members.

4. The Copenhagen Gospel Festival (CGF) was inaugurated in 1992 and since then has been held annually during the first weekend in October. The event attracts some of the world's most well-known gospel artists, usually from the U.S. and Britain, and provides area choirs and singers an opportunity to receive intensive training during the weekend by these artists. The event concludes with a Sunday evening concert featuring the artists and registered participants, singing together as a mass choir. In 1994, the num-

ber of participants was limited to six hundred. In October 2005, the capacity was extended to eight-hundred and fifty registrants. The concert was held in Copenhagen's largest concert hall (*Circus Bygning*) until recent years, and tickets are often sold out in advance.

5. Gospel music in Denmark is sung almost exclusively in English. However, this is not always the case in other non-English speaking countries. An interview with Jonas Engström, a gospel music leader in the neighboring country of Sweden, reveals that some texts are translated while a growing number of indigenous gospel songs are being composed and performed.

6. Diffusion and contextualization are themes that figure prominently throughout this thesis.

7. The assertion that Danes are dispassionate about religious matters is backed up by the European Values Study (EVS), which shows Denmark to have the lowest percentage of church worship attendance in all of Western Europe.

8. The Danish National Church, or as it is generally called "Folk" Church or "People's" Church, is the largest church in Denmark, comprising around 85 percent of the population. It is part of the Evangelical Lutheran Confession, and was, from 1536-1849 the only state sanctioned church in Denmark. The Danish Constitution of 1849 made provisions for religious freedom, which led to the approval and establishment of other denominations, such as the Baptist and Methodist Churches. However, the Danish Folk Church still enjoys a sort of monopoly status, in spite of its very passive membership, in which only two to three percent of its members are active on a weekly basis.

9. Throughout much of the dissertation I will adopt the appellation "Cultural Christians" in addition to pre- and post-Christians, and secularists. The expression "Cultural Christian" is often used in Denmark to describe the majority of the population, who are baptized and confirmed members of the National (Folk) Church, but are otherwise not active participants in the church. The term has been employed by Prof. Hans Raun Iversen, Dean of the School of Systematic Theology, University of Copenhagen, who has written extensively on issues of church and culture in Denmark. Iversen contends that the negative results of tangible Christian measurements, such as church attendance, does not necessarily mean that Christianity has no influence in Danish society, or is completely rejected. He propounds that the nearly eighty-five percent of Danes who are baptized members of the Danish Folk Church yet do not attend, otherwise known as Cultural Christians, cannot always be assumed to be non-Christians. I do not want to make that blanket assumption either. The intent here is not to be polemical, but rather to utilize a nomenclature that avoids unintended pejorative connotations.

10. Peter Steinvig is a Methodist musician and leading innovator and change agent in the gospel music movement in Denmark. In addition to being founder of the Copenhagen Gospel Festival, Steinvig is an organist in a Danish Folk (Lutheran) church and leads three gospel choirs, including *Kefas,* which is one of Denmark's best known groups.

Chapter 1

The Value of Diffused Gospel Music to Research and Reflection

Although this study deals specifically with the diffusion of Black gospel music in the particular country of Denmark, the ultimate aim is inductive in nature. Gospel music, whether performed strictly in an African-American context or contexts foreign to the original culture, is a dynamic genre that is spawning a secondary movement in locations around the globe,[1] and thereby merits scholarly consideration from various vantage points. However, the overriding focus of this particular contribution is to explore whether or not gospel music constitutes a model signifying how the Christian message can be re-contextualized in areas of the world where historical Christian contextualization has gone so far that, ironically, it serves as a hindrance to the effective communication of Christianity. Denmark, for example, has been home-soil for evangelical proclamation for roughly one-thousand years. Christianity is today inseparable from Danish culture itself – a fact that is no less true if one is a professing atheist. And, that is the problem. One particular Danish bishop even suggested that all indigenous Danes at heart are "scratch ticket" Christians (*skrabelodskristne*), implying that no matter what appears on the exterior, it is Christianity that "pulsates" in their inner being (cf. Mortensen 2005:40, Højlund 1999:53). Yet it is this very sort of contextualization that arguably serves as an "inoculation with a mild form of Christianity" which causes people to become immune to a more substantive faith (Hauerwas and Willimon 1993:90). The gospel music movement is somehow circumventing traditional models of contextualization and raising issues regarding evangelization and Christian identity-formation in a part of the world where Christianity is often regarded as a spent force.

In and of itself, the diffusion of Black gospel music across boundaries of culture, ethnicity, and religion is intriguing for a number of reasons. First, it exists as a musical and theological expression that is unambiguously connected to the specificity of African-American history and ethnicity, and yet the degree of enthusiasm and support given to it outside the African-American context is striking.

Second, the texts and themes in gospel music fall definitively in the Christian "praise" music genre (Spencer 1990:198), and yet many who are attracted to choirs, concerts, and such do not adhere to any Christian Confession, or are Christians of a completely different theological persuasion. This does not seem to create any sort of general "disconnect" for these particular gospel music adherents.

Third, many gospel choirs are fulfilling the role of "congregation," thus raising questions about the potential emergence of a new ecclesiological expression, which centers on a distinct (missio-) musical genre. Choirs constitute *koinonia* for many, as a number of interviewees state that their choir is their primary source of fellowship. *Kerygmatic* expressions, such as devotionals and sermons are common during rehearsals and gospel events, in addition to the message in the song texts. *Diakonia* is expressed both outwardly – via singing in venues such as nursing homes, prisons, homeless shelters, benefit concerts, and the like, and inwardly – through nurture and support offered to fellow choir members in need. Gospel songs become, according to Hans Christian Jochimsen, prayers for those who otherwise would not know how to pray.[2] Gospel choirs and music are sometimes present at the primary rite of passage experiences normally associated with the church, including baptisms, confirmations, marriages, and funerals.[3] Liturgies employing gospel themes and music are also being formed and utilized in some churches.[4]

Against the backdrop of Danish religiosity, the widespread adoption of gospel music is somewhat curious. As stated, church attendance during normal Sunday services in Denmark is only around two to three percent of the population, in spite of the fact that close to eighty-five percent of the population are baptized members of the Danish Folk Church. Though conventional measuring devices do not always provide an accurate picture of the situation, one could in all fairness conclude that Christianity (as it is defined in the Danish Folk Church context) is integral to Danish culture, but is not tangibly practiced by many on a personal level. If one were to tally the several thousand attendees who meet weekly for choir rehearsals, concerts, and gospel worship services where Christian music is sung and the Christian message is on some level proclaimed, then one might conclude that the overall percentage of church attendance in the country has experienced resurgence.

The Main Issue(s)

Before delving into the main body of this work, a brief sketch involving what this research is and is not about is in order. In light of the preceding information, the primary issue (or issues) I am addressing can be stated in the following way: Black gospel music is diffusing rapidly into locations around the world that have a significant cultural differential from African-American culture, which includes their history, ethnicity, and religion. This includes Denmark, where Danish people are reputed to be reserved and church attendance is among the lowest in the Western world. In light of these realities, this research is designed to discover the reasons for gospel music's appeal to many Danes, the effects that gospel music has on participants and concert-goers, and the possibilities that the gospel music movement might present for the evangelization of the Danish unchurched and nominal church members known as Cultural Christians.

Implicit in this thesis are a number of hypotheses, including (but not limited to) the following:

1) Christian themes and symbols are present in gospel music and performance, and are playing a consequential role in the religious belief patterns of many participants. These themes and symbols are found not only in the song texts, but also in many of the rituals that are enacted during gospel gatherings, as well as the general gospel ethos.
2) Participants react to these Christian symbols and themes in a variety of ways. With regard to these Christian elements, participants are either: (a) unaware, (b) aware yet apathetic, (c) aware and considering, (d) receiving for the first time, and/or (e) aware and in agreement (i.e., consciously committed).
3) The presence of Christian symbols and themes is a fact that attendees of gospel concerts and other events also react to in a variety of ways, including: (a) unaware, (b) aware yet apathetic, (c) receiving for the first time, or (d) aware and in agreement.
4) Thus, *meaning*, as it pertains to the interfacing of Christian symbols and Danish cultural factors in the gospel music context, is being rhetorically constructed.[5] This is a topic of central importance to this study.

My work endeavors to ascertain what is undergirding the behavior and symbols of gospel music participation, as the music genre is transported from the socio-religious context of African-American ethnicity to a distinctly postmodern cultural milieu. It thus explores whether Black gospel music, as it is transferred to participants in the Danish cultural climate, represents a contextual (or re-contextualized) construction of Christian meaning in a context characterized by a diminishing sense of common truth and a "rising tide" of religious pluralism (Biesecker-Mast and Biesecker-Mast 2000:12).

By contrast, the project will naturally address the inverse proposition, which inquires whether or not the emerging popularity and fecundity of Black gospel music within the "religious supermarket" climate of a Western/Northern European country represents the cooptation of a Christian art form/expression by a non-Christian socio-political agenda. This would imply the possibility that the utilization of Black gospel music by those outside the realm of Christian confession constitutes a contemporary example of syncretism. By this, I am referring to the employment of Christian symbols and forms coupled with the attachment of or "bonding" to meanings that ultimately contravene the particularities of Christian truth (Zahniser 1997:113).

The thesis is addressed through the exploration of several sub-problems, which include the following:

1) A review of pertinent literature and resources dealing with the ethnohistorical development of gospel music in the African-American context *in order to* discover/identify themes that might be parallel to the Danish context. It will be determined whether or not any parallels do exist between gospel music in its original context and gospel music as it is transferred cross-culturally and constitutively reenacted. The aim here is to explore developmental factors which might shed light on the cross-cultural transition of Black gospel, as well as identify concepts germane to the gospel music identity, such as "liberation," "good news and bad times," and "praise." It is interesting that these themes are likewise being adapted by Danish gospel adherents, but their actual meanings might be something entirely different. How these themes are being deconstructed and reconstructed in ways that make Black gospel music adaptable to the new context necessitates a working knowledge and understanding of Black gospel music in its ethnohistorical context.
2) An analysis of the diffusion of the gospel music movement as an innovation which has been transported from a distinct ethnic and religious context to a radically different culture. This will include a systems study on the rate of adoption and methods of communication utilized in proliferation of gospel festivals, choirs, etc., insights from interviews with primary innovators and change agents, and assessment of the movement's continued popularity and continuity.
3) An analysis of the religious/spiritual inclinations of Danish gospel choir adherents, including confession or possible rejection of Christian faith as a result of gospel music involvement. Since Christianity has been an integral part of Danish heritage and culture for close to a millennium, the problem involves determining what Christian faith itself means in such a complex religious milieu, in addition to changes in perception of Christian meaning that gospel choir participation may be engendering. This section will draw from religious and cultural analysis of the Danish situation, as well as interviews with gospel choir participants.
4) An assessment and critique of global currents, including the postmodern condition, as salient factors in the dissemination of Black gospel music. The major epistemological paradigm-shift[6] known as postmodernism is now regarded by many scholars in the West as a ubiquitous interdisciplinary construct,[7] and thus cannot be ignored. It would be overstated to suggest that cultural diffusions, such as Black gospel, are occurring at an unprecedented rate since the advent of the postmodern age. However, it is becoming clear that the current cultural condition has created a climate favorable to the sort of "irony" involved in the importation and homogenization of an ethnic spirituality (Snyder 1995:218).[8] Understanding the postmodern condition may be a key to determining how and why, at this particular time in history, it is possible for a musical

genre and style containing strong ethnic and religious underpinnings to be diffused cross-culturally.
5) An investigation into the formation of a "gospel identity" as it is forged by way of participation in gospel choirs, including rehearsals, concerts, worship services, festivals, camps, and the like. By looking at the development of identity through the epistemological lens of ritual process theory as promulgated by Victor Turner, Mathias Zahniser, and others, as well as the practice of *mimesis*, it may be possible to explore not only how this identity is socially constructed, reinforced, reified, and adopted, but likewise whether or not the identity being formed qualifies as an appropriation of Christian meaning.

Data and Methodology

Since very little scholarly reflection has been applied to the cross-cultural diffusion of gospel music, especially from a missiological perspective, the study for the most part is grounded in the worldview of the performers. In other words, the nature of this study is not about graphs, charts, and other quantitative measuring devices; instead, the research and methods are decidedly qualitative. This means that a great deal of the data come primarily from the participants themselves. Of course, the data do not appear in these pages in their "raw" form, but have been selected, arranged, and interpreted through the various lenses that comprise the theoretical frameworks for the project. There are other written records, including websites that by their sheer existence offer documentation of gospel music's impact and continued advancement in Danish society.

Yet the most important methodology is ethnographic in nature – more specifically, participant observation. As James P. Spradley acknowledges, the method of direct involvement provides an interpretive framework that "takes meaning seriously" (1979:9). The participant observation methodology likewise presupposes (according to Spradley) the theoretical framework of symbolic interactionism – a framework that girds an approach that ventures to unpack the layers of meaning associated with the gospel music culture (Spradley 1979:9; cf. Blumer 1969).

My own involvement with gospel choirs since 1996 has provided the foundation for a number of hypotheses, and has lead to countless hours of conversations over the past decade. In specific connection with this project I have conducted close to two-hundred interviews of both a formal and informal nature. Informal interviewees have by and large been members of my own choir in Rønne and former choir in Copenhagen, church members, audience participants following concerts, festivals, or gospel worship services, and colleagues. Gospel leaders, contributors to gospel lore, and select participants who are able to articulate the gospel music experience in an exceptional manner have been interviewed formally.

In addition to the ethnographic approach, other methods figure into the overall research, including the following:

a. Sociological Method: Regarding the cross-cultural diffusion of gospel music and choirs (subproblem one), available information dealing with the origins of choirs in Denmark, the timeframe and rate of growth involved, the catalyzing events, such as festivals and workshops, and other pertinent factual data have been gathered, primarily from existing databases. Interviews with key leaders and participants have also been helpful in gaining a more complete understanding of "the big picture." Peripheral documentation, such as flyers, advertisements, and articles in newspapers and journals has also been collected. This portrays an objective account of gospel music's diffusion, especially in Denmark. The purpose of the data is to provide some quantitative evidence of the rapidity in which gospel has proliferated, the rate of adoption and defection, and the means by which the movement is securing its continuation through the founding of children's gospel choirs, the multiplication of workshops and festivals, the attempts to plant gospel congregations,[9] and the like.
b. Historical method: Relevant literature relating to the ethnohistorical development of gospel as it pertains to cross-cultural diffusion (subproblem two) is explored. The legacy of gospel music – from its emanation from African-American culture, to precursory developments, such as Negro spirituals, to the birth of gospel music with Thomas Dorsey during the Great Depression, and up to the contemporary era – has bearing on the overall topic. Therefore, familiarity with gospel music lore, particularly recent studies, provides necessary groundwork in making further assessments regarding the factors which are enabling gospel music to disseminate across cultural boundaries. A major data source comes from contacts among the Black gospel headliners who, by virtue of responding to invitations to lead and teach gospel performance, style, and worship, are acting as bridges between the "authentic" milieu and the "surrogate" versions. Their stories provide an important cog in the overall understanding of gospel music's meaning in its original context, and the assessment of its construction in new contexts.
c. Anthropological Method: In terms of the analysis of the religious/spiritual constitution of choir adherents (subproblem three), data has been gathered through participant observation (as previously mentioned). Interviews and personal involvement have been important elements in ascertaining the perceived spiritual meaning behind the gospel ethos; likewise, records of conversations, description of behaviors, interactions, and collections of oral histories play a central role in conveying the narrative which is being constructed. Since one of my "roles" while living and working in Rønne (as was previously the case in Copenhagen) is "pastor," I have had to become aware of how my position possibly has had a "tainting" effect on some of my interviews; therefore, it has been important to conduct interviews with gospel adherents with whom I have not had a pastoral relationship.

Regarding investigation into the formation of the distinct gospel identity (subproblem five), data has been derived from participation and observation of the transformations that are taking place as a result of gospel involvement. Such information can not really be ascertained apart from the sort of emic (participant) and etic (observation) interplay upon which most viable ethnographic investigation is based. My own research has been no different since the data collected has oscillated between intimate involvement in gospel choirs and the lives of its members, and usage of theoretical sources that have facilitated interpretation of their stories.

d. Literary Method: In addition to the resources dealing with gospel music and the theories employed in the overall research, there is another database consisting of gospel song texts. Since the songs themselves convey particular theological themes, it becomes important to determine what sort of relationship or associations gospel participants connect with the content of the songs they sing. Even though the widespread appeal of gospel music is understood more in terms of affectivity rather than conceptualization (in other words, how it makes them "feel" rather than "think"), the actual textual formulations are at least marginally important. The overall determination of whether or not the gospel movement is ultimately Christian is contingent upon some sort of assessment of the cognitive and conceptual expressions emerging from the deeper affective experience. Interviews and observations are employed to determine the extent to which song texts provide a key to understanding the actual meanings that are associated with gospel music expression.

Definitions

As is true of most every research topic, understanding the subject matter is contingent upon familiarity with the associated vernacular. Several key terms are used repeatedly throughout this study, and grasping their precise meanings is critical to the overall project. The insights of *symbolic interactionism*[10] remind us that the meanings which are attached even to the most commonly used terms cannot be taken for granted. Attitudes and actions are often determined on the basis of the meanings that one attaches to certain words and concepts, and the attached or "constructed" meanings involve interplay of social interaction and individual thought-processes. Research into the world of Black gospel music as it is being reconstructed in differing cultural contexts likewise elicits certain key terms, such as the following:

* Gospel music – Though the term has a wide variety of connotations, it is used here to denote the particular music, aesthetic, and performance style that germinated from African-American culture and was born around 1930 through the song-style innovations of Charles A. Tindley, Lucie Campbell, Thomas A. Dorsey (considered the "Father of Black gospel"), and others. Usually referred to as "Black gospel," at least in the American context where gospel music is divided into many strains and therefore requires some qualification,[11] the hymns

of Dorsey and others find antecedents in early black hymnody, "sorrow" or slave songs (also generically known as spirituals), and "jubilee" spirituals (Eskew 2001:177). The deepest roots of gospel music relate to song and rhythm traditions of Equatorial Africa. Musicologists have determined this region to be the most homogeneous song style area in the world, meaning that striking similarities in musical patterns and style can be experienced throughout an inordinately broad geographical expanse (Darden 2004:14). Gospel music has since evolved into more contemporary styles, of which Edwin Hawkins' 1969 hit *O Happy Day*, has become emblematic for the type of gospel that currently is experiencing mass cross-cultural appeal.

* Gospel festivals and workshops – These are events that feature headliners in the gospel music industry, and often utilize mass choirs, which consist of local choirs and individual singers who are brought together for that particular occasion, in a concert setting. Usually, large crowds are attracted to gospel festivals, and the music is generally accompanied by preaching and testimonies. Festivals are a primary catalyst in the spread of gospel music. Workshops are similar to festivals in that participants are registered and then trained by a gospel artist in select songs for the purpose of a larger concert, usually held at the end of a weekend. In comparison to festivals, workshops are smaller in scale and tend to employ one particular gospel artist rather than several. The impact in terms of catalyzing gospel music involvement, however, is quite similar.

* Gospel worship services – Although the expression may have particular connotations in some church circles, it is used here to describe a peculiar phenomenon, where the performance of gospel music constitutes the primary agency of Christian proclamation. Typically, a gospel choir will sing a repertoire of five or six songs, interspersed with testimonies, prayers, words of encouragement, and other contextually appropriate expressions. A short homily is often held, and the service may conclude with communion, candle-lighting, or some other ritual. The primary characteristics include the presence of "energy" and rhythm," which are integral to gospel music, and attendance by people drawn to gospel music from a wide spectrum of religious and non-religious perspectives.

* Gospel choir rehearsals – Though rehearsals are nothing extraordinary in the world of music, the (usually) weekly gatherings take on another dimension as they provide a primary arena for social bonding, connection with the church that houses the choir (if the choir meets in a church location), exposure to Christian content through devotionals and prayers (in contexts where they are offered), and the general reification of the gospel identity through ritual re-enactment and *mimesis*.[12] It is within the context of weekly rehearsals that many choirs arguably are assuming the role of "congregation," thus adding a symbolic dimension that normally is not consciously associated with practice sessions.

* Gospel ethos – Though "ethos" is often used generically to connote the character, values, and dynamic of a culture or people, the term also applies to the specific connection with the persuasive and dynamic demeanor of the gospel music experience as proliferated by its leaders and innovators. Within the gospel music culture, there is a distinct "energy," "style," and "character," which is embodied by the primary communicators, such as choir directors and other par-

ticipants, thus contributing to its "contagious" and persuasive nature. The evolution of the word ethos is summarily detailed by James Baumlin in *The Encyclopedia of Rhetoric* (2000). Though ideas of "credibility," "good will," "virtue," and the like, are integral to the gospel ethos, the term is broadened here to include the emotions (*affectus*), and style (Baumlin 2000:269), as well as the "imaginative identification" promoted in Søren Kierkegaard's notion of indirect communication (Kierkegaard 1992:75; cf. Hunter 2000:61-62).[13] One should not forget that the concept of ethos according to rhetorical analysis is part of a tripartite concept, which includes *logos* and *pathos*. This implies that the character and influence of a person or group cannot be neatly dissected from the nature of the message and the condition of the receptors. Although this study will suggest that a distinct gospel ethos does exist, factors involving the nature and character of the message it communicates, as well as the conditions of culture and other social factors related to receptivity of gospel in a specific context are implied, if not stated explicitly.

* Missiomusicology – The kind of impact rendered by Black gospel music, especially cross-culturally, provisionally suggests a new concept in both missiology and musicology. The term I am proposing is "missiomusicology." Jon Michael Spencer has coined the word "theomusicology" to depict a type of musicology that functions as a theologically informed discipline. There is, of course, a great deal of music used in religious settings that reflects on issues of faith, ethics, and mortal existence, and thus merits a unique form of classification. Research into music that has made an impact culturally and interculturally in the domains of religion, mythology, and ethics entails an in-depth probe of the music "created, performed, and listened to in the domain or communities of the sacred (the religious), the secular (the theistic unreligious), and the profane (the atheistic irreligious)" (Spencer 1991:xi). According to Spencer, this is the task of theomusicology – a discipline that dialogues with other disciplines, including anthropology, psychology, sociology, and philosophy in an endeavor to understand the peculiar relationship between music, culture, and theology (Spencer 1991:xi). Missiomusicology would go a step further by suggesting that some musical genres have inherent missional capacity. By this, they have the ability to breach the barrier between faith and unfaith and shape a distinct religious identity, not only by supplementing a particular brand of theological proclamation, but by actually serving as the primary *kerygmatic* source. Black gospel music is hypothetically providing just such an example by virtue of the numbers of people who profess a new or renewed faith as a result of gospel music involvement.

Delimitations

Since the diffusion of Black gospel music is a global phenomenon that even now is "flying under the radar" of scholarly attention, the temptation exists to incorporate research angles that are peripheral to missiological consideration. Since the focus deals predominantly with issues of Christian meaning and faith-identity formation, the parameters of the research project are naturally limited, though not exclusively, by the contours of missiological reflection in these areas – more specifically, the reflections of Christian anthropology, contemporary mission theology, and evangelization theory, in addition to musicological insights.

However, several researchable tracks within the scope of missiology are, out of practical necessity, either undeveloped or truncated altogether. One such topic involves a comprehensive analysis of Black gospel in its original context, entailing a detailed ethnohistorical analysis of the music as it pertains to the religiosity and ethnicity of African Americans. Such research, though not voluminous and exhaustive, has been undertaken by a number of competent authors and scholars. It would be presumptuous to think that this project could expand substantially on gospel literature as it relates specifically to African-American culture. Ethnohistorical analysis will not and should not be ignored in this project, but the overriding agenda is the relevance of ethnohistory as a component in what the gospel movement is engendering cross-culturally. Literature and ethnomusicological analysis dealing with gospel music, as well as the origins of the song and rhythm traditions of the African continent, are indeed relevant; however, the project's ultimate focus is on gospel music's effect internationally, as it becomes disengaged from African-American culture. The original "plant" is indeed important; the ultimate focus, however, is on the new "hybrid species" that is taking shape in a cultural soil that is incongruent from the one in which Black gospel music historically emanates.

Another line of demarcation involves detailed reference to other styles and genres of Christian music, which in some distinct cases are likewise harvesting a global impact. The *Praise and Worship* music expression, for example, is worthy of scholarly attention in terms of its global appeal, ecclesiological impact, and missiological impulse. The same perhaps could be said for Southern (White) gospel and Contemporary Christian music. The point of departure is that Black gospel music has its own distinct ethos and is particularly unique due to its ability to attract and elicit the support of non-Christian people.[14] Some comparative data may be warranted, especially as music from every conceivable cultural "nook and cranny" is readily diffused in the global marketplace, of which Black gospel music is clearly a part. Yet each style and genre entails a distinct narrative that is not wholly understood by comparison or contrast within otherwise comparable musical systems (Gutting 1998:596-604). Therefore, Black gospel music and its appeal is treated here as a unique entity and not used as a point of reference with other contemporary religious music genres.

In a similar vein, the project will not delve extensively into other Christian music movements of the past. Exceptions may otherwise be warranted, as in the case of the Methodist Revival and the hymns of Charles Wesley, and the hymns of Isaac Watts, given the sublimity of the emergent hymnodies and their accessibility to other Christian social movements, including Christianized African-American slaves (Darden 2004:39). However, one area where the proliferation of gospel choirs internationally tends to diverge from other antecedents is that the music is central, not subsidiary to the movement itself. In addition, the gospel movement as a global commodity is not unambiguously Christian, and is emerging from very different cultural patterns than earlier hymnody expressions. The global and instantaneous flow of information arguably is changing cultures in ways that uniquely facilitate the spread of social-religious movements, which would include the gospel music subculture. This means that, in the context of globalization and postmodernism, Christian meanings and constructs are often coopted by some other agenda. Although one can debate whether or not postmodernism constitutes something unprecedented or signifies the inevitable historical "recycling" of the creative antithesis to hegemonic social structures and categories, enough evidence does exist to posit that comparative studies with past movements ultimately could not address issues involving current trends, in Western culture or elsewhere.

Another area that will not directly be addressed is the impact of gospel music on the renewal of traditional churches. Although the gospel movement is challenging extant traditional churches to "open their doors" to groups of people brought to them via an "untraditional" source, there is yet little evidence suggesting that gospel affiliates are becoming incorporated at any significant rate into mainline or traditional ecclesial systems. Current developments at this point indicate that the gospel movement is more likely to give birth to a new ecclesiological structure rather than constitute "new wine in old wineskins." At any rate, as is true of all extensive studies, the researcher will come to the proverbial fork in the road where a choice must be made; in this case, the study veers in the direction of evangelization and gospel music's appeal to pre-Christian people and Cultural Christians, rather than exploring the relationship of gospel choirs and existing churches.

Another research angle that is to some extent implied but not developed in these pages revolves around social movement theory. Although I refer to the gospel music phenomenon as a secondary movement, meaning that it relates to certain groups of people within a cultural context but is not as primary as, say, feminism, unionization, or civil rights, I am using the term in a more generic sense. Future research on gospel music may utilize, for example, revitalization theory and demonstrate that it constitutes, in some small or large way, just such a movement. Given the centrality of social movement thought to missiological consideration of Christian renewal and revitalization, it is hopefully only a matter of time before this angle is adequately explored.

A final and personally regrettable delimitation entails an exhaustive comparison of the burgeoning gospel movement in cultural contexts where the cultural scripting of Christendom has not taken place. Although the diffusion of gospel in Denmark is with high probability comparable to other Western and Northern European nations due to commonality in cultural heritage, this study will not address the issues swirling around the proliferation of gospel choirs, for example, in countries like Japan, China, and other areas outside the realm of Christendom. It would be exceedingly interesting to cross reference information with studies from countries where there is no widespread existence of Christian memory in order to determine the sort of meanings that are being constructed in connection with gospel music participation. This particular "stone" must remain unturned for now, at least until future discourse and research by missiology scholars from these areas begins to yield data and provide assessments.

Notes

1. Although I am categorizing gospel music as a movement, the project does not really delve seriously into social movement theory. The work of Anthony F.C. Wallace (1956) and subsequent research of Greg Leffel (2004, 2007) could provide an intriguing theoretical framework for the study of gospel music proliferation. However, the particular research foray grounded in social movement theory has been, of practical necessity, truncated in this particular project.

2. Major Danish gospel music innovator, change agent, and leader, Hans Christian Jochimsen provided this insight into prayer during a July 2006 interview. Jochimsen leads four gospel choirs and is the impetus behind several workshops, festivals, and the Gospel Factory website.

3. Danish Methodist pastor, Ole Birch, reported that he officiated at a "gospel funeral" at the request of a dying choir member. This demonstrates that gospel music is beginning to make an impact at every stage of the life cycle. I have officiated several times at baptisms, confirmations, and weddings, where gospel music was thematic.

4. Swedish gospel leader, Jonas Engström, reports that gospel liturgies are being written in Swedish.

5. Since the meaning of gospel in places like Denmark is a social construct, the role of <u>constitutive rhetoric</u> will be utilized as a model of communication. As a theory which maintains that "Subjectivity and consciousness of self are made up, or constituted, through the process of rhetorical exchange" (Radwan 2004:191), constitutive rhetoric applies very conveniently to the association of meanings and feelings to musical expressions.

6. The language of paradigm shift is borrowed from Joel Barker, *Paradigms: The Business of Discovering the Future*, which he in turn adopts from the seminal work of Thomas Kuhn, *The Structure of Scientific Revolutions*.

7. Walter Truett Anderson's book, *The Truth About the Truth*, includes a variety of articles and excerpts which demonstrate that postmodernism is a category that is acknowledged in virtually all disciplines.

8. Snyder characterizes postmodernity as signaling "the triumph of the contingent, the transitory, and the ironic" (1995:218).

9. The concept of gospel congregations or gospel churches is quite new, at least in Denmark. According to the Gospel Factory website (2004 statistics), an attempt was made to start a congregation formed around the theme and ethos of gospel music. Another gospel congregation was formed in 2006 in connection with Copenhagen Free Church, under the leadership of Julie Lindell and Pastor Jørgen Mortensen. Whether these cases constitute an oddity or the beginning of a new trend is yet to be seen.

10. The work of George H. Mead on symbolic interactionism as filtered through the writings of Herbert Blumer has proven to be an invaluable asset in determining the nature of meaning.

11. Gerome Bell, who is a well-known gospel choir leader in Chicago and frequent guest artist at CGF pointed out to me in a 2005 interview that "blacks" usually refer to "gospel," whereas "whites" typically use names like "Christian music" or "contemporary Christian music."

12. Mimesis is a term that originates with the literary theories of Plato and Aristotle, describing the relationship between the words of a literary work and the actions they recount (Most 2001:381). For Plato, the term means "imitation," taking on a pejorative connotation since imitation is by nature inferior to reality itself. Aristotle, for whom mimesis connoted "representation," interpreted the term in a more positive light by suggesting that some similarity between the word and the representation of the word does exist (2001:381). In relation to gospel music, the term encompasses the behavior, style, and ethos that choirs are replicating and endeavoring to actualize. Whether European gospel choirs, for example, are merely mimicking the Black gospel style or are in fact capturing some of the essence of it, is a matter of intense debate. However, I tend to side with Aristotle in that meanings are often learned through participation and apprenticeship, thus corroborating another salient hypothesis believed to be inherent in the gospel experience – namely, belonging is antecedent to believing (Hunter 2000:55).

13. Kierkegaard's notion of indirect communication is expanded upon in Chapter Eight, in a section dealing with the nature of "the sublime."

14. One particular interviewee reminded me that our gospel choir on Bornholm is the only Christian or church group on the island, including Praise and Worship bands, which expressly attracts people outside the church. This is a typical observation and something that renders gospel music's identity distinct from other genres.

Chapter 2

The Framework of Missiology in the Study of Black Gospel Music

Missiology provides an ideal framework for the study of and reflection on the diffusion of Black gospel music. As a multidisciplinary discipline, missiology both analyzes and catalyzes the church's participation in the ongoing mission of the Triune God through the use of tools and insights from a number of other academic fields. Some of these fields include cultural anthropology, religious studies, interreligious dialogue, mission history and theology, church growth and evangelization, leadership studies, sociology, contextualization, linguistics, and more (Van Engen 1996:19). Missiological consideration endeavors to utilize these resources in a concerted attempt to explain how the Christian message traverses the boundaries between faith in Jesus Christ and its absence, as well as suggest ways that it can be done in manners that are cognizant of and sensitive to culture and context. Given the missionary or "sending" nature of the Christian *evangelium*, as well as the crises and conflicts that often arise as a result of intrusive and culturally insensitive approaches to cross-cultural communication (religious and otherwise), the role of missiological reflection is critical. Especially in the West, where the onslaught of secularization, religious pluralism/relativism, growing awareness of the complicity of religion in the exploitation of peoples of color, and the increased sense of fragmentation in life has arguably diminished or displaced Christian witness (Bosch 1991:3-4), the need arises to understand how Christian faith is and can be propagated in light of the emerging contexts.

Although gospel music lends itself to a number of different analytical angles, the inherent meeting between faith and culture in choirs and among individual participants renders the phenomenon keenly suitable to missiological reflection. In this particular case, attention is given to how the kind of faith engendered by the gospel music ethos is impacting the listeners and participants in the movement, and how the cultural dispositions of those involved may be shaping the perception of the faith-element in the music. However, before continuing, a brief survey of some of the key missiological constructs and presuppositions in this study is in order.

Missio Dei

A central theological pillar in missiological reflection is a concept that missiologists refer to as *missio Dei*. This driving concept is based on the supposition that the breaching of boundaries, cultural and otherwise, by the message and heralds of the Christian faith is initiated by the "missionary God," who both wills and facilitates the spread of the Good News via interpersonal and cross-cultural relationships. The implication is that Christianity is expansive in nature – that is, communicated from person to person, group to group, and culture to culture – rather than being self-contained or privatized. From a biblical perspective, the directional or "sending" nature of Christianity is succinctly encapsulated in John 20:21. As Jesus is encouraging and motivating his followers, he says to his disciples: "As the Father has sent me, so I send you."

The reason for alluding to *missio Dei* (i.e., mission of God) in this context is not rhetorical; rather, it is to state matter-of-factly an underlying assumption in missiological consideration which can be objectively observed throughout church history – namely, the ongoing centrifugal (and centripetal) movement of Christian proclamation and influence from center to periphery, or from periphery to center.[1] As one explores the specific movement of Black gospel music as an instrument of Christian evangelical expression across cultural divides, it is helpful to keep in mind the "movemental" or "directional" nature of faith as implied by *missio Dei*. One might add that, since *missio Dei* is inherently Trinitarian, the concept of "communion" or relationship can likewise be employed to supplement the idea of direction. As we shall see, the Black gospel movement is reputed not only for crossing boundaries of culture, ethnicity, and the like, but also for forging relationships in the process – among the participants, and between participants and something more transcendent.

Gospel Music and the Joseph Narrative

Missio Dei is, of course, clearly expressed in the Bible itself, which provides a central hermeneutical lens and constitutes a critical starting point in all missiological reflection. A number of biblical-missiological themes are relevant to the study of gospel music. However, the story of gospel music, from its rootedness in African-American ethnicity and history to its cultural transference, could especially be noted for sharing a keen affinity with the story of Joseph (cf. Genesis 37-50).[2] As one of the younger sons of Jacob, Joseph was both gifted and favored by his father, which incurred the jealousy of his older brothers. After sharing with his brothers a dream, in which Joseph's siblings were bowing before him, they conspired to do away with him. While shepherding the flocks, Joseph was attacked by his brothers, thrown into a deep well, and then later found by merchant traders from Midian, who subsequently sold him into slavery. While in Egypt, Joseph suffered the injustice of a false accusation from the wife of Potiphar, an officer of Pharaoh, and resultant imprisonment. It was there, while enduring the indignity of slander and abuse in an Egyptian dungeon that Joseph's fortunes turned. Having developed a reputation as an accurate interpreter of dreams, he was eventually beckoned to the house of Pharaoh, where he successfully recognized Pharaoh's dreams as forebodings of an impending famine. He was hence appointed as a ruler in Egypt, in charge of stockpiling the granaries in preparation for the coming food shortage. The ironic twist comes when Joseph's brothers – the very ones who were deviously responsible for his fate as a slave in Egypt – found salvation at the hands of their lost brother, who was able to distribute grain to them during the famine. This led to the emotional climax of the story, as Joseph became reunited with his entire family, including his father, Jacob, in Egypt.

The parallel between the Joseph story and the impact of Black gospel music becomes clear when considering the plight of African Americans and the global impact of African-American culture. The devastation wrought by the European and North American slave trade cannot be measured. During the passage of four-hundred years between the fifteenth and nineteenth centuries, the African continent lost an estimated forty million people, of which around twenty million ended up in the New World (Bennett 1983:30). Subjected to the worst forms of cruelty and inhumanity, African slaves in the New World eventually attained emancipation, although conditions were not greatly improved. The reality of institutional racism, discrimination, economic disparity, and the like perpetuated the injustice that began when slave traders first invaded African shores. The "African Diaspora," coupled with the Christianization of slaves on the North American continent led to the emergence of the Black church, which would become the primary voice of African Americans throughout their history (Raboteau 1978:5-42). The musical and worship expressions emanating from the early Black church are antecedent to gospel music. The paradox involves the reality that gospel music is now serving to rejuvenate Christian faith, especially among peoples of the world whose ancestors were complicit in the slave trade, and where Christian faith is in decline. The very conditions that gave birth to musical genres such as gospel music ironically are making it possible for thousands of people in postmodern and post-Christian contexts to rediscover the joy and vibrancy that are inherent elements of the Christian message.

As an integral part of the mission of the church, the concept of "election" relates cogently to both the particularity of African-American history and the universality of the Kingdom of God that is being communicated through the specific conduit of African-American religion. Of course, election in a biblical sense does not imply the conferring of privileged status, special blessing, elitism, or divine favor over non-believers (Newbigin 1995:77). The history of the Israelites reveals that God's purpose is often conveyed through the suffering and even ignominy of the "chosen people," which is a far cry from what is commonly associated with being of the elect. Election is indeed a paradox according to biblical accounts, as God often sees fit to use the weak, oppressed, and marginalized to achieve God's salvific purposes. The idea of salvation coming to the masses through the "rejected and despised" is a pattern articulated in the songs of the suffering Servant (cf. Isaiah 52:13-53:12), which is interpreted to reference both the Israelite community in the Old Testament and the messianic motif fulfilled through Jesus of Nazareth in the New Testament. This particular pattern is perhaps being played out in some modest way through the proliferation of gospel choirs cross-culturally, as people from varying contexts are discovering faith as a result of their association with the unique African-American ethnic, religious, and aesthetic expression that is gospel music.

Constants in Context

Aside from biblical themes and motifs, missiology offers a number of other interpretive frameworks that can help to determine the nature of the Black gospel movement. The recent (2004) work of Stephen B. Bevans and Roger P. Schroeder, *Constants in Context*, is a helpful tool in assessing the missiological value of this movement. The book, which very ambitiously weaves the constructs of classical or systematic theology together with contextual theological interpretations of Christian mission history, actually owes a great debt to the work of Justo González, *Christian Thought Revisited*.[3] González discerns three distinct theological expressions throughout the history of Christian theological expression, referring them to types A, B, and C, and relating them both to archetypal figures from early church patristics and the geographical areas to which they are identified (cf. González 1999:16). In referencing the law-oriented conservatism of Tertullian (type A), the truth-oriented speculative approach of Origin (type B), and the history-minded liberationism of Irenaeus (type C), González is able to provide a framework for understanding the summation of Western Christian theology according to three unique strands. Bevans and Schroeder adopt these categories while adding a distinctly missiological slant by demonstrating the changing nature of theological expression according to the historical context within the framework of González's typologies. Although a "types" or models approach will always have limitations given the proclivity to "caricaturize" certain perspectives (González 1999:35) while de-emphasizing the fluid character of thought and knowledge, the typologies expounded upon by Bevans and Schroeder are helpful in assessing the place of the gospel music movement within known theological categories.

Where does gospel music fit in according to the categorizations of González, Bevans, and Schroeder? At this stage of reflection, any kind of response may be perceived as speculative. However, as the proliferation of gospel choirs and gospel music interest continues to impact the faith confessions of many participants, there is good reason to consider the gospel ethos as engendering a nuanced contextual theology. Since theological discourse regarding the impact and influence of gospel music globally is in a nascent stage, the relevance of this movement for theology and cultural context has not yet been articulated. It can be stated, though, that the existence of Christian themes and symbols wherever gospel music is practiced or performed, the distinct manner in which they are mediated to the participants, and the sheer numbers of people amassing around this expression are suggesting that the movement is giving voice to some aspect of Christian meaning in a way that is synergistic with culture and context. These factors point to a missiological dimension inherent within gospel music as this expression facilitates the dialectic between the Gospel[4] and the culture in which it becomes imbedded.

Since some aspect of Christian meaning is being communicated through gospel music, then the typologies propounded by Bevans and Schroeder appear germane to this discussion. Whether gospel music is indicative of the emphasis on "law and salvation" in type A theology, the "general revelatory and human experience hermeneutic" of type B, or the primarily "this-worldly transformation and liberation commitment" of type C, the point is that this Christian aesthetic, worship, and performance expression is addressing the so-called "constants" of mission, such as Christology, ecclesiology, eschatology, soteriology, anthropology and culture (cf. Bevans 2004:35-72). The difficulty of classifying the gospel music movement in accordance with specific theological types is exacerbated by the fact that gospel music in all likelihood mutates meaning as it is deconstructed and reconstructed in cultural transition. This means that gospel music might be categorized one way in the context of African-American religion and ethnicity and then differently in the context of a Western European country. The intriguing aspect here is that the texts are mostly the same, no matter where they are performed, but the associations of meaning with the actual texts are determined by varying factors.

In a sense, the overt emphasis on salvation, heaven, substitutionary atonement, and the malaise of "this world" in relation to "the glory to come" indicates characteristics of a type A theology, especially in the African-American context. However, the fact that gospel music and the antecedent genre of Negro spirituals are famously laced with double meanings renders categorization a complex matter. Since "freedom" and "liberation," spiritually, individually, and sociopolitically, are axiomatic in gospel songs and to the gospel ethos in general, one might provisionally categorize gospel music as a type C theological expression in all contexts. However, what themes such as "freedom" and "liberation" might mean and how they are perceived in the varying cultural locations is a debatable matter. In contexts that share very little commonality with the authentic origin of gospel music, for example, these themes are in part allegorized, although one should not underestimate the existential need for liberation which gospel music articulates across boundaries of culture and ethnicity. The fact that it is being discussed at least points to the notion that gospel music deserves to be considered as a valid contextual theological construction.

Further Missiological Implications

Apart from the musings of Bevans, et al., the nexus of missiological reflection and the diffusion of Black gospel music cross-culturally open up a number of other avenues for consideration, which will at least be implied throughout this study. One such avenue involves the transcultural proliferation of a Christian art form. In a sense, the capacity for a particular music genre to translate across cultural boundaries is not a new phenomenon. Other African-American musical expressions, such as spirituals, ragtime, jazz, and blues were reaching global audiences long before the onset of globalized pop culture. It is gospel music's impact on spirituality and the church that sets this particular art form apart. As mentioned, gospel choirs themselves are creating a type of *ecclesia*, which revolves around the community and rituals indigenous to the gospel scene. As several interviewees explicitly expressed it, "Gospel is my church." The fact that an artistic and religious expression emanating from African-American culture and ethnicity is able to breach cultural boundaries and convey Christian meaning within contexts that are substantially different from the host context strongly suggests the presence of impulses that defy the way many traditional churches understand mission and evangelization.

Another missiological characteristic inherent in the impact of gospel music revolves around the formation of Christian disciples. A primary interest of this study relates specifically to the area of evangelization, which includes the communication and construction of Christian meaning, and the process of conversion.[5] Even though many who participate in the gospel music movement are not professing Christians, the structure and dynamic of gospel choirs and events engender a dynamic that appeals to non-Christian people. This impulse demands attention by virtue of its attraction to people of all religious and non-religious backgrounds, as well as the Christian transformation that often does take place. As people are incorporated into the gospel music milieu, opportunities for (re-)discovering a vibrant form of Christianity emerge because Christian meaning and identity are, at least hypothetically, present. Though this study also explores the extent to which Black gospel music, as a Christian music genre, is being co-opted in order to serve a non-Christian agenda, the contention remains that "Christian meaning trickles through" (Lubbock on Line 2005). An exploration of the anthropological categories of "form" and "meaning" in relation to gospel music may suggest that Christian symbols in gospel music diffusion constitute outward manifestations which belie the non-Christian meanings attached to these symbols; however, observations and interviews reveal that new Christians are produced via gospel music participation and influence. Since gospel crowds regularly amass around themes and events that have Christian content, even when many who gather do not share that faith, the tools of missiological analysis become important in order to ascertain the nature of the appeal of the music and message to non-Christian people.

Another missiological avenue of consideration focuses on the contextualization of Christianity in a part of the world that already is saturated with Christian information.[6] Another primary axiom in missiological education centers on the need for Christian communication to be "relevant" to the cultural context where it is being applied, that is, to adopt known forms and symbols as the conduits for conveying Christian meaning. The biblical model often endorsed is the Incarnation – the example of how God in Jesus Christ assumed the limitations of a particular space, time, and culture in order to embody and spread a message that ultimately is for all peoples in all places (Whiteman 2003). As important as the contextual approach is in terms of Christian mission, especially in an era of globalization, it does not always adequately address contexts where Christianity has been so thoroughly contextualized that it has become culturally coopted. A number of contemporary theologians, most notably Lesslie Newbigin and Stanley Hauerwas, offer caveats to the contextualization approach in the Western world through analyses that view Christianity as essentially domesticated, subverted, and commodified by the dominant culture (cf. Hauerwas 1983, 1991, and 1989; Newbigin 1986, 1989 and 1995; and Bevans 2002:117-120). An intriguing feature of the gospel music movement is that it employs forms and expressions that are not indigenous to the contexts where gospel music is being diffused. The "cultural distancing" that takes place in the gospel music scene, as evidenced in the general unwillingness to translate the songs into the indigenous languages of the new contexts, for example, may present a notable example of *recontextualization*. In this case, gospel music constitutes a process of bringing Christianity to "Christianized" people in a way that is not so culturally familiar as to impede receptivity, or to fit too "neatly" into religious categories that have become cliché and coopted.

A final consideration implied by the study entails the impact of music and its significance to missiological consideration. Writings on missiology which directly address whole areas of human life, such as music, the arts, aesthetics, and affectivity, are hard to come by. This has been the case in theological circles in general. Jeremy Begbie states in his book *Theology, Music and Time*:

> Much has been written about the bearing of literature upon theological disciplines . . and the same goes for the visual arts. There have been some courageous forays into theology by musicologists, but apart from a few notable exceptions, twentieth-century theologians paid scant attention to the potential of music to explore theological themes. (2000:3)

Spencer's book, *Theological Music: An Introduction to Theomusicology* (1991), is a noteworthy attempt at addressing this void. The cross-cultural dissemination of the gospel music ethos raises issues germane to the relationship of music and missiology, thus potentially giving birth to a new field, which I for the time being have dubbed *missiomusicology*. The emergence of Black gospel music as a global phenomenon indeed constitutes an opportunity to explore issues in mission (and theology) that circumvent common conceptual approaches to the cross-cultural communication of the Christian message. It is my contention, at any rate, that music and the arts are matters of missiological importance – a contention based on the hypothesis that Christian identity is often formed as a result of gospel music involvement.

Although I have devoted this chapter to an explanation of the missiological nature and intent of this project, as well as a presentation of salient themes in missiology, it should be noted that the missiological parameters are not limited to this chapter. The subsequent chapters, dealing with ethnohistorical explorations, cross-cultural diffusion of innovations, cultural exegesis and transcultural trends, meaning construction, aesthetics, and ritual theory all are imbued with missiological content. It is now the task of illuminating the cross-cultural diffusion of gospel music through various theoretical frameworks for the purpose of broadened missiological understanding that this project now turns.

Notes

1. Jung Young Lee has written a profound book, *Marginality: The Key to Multicultural Theology*, in which he argues that some of the most noteworthy theology involves the movement from the periphery to the center. This does not contradict my intent. I am merely pointing out that *missio Dei* implies an outwardly directional movement.

2. The parallel between gospel music and the Joseph story was first brought to my attention by my friend and colleague, Rev. Randy Smith of South Carolina.

3. Bevans and Schroeder also acknowledge the pivotal work of Dorothee Sölle, *Thinking About God: An Introduction to Theology*. Since the theological typologies utilized by Bevans and Schroeder are more closely aligned with those first proposed by González, I have chosen not to emphasize Sölle in this context.

4. Use of the upper case "G" in the word Gospel is used to distinguish the Christian "Gospel" from "gospel" music. Since most gospel music participants simply refer to the music style as "gospel," such a distinction is likely necessary to outside observers.

5. For a more comprehensive understanding of conversion as a process that involves several distinct phases, see Lewis R. Rambo's, *Understanding Religious Conversion*.

6. In his book, *Overhearing the Gospel*, Fred Craddock quotes Søren Kierkegaard: "There is no lack of information in a Christian land; something else is lacking, and this is a something which the one man cannot directly communicate to the other." Although Craddock never footnotes this quote, it is nevertheless thematic in understanding the dilemma of communicating the Christian message in cultural contexts inundated with Christianity. This is a missiological issue that gospel music inadvertently seems to be addressing.

Chapter 3

Gospel Music in Ethnohistorical Perspective

The diffusion of Black gospel music across cultural, ethnic, and religious boundaries and its widespread popularity is a phenomenon. Since the music is indelibly linked to the plight of African Americans – from slavery to Jim Crow, to economic hardship, to many forms of oppression – and their specific ethnic/religious response, one immediately wonders why this particular musical genre lends itself to such a high degree of transcultural adoptability. Of course, some have argued that gospel music is too indigenous an African-American expression to be disengaged from it. Lisa C. Jones has articulated this concern most honestly in an article entitled, "Are Whites Taking Gospel Music?" Noting the fact that the music industry has historically snubbed Black gospel artists during awards ceremonies, Jones conveys the irony of how the music of black urban churches, which "changed the tone of American music forever," has only recently become popularized because of the involvement of white Christians. The irony lies in the knowledge that the "African-American experience adds true meaning to this musical form" (L. Jones 1995:30). Jones' charge is that the diffusion of gospel music beyond African-American religion and ethnicity mutates the meaning and therefore causes it to become something that it is by nature not intended to be. The mere notion that gospel music should become coopted by Anglo-Saxon culture in a vein similar to jazz, ragtime, and blues is perceived by a number of gospel "purists" as a form of "prostitution" (L. Jones 1995:30).

Since gospel music is inexorably and essentially connected to the sociopolitical and religious ethos of African-American culture, it is understandable that gospel music scholars on the whole have not yet begun to record its impact beyond the host culture. In his book, *The Spirituals and the Blues*, James Cone states that black music is essential for the identity and survival of the black community, and "Must therefore be lived before it can be understood" (1972:1,4). Melonee Burnim asserts in her 1980 dissertation, "The Black Gospel Music Tradition: Symbol of Ethnicity," that "Gospel music persists within Black culture as the single existing genre of Black music still being produced and performed primarily for and by Black people themselves" (1980:1). Though more than a quarter century has passed since Burnim's thesis was published (and even longer since Cone's analysis), there are still many in North America who believe that this nexus ought to be meticulously guarded. A February 2005 broadcast on the *Black Entertainment Television* (BET) channel entitled "A Celebration of Gospel," reinforced the inherent interconnectedness between gospel music and its African-American cultural heritage, while validating Burnim's contention that gospel music constitutes a juncture in an ongoing Black music continuum. The perception here is that it could not properly be understood apart from the collective experiences, values, and beliefs of African Americans (Burnim 1980:2-3).[1] Joyce Marie Jackson expands on the notion of "continuum" in African-American music, referring to it as a "continuity of consciousness" (1995). The common denominator, of course, between the statements of Cone, Burnim, Jackson, and others, is that gospel music's rightful place is among the people from whom the music has emerged and to whom the music directly speaks. Yet it is precisely this "continuity of consciousness" that the global diffusion of Black gospel music is now, for good and/or ill, beginning to challenge.

Although the existing research on Black gospel music does not focus on its diffusion outside of the U.S., the work that has been done does nevertheless offer guidance in assessing the constitutive nature of gospel music in culturally diffused forms. As meanings are being deconstructed and reconstructed in various contexts, a debate emerges regarding the degree of similarity or dissimilarity in attached meanings between white European gospel participants, for example, and participants from the host context. Ethnohistorical analyses of gospel music offer invaluable components in drawing certain conclusions by elucidating the themes and symbols that are being imported. Even though a gospel theme, such as "liberation" or "good news and bad times" may mean something specific in a socio-political context characterized by oppressive racism, economic hardship, and discrimination on every level, it is still important to ascertain what these themes and symbols actually are, especially since the cultural conditions among most European gospel participants are quite different. Even if the meanings that are attached to these symbols are radically divergent, ethnohistorical analysis provides the framework needed to understand the comparisons and contrasts between "domestic" and "foreign" gospel music.

Gospel music itself is still an under-researched topic. Even less material exists on gospel music's cross-cultural dissemination. Scholarly works do exist, but there is hardly an abundance of material to work with. This is odd considering the profound impact of gospel music on American culture in general. Ray Pratt acknowledges that "gospel is at once the most influential and yet least-known American music," in addition to noting that gospel music's influence is unavoidable in popular music (1990:59). This insight was perhaps inspired by Wyatt Tee Walker, who purports that the Black religious experience is a primary root of all music born in the U.S., in spite of the lack of public awareness (Walker 1979:15).

The reasons for the neglect among scholars are cause for speculation. Walker points out that gospel has been the musical expression of people of low-status, which possibly suggests that many "educated" scholars have lacked the kind of exposure that might pique research interests (Walker 1979:19). Burnim acknowledges a certain disdain for gospel music due to its "low culture" associations – a judgment that likely reflects white attitudes toward black art in general as inferior to white European/American intellectual standards. This form of prejudice perhaps has impeded a fair assessment of gospel music's genius and impact (Burnim 1980:5).

Rosalind Hackett understands that the study of gospel music by nature demands a multi-disciplinary approach, which would combine the insights of musicology, cultural anthropology, sociology, and religion, among others (Hackett 1996). This would preclude a formalist approach, which might be able to analyze "the parts" while failing to capture "the whole." Jackson offers another viable explanation. By pointing out the complexity involved in analysis of this musical genre, she contends that it is the evolving and dynamic nature of this "vernacular art form" which renders it difficult to classify chronologically and delineate stylistically, thus making it difficult to research (1995). This is indeed a critical observation since it is possible that the very changing nature of gospel music (i.e. its adoptability) ultimately has led to its eventual expansion beyond, or detachment from, its African-American origins. This leads one to consider the fact that gospel music at its core is an innovation that is predisposed to both ethnic continuity and cross-cultural diffusion.

African Origins

It seems to be the overwhelming consensus among scholars that the character of gospel music in terms of both ethnic expression and universal appeal can be traced to the African continent. In one of the most recent and comprehensive books to date on the genesis and development of Black gospel music, entitled, *People Get Ready*, Robert Darden offers the astute observation: "It begins where it all began – Africa. The unique combination of music, religion, and worldview necessary to create both spirituals and gospel began thousands of years ago on the African continent" (2005:12).

In an interview with gospel music scribe Michael Harris, an "old-line" gospel choir director, James Mundy, expresses it in this way: "The Negro people like gospel 'cause it goes back to Africa. That's why it got hold of them. It's indigenous..." (Harris 1992:180).

There are some scholars, however, who refute the idea of African origin for gospel music. Historically, the denial of an African continuum was based on the racist attitudes of "unknowing European pedants," who could not believe that slaves or ex-slaves were capable of the musical genius engendered by black music (Katz 1969:vii). A few contemporary scholars have been more honest in their assessment of the musical origin of "so-called" black genres. In his book, *The Sound of Light: A History of Gospel Music*, Don Cusic contends that black spirituals and their offspring are primarily from white culture, from the British and European folk song tradition brought to America in the seventeenth and eighteenth centuries. Cusic also believes that tracing music to African roots is problematic because of the sheer size and diversity of the continent, which precludes (for him) the possibility of a singular source (1990:84).

Darden takes direct aim at this argument by noting ethnomusicological analyses which demonstrate musical similarities over a broad expanse of the African continent, especially in coastal areas south of the Sahara, which not coincidentally are the areas most impacted by the slave trade (2004:13). In fact, the musical style of equatorial Africa has been determined to be the most homogenous song style area in the world – an assertion that is based on the almost universal use of this particular music form by sub-Saharan Africans, in spite of the number of languages, tribes, and cultures extant within the region (Darden 2004:14-15). Although white hymnody was a component in the development of black music (cf. Raboteau 1978:243), the influence of African heritage, the re-appropriation of meanings connected with white hymns within slave culture, and the remarkable musical innovations which emerged from the black church strongly suggest that gospel music is part of an African continuum.

Joyce Jackson argues that there has been very little deviation in gospel music from the traditional music of West Africa. She notes that the African-American church is conservative in nature, thereby assuming that it would be the one institution more prone to preserving the rituals, styles, and musical functions of their African forbearers. She articulates it this way:

> Many of the ritual practices which we commonly associate with the African American folk church, such as freely structured services, dance, improvisational music, the emotional and musical delivery style of sermons and prayers, and spontaneous verbal and non-verbal responses by preachers and congregations, have essentially emerged from African values and aesthetics. ... The structural form and performance style associated with folk spirituals are derived from West African musical practices. In West Africa, the geographical origin for a large number of the slave population, cultural mores govern group singing at a musical event. These principles require the participation of group members who are present. Individuals become involved either by singing, dancing/shouting, hand-clapping, foot-stomping, or some combination of these rhythmic textures, which also provide the accompaniment for the layered voices. ... This type of animated and emotional ritual was valued by the slaves so much that many would risk being beaten or killed in order to continue to worship in a manner which represented a continuity with African performance aesthetics. (Jackson 1995)

In addition to some of the stylistic characteristics mentioned by Jackson, one can summarily point out that the African-American church experience in general,[2] which has given rise to a number of musical forms, demonstrates continuity with their African heritage[3] in the following ways:

First, there is, in the most fundamental sense, the presence of <u>rhythm</u>. Although the use of drums and other rhythmic devises is common also among non-African indigenous peoples, the widespread impact of African rhythm upon much of Western music renders it unique. As Darden asserts, "Among the richest of the lavish gifts Africa has given to the world is rhythm. The beat. The sound of wood on wood, hand on hand. That indefinable pulse that sets blood to racing and toes to tapping" (2004:1). Perhaps everyone who has truly experienced gospel music intuitively knows that rhythm is its driving force. It is, in its truest sense, "religion with rhythm" (2004:1). Since kinetic movements, such as clapping and swaying, are also integral features of gospel music, it is obvious that the kind of syncopations, cross-rhythms, and improvisational elements that drive these movements defer to African origins (Hillsman 1990:1).

Second, music in African culture is *functional*. In contrast to the Enlightenment worldview of the West, where music is classified as "art" and thereby segmented from other dimensions of life, music is integral to every aspect of human existence. In the African context, all music has a function. Songs are used to please the gods, to make work go better, and to relate to various aspects of daily life (Darden 2004:19). Music is sung by young men for courtship, by workers toiling in the sun, by old men preparing adolescents for manhood, by women in various states of childrearing, by all in recreational contexts, and so on (A. Jones 1993:3). In the African context, music is not art; it is a way of life (Hillsman 1990:1). The functional nature of music is clearly a defining characteristic that has imprinted the African-American music culture and has provided the soil from which black music has germinated.

Third, there is, in the traditional African mindset, the unbroken connection between the *physical and spiritual worlds*. Studies in the folk and primal religions of African people groups reveals certain distinguishable patterns of belief, such as the perception-impact of deceased ancestors and other spiritual beings upon daily life (Burnett 2000:62). Arthur Jones points out that the adoption of the name "spirituals" to classify the music genre of African-American slaves is a misnomer since all music from African tradition is spiritual (1993:9). The polarization that exists in Western culture between 'body and spirit', 'faith and reason', 'science and religion', and 'secular and sacred' did not substantially affect the worldview from which gospel music was born. A peculiar byproduct of the African "holistic" worldview is that meanings attached to various symbols, including music, are often layered and multifarious (Risher 1997:46). This characteristic of African music would subsequently become integral to understanding the "spirituals" and other expressions emanating from slave culture. The point is that the ability to attach multiple meanings to certain symbols without creating a sense of ambiguity was already present in early African culture. This feature translates astoundingly well in postmodern contexts, where meaning is generally regarded as socially constructed and rhetorically constituted.[4]

Fourth, an area in which the early African-American church experience and gospel music demonstrate continuity with African heritage revolves around oral culture. According to Burnett, oral transmission is the primary way that folk religious cultures protect and propagate their group identity since they do not rely on written texts or documents (2000:23). Of course, one of the primary methods of conveying the sense of identity, particularly in oral cultures is through song (Risher 1997:47). In analyzing the musical lineage from African origins to gospel music, this point cannot be overemphasized, in part because many of the precursory music styles and techniques, such as the "ring shout," "call and response," story telling, linguistic colorations, and improvisation are byproducts of a worldview that is transmitted orally (A. Jones 1993:6). The religious dynamic engendered by the vanguards of gospel music reflect the influences of oral culture. This is obviously not the case for diffused gospel music, and one wonders how the background of literary culture in itself might alter the perception of gospel music in diffused contexts. However, the cultural affects of the global information flow (globalization) and postmodernity are possibly creating a phenomenon referred to as "secondary orality,"[5] which may be impacting the proliferation of gospel music cross-culturally. This might suggest that the connection between the orality of African culture (historically) and postmodern Western culture is not so far-fetched.

The Spirituals as Precursor to Gospel Music

As African culture diffused to the North American continent within the context of slavery, a distinct musical genre emerged, standing as a living scion of gospel music – namely, spirituals. Darden states it: "The spirituals are an uncensored, unedited glimpse into the hearts and minds of slaves" (2004:2). This is indeed significant since the music provides a testimony of how slaves responded to their dehumanizing context. Cone articulates the African-American struggle in this way: "The black experience in America is a history of servitude and resistance, of survival in the land of death. It is the story of black life in chains and of what that meant for the souls and bodies of black people" (1972:20). This must be understood as the background of spirituals, and subsequently for the emergent gospel music genre. Although American slavery is well-documented, the ongoing psychic repercussions caused by institutional and systematic oppression are often misunderstood. Darden points out that spirituals and gospel music provide the most powerful contemporary folk expression of the people most affected by it; therefore, studying the music becomes necessary to understanding African-American culture and ethnicity (2004:6).

According to the research of Walker, spirituals contain three fundamental elements: 1) the obsession for freedom, 2) the desire for justice, and 3) a strategy to gain an eminent future (1979:32). Walker, among others, notes that spirituals themselves are an antecedent of "slave utterances," including "moans," "chants," and "cries" (1979:129). These early sublime expressions of longing for deliverance melded an African worldview with the new conditions of African slaves on the North American continent. Out of these moans, chants, and cries emerged a new hymnody that was birthed primarily in the farmlands of Colonial America (Burdett 2006). As slaves met in illicit gatherings referred to as "invisible" churches (that is, in brush arbors, ravines, forests, fields, or anywhere they could gather that was beyond the earshot of their European-American "masters"), they were able to preserve elements of African culture combined with their growing knowledge of Christian faith. The meetings consisted of prayer, which often turned into singing. As the congregation was encouraged to respond, the songs would break into a call-and-response pattern, which reflected a cultural trait inherent within Western and Central African music (Burdett 2006). The texts themselves were often taken from European hymns. Together with the rhythmic preaching, moving, and dancing, the emerging "spirituals" demonstrated a link to African religion that was condemned by white observers, often judged as "barbaric" and even indicative of voodoo practice and demon-possession (Raboteau 1978:65).

As slavery gave way to post-Civil War Reconstruction, the plight of African Americans did not noticeably improve. Though the Emancipation Proclamation was signed into effect, lynching, the Ku Klux Klan, Jim Crow Laws, and "Black Codes" merely perpetuated the repression of blacks (Darden 2004:113). The only institution where African Americans were allowed to assemble was the established church, which enabled the church to become the center of all social and spiritual life (Darden 2004:113). This, however, did not preclude the formation of non-sanctioned gatherings. As a way of escaping the emphasis on servitude, which characterized much of white preaching, blacks met secretly in enclaves, where the pronounced longing for freedom was nurtured (Walker 1979:31). Due to the inordinate psychological strain associated with their overall plight, "invisible" churches likewise served a therapeutic role, providing opportunity for oppressed blacks to vent emotions. Thus spirituals, which among other things provided emotional release, were cathartic in nature. It was the ability to cope with hardship through the use of indigenous religious music that would come to characterize much of black music on the North American continent – including the gospel music genre.

Spirituals themselves underwent a great deal of change as time passed. This was also true of the perception of them, even among African Americans. Darden, among others, notes that the rise in educational status among blacks caused some to distance themselves from them, perhaps because of their association with a painful past (2004:114). As a result, many black churches preferred white European hymnody and psalmody – a preference that reveals a cultural divide among African-American churches still. Bishop Daniel A. Payne of the American Methodist Episcopal Church was an outspoken critic of spirituals. As America's first African-American college president, Payne was influential in his articulation of disdain for the music of bush arbor meetings, dismissing the songs as "cornfield ditties" and "heathenish" (Darden 2004:114-115; Harris 1992:3). Of course, the rejection of spirituals by a segment of the black community due to factors related to social class, educational standard, and "sophistication" finds a direct parallel to the divergent reactions to gospel music, when this genre subsequently burst onto the scene.

Although the spirituals changed over time, certain characteristics remained constant throughout its development. Walker pinpoints eight defining qualities of a true spiritual, including: 1) deep Biblicism, 2) the eternity of the message, 3) rhythm, 4) improvisation, 5) antiphonal or call-and-response nature, 6) double or coded meanings, 7) repetition, and 8) unique imagery (1979:52-58, cf.

Darden 2004:75). Darden points out that the simplistic characterization of spirituals in terms of the beat or rhythm, especially the use of simple duple meters (the time kept by the "patting of a hand or a tapping of a foot") errs by focusing too narrowly on a singular feature (2004:75). Other characteristics might be added to Walker's list, including use of syncopation (in melody and rhythm), heterophony (wandering away from the lead melody in favor of variety, individual creativity, or the need to sing notes that fit ones personal tonal register), and the overwhelming preference for singing in an ordinary major key (though not exclusively), particularly in a pentatonic scale (Darden 2004:75).[6] These characteristics remained relatively true of spirituals in various forms, including the later developments of anthemic and concert (performance) spirituals, although they are clearly more indicative of the earlier folk expression.

One of the more intriguing aspects of spirituals involves the employment of double or coded messages in the songs. The use of language in a way in which overt and covert meanings are incongruous does have some biblical precedence, especially in the apocalyptic genre. It would be erroneous to assume that the cosmic dualism inherent in some of the literary works of post-exilic Judaism and early Christianity and the worldview of African Americans during slavery and reconstruction are coterminous. However, there are a few striking similarities, beginning with the ontology emerging from and shaped by conditions characterized by extreme persecution and the emergent linguistic responses. In these texts the intended meanings of the oppressed communities eluded the mainstream, even when the texts or writings were publicly accessible.

The spirituals often provided encrypted messages, which addressed specifically the social condition of the oppressed while giving the impression, especially to white masters that the songs referred exclusively to eschatological themes. The well-known spiritual, "O Canaan, my Canaan (I am bound for the land of Canaan)," for example, was more than a utopian dream; it meant escaping the South and reaching the North (Raboteau 1978:247). References to "Father Abraham" were not just allusions to the biblical patriarch, but also the signer of the Emancipation Proclamation and freer of the slaves, Abraham Lincoln (1978:249). Spirituals singing about "death," particularly as a passage to heaven, were meant to inspire and signal the literal passage to freedom (1978:261). While sermons by white masters repeatedly admonished slaves to remain docile and compliant, the slave response was "Steal Away," which was a coded message referring to escape (1978:213). Harriet Tubman, the remarkable abolitionist, and others, who effected emancipation via the Underground Railroad, figure prominently in several spirituals, including the ubiquitous "Swing Low, Sweet Chariot." Tubman is particularly noted for using spirituals, such as "Swing Low" and "Go Down Moses," as "signal songs." The reference in "Swing Low" to "a band of angels coming after me," for example, signified the coming of the Underground Railroad and the imminence of freedom. This meaning eluded those who assumed that the text alluded singularly to the biblical story of Elijah's ascension into heaven on a chariot, recorded in II Kings 2 (Darden 2004:95-96; cf. Job 1989:703).

The presence of coded and double meanings in spirituals contradicts the assumptions of those who complain that the texts are purely otherworldly and utopian in nature (Darden 2004:96). As Darden contends, whites have had trouble understanding the underlying meanings since they are often layered, while incorporating proverbs as well as the language of the slaves (2004:79). Of course, the advent of gospel music over a century after the death of Tubman would elicit the same misconceived critique, since the texts in gospel songs are no less complex. The kind of metonymic overlay implied in the common figures of spirituals, such as "King Jesus" (slave benefactor), "Satan" (slave master), "Jordan" (first step to freedom), "Israelites" (enslaved African Americans), "Egyptians" (slaveholders), and "heaven" (North) are equally implied in gospel texts (Lawrence-McIntyre 1987:389). This raises not only the question of meaning as songs are diffused across boundaries of ethnicity and social class, but (germane to this dissertation) also across cultural boundaries where the adopting context shares no historical connection with the culture of origin. How Danes, for example, understand "Steal Away," "Wade in the Water," and "Swing Low" may be determined by how well-acquainted they are with American history and culture, as well as idiomatic and parabolic expressions in English – factors which can not be taken for granted in any context. The enduring power of spirituals within black culture relates to the ability of the composers to bring the characters of the Bible to life while relating to the distinct circumstances of the immediate audience (Darden 2004:84-87). This assumes a common knowledge of biblical stories as well as empathy both for the biblical characters and the victims of socio-political injustice. The fact that spirituals and gospel music enjoy the same kind of universal popularity among people for whom the original messages remain encrypted suggests that the metonymic nature of the texts perpetuates the rhetorical reconstitution of meaning as the music is deconstructed and reconstructed in foreign contexts.

The diffusion and popularization of spirituals among predominantly white audiences is noteworthy. During the period of Reconstruction, a band of former slaves and children of slaves affiliated with Fisk University in Nashville, Tennessee formed a seminal group called "The Fisk Jubilee Singers." As a university chartered by the American Missionary Association in 1847, Fisk, like other African-American schools, was not financially solvent, and was forced into a desperate attempt to raise funds. The school solicited the support of First Sgt. George Leonard White, a Union veteran and music teacher. Realizing the level of musical talent enrolled at the University, White recruited singers from the talent pool and afterwards arranged a fund-raising tour. As one might imagine, the group was often rejected and subjected to numerous hardships. However, after receiving support from powerful opinion leaders, such as Reverend Henry Ward Beecher, the Fisk Jubilee Singers eventually received widespread acclaim and are today acknowledged for bringing spirituals to the mainstream (Ward 2000:73-81; cf. Darden 2004:116). By bringing the music to concert venues and adapting the sound to appeal to white audiences, the Jubilee Singers constitute a nineteenth century example of missio-musicological contextualization.[7]

Another factor involved in the diffusion of spirituals was minstrelsy. The concept of the blackface minstrel tradition by today's standards is, of course, repugnant. This form of entertainment, which remained popular in the United States and Europe well into the twentieth century (at least in vaudeville settings), often ridiculed African Americans and reduced their culture and ethnicity to a "twisted caricature" (Darden 2004:121). It is likely that the popularity of this entertainment form (the most popular in the United States up to the dawn of the twentieth century [Darden 2004:122]) was largely pathological in nature. It has been suggested that the portrayal of blacks as "happy, shiftless darkies" allayed the guilt of whites, who otherwise thought they were advancing the cause by perpetuating the stereotype of black musicality (Rublowsky 1971:101). Nevertheless, black minstrelsy did provide a formidable conduit by which black music, particularly spirituals, was exported cross-culturally. As a medium, it did give African Americans an opportunity to perform before a varied public (Darden 2004:125), which in turn provided an essential stepping stone toward the legitimization of black culture in a paternalistic/racist context. In a sense, minstrelsy demonstrates the missiological character of African-American spirituals by virtue of the fact that the Christian message inherent in the music and culture could not be assuaged by the debasing nature of the medium itself. One wonders if the caricaturing of black culture, which *de facto* would include black religious expression, somehow unleashed an expression of faith that would quietly begin to influence the mainstream. At any rate, the phenomena of the Jubilee Singers and blackface minstrelsy would effectuate developments in spirituals which eventually led to the unparalleled musical and spiritual innovation of Black gospel (Darden 2004:125).

Black Gospel: "Good News and Bad Times"

The emergence of Black gospel music coincides with the beginning of ragtime, blues, jazz, and the rise of Pentecostalism (Eskew 2001:177). The economic backdrop during the breakthrough of traditional gospel music in the early 1930's was not coincidentally the Great Depression (Harvey 1987:25). During the early twentieth century, a great northward migration of African Americans took place, commonly referred to as the "Black Exodus" (Darden 2004:131). The migration was primarily urban, as blacks fled the Southern states *en masse* due to the prevalence of Jim Crow laws, the KKK, daily humiliation, lack of justice, lack of educational opportunities, inadequate health care, and deprivation of the right to vote in hopes of improving their fortunes. Notably, some of the migrants were musicians, and cities such as Chicago and Detroit provided the optimal testing ground for their talents (Darden 2004:131-133). This likely explains, at least in part, why gospel music continues to be construed as an urban development and expression, whereas other African-American musical genres, such as spirituals and blues, are largely associated with the rural South.

There are indeed a number of other precursory influences that helped to shape the gospel sound and expression. One such expression was the

"Barbershop Quartet." Although this phenomenon is still perceived as an outgrowth of the "Gay Nineties" and remains indelibly linked to white aristocracy, Lynn Abbott argues convincingly that Barbershop harmonies originated from the black community (Abbott 1992). Since three and four part harmonies are integral to gospel choir performance, it is highly probable that the Barbershop sound influenced a number of subsequent musical innovations, including gospel music. The Black exodus also paved the way for a somewhat eccentric figure: the "jack-leg" or singing street preacher. The term "jack-leg preacher" refers to someone with little or no education, as well as no mainline church affiliation, yet who is recognized as an avant-garde musical missionary (Darden 2004:142). Although some were transient street-evangelists, jack-leg preachers often developed stable audiences and formed store-front churches, usually in the larger northern cities (Darden 2004:142). A final notable influence in the development of gospel music was the rise of early recording artists. It was the advent of recorded music, together with the street-style of the jack-leg preacher and the harmonic quality of the Barbershop sound that likely added to the cauldron from which the gospel sound and ethos emerged.

The ecclesiological foundations of early gospel music were somewhat varied. Perhaps the leading harbinger was Charles Albert Tindley (ca. 1851-1933), a well-known Methodist minister. Some of Tindley's better known religious songs/hymns, such as "Stand By Me" and "I'll Overcome Someday" (later rechristened "We Shall Overcome") constituted a watershed in black church music, and are now classified as "transitional gospel" (Spencer 1990:208). The lyrics, which focused on the concerns of the African-American community, together with stylistic musical innovations, notably the employment of flatted thirds and sevenths, brought together elements that still render his songs unique in relation to other musical genres (Darden 2004:162; Heilbut 1969:23). Other significant influences came from the Baptist church, such as Lucie Campbell and the National Baptist Convention Publishing Board. It was the latter's discovery of a hymnal composed of songs by William H. Sherwood that parlayed the "simple and repetitive, easy to sing and catchy" songs of Sherwood into the public arena (Boyer 1995:26; Darden 2004:160). Since the music of Tindley, Campbell, Sherwood, and others reflected daily life in the respective churches in which these artists were embedded, there is no doubt that ecclesiological orientation played a role in the development of gospel music.

However, the church movement that provided the most fertile soil for new musical innovations was Pentecostalism. The Pentecostal movement together with the Holiness Church have clearly had a global impact, with the number of church members today amassing into the hundreds of millions (Jenkins 2002:7). The rate of proliferation of Pentecostal churches in the two-thirds world is the subject of much research and analysis. Some of the basic reasons include the emphasis on the supernatural, the de-emphasis of ecclesial structure, and the ability to empower the laity, who often are among the poor and marginalized, through unwavering stress on personal salvation and glossolalia (Jenkins 2002:7).

When Pentecostalism began to soar in the United States following the Azusa Street Revival in 1904-1905, prompted under the leadership of an African American, William J. Seymour, the movement made particular headway among African Americans (McGee 2000:739). Darden cites the way in which this "new religion" gave status to ordinary people, especially the socially underprivileged, in addition to the emotional nature of worship, as key factors in the gravitational pull of Pentecostalism among disenfranchised blacks (2004:138-139). Above all, it may have been the encouraged use of musical instruments in church that legitimated the implementation of musical innovation (Darden 2004:140), which not only would nurture the birth and growth of gospel music, but would assure its rootedness within the Christian church. In the early twentieth century, a number of instruments were employed to provide accompaniment to church singing in Pentecostal and Holiness churches. This included an array of percussion devices, such as bass and snare drums, the triangle, tambourine, and washboards, and also featured the banjo, at least until it was replaced by the guitar in the 1920's (Eschew 2001:181). Eventually, the piano would become the dominant instrument in gospel music, especially because one could play syncopations with the right hand while playing bass note octaves with the left (Eschew 2001:181). All in all, the rhythmic sound of church singing with instrumental accompaniment in churches that fostered passionate and ecstatic expression in worship provided the primary framework for the development of gospel music.

Thomas A. Dorsey and Beyond

In the early twentieth century, the convergence of musical and performance styles together with ecclesiological innovations issued in the gospel sound, which commenced around 1930. Though gospel music emerged gradually rather than meteoric, the name Thomas A. Dorsey (1899-1993) has singularly come to symbolize its genesis. Dubbed "the Father of (Black) Gospel Music," Dorsey was raised in a religious and musical family. His father, himself the son of former slaves, was a flamboyant evangelist, while his mother, who was a spiritual mentor to her family, also mastered the portable organ, which became pivotal in Thomas' musical development (Darden 2004:166; Harris 1992:19). As part of the Black Exodus, the Dorsey family migrated from rural Georgia to Chicago.[8] Thomas quickly developed a reputation as a gifted blues and jazz pianist, playing bars and nightclubs as his primary source of income. After an apparent nervous breakdown, which prompted his return to Atlanta for convalescence, he attended the National Baptist Convention in Chicago in 1921. It was there, while listening to the powerful singing and preaching of "Professor" W.M. Nix that Dorsey received what Methodists might refer to as an "Aldersgate experience," that is, a heart-warming epiphany that brought about some form of conversion (Harris 1992:75). Although he continued to play secular music in secular venues, his passion became the composition and performance of gospel music (Harris 1992:75). It was through this genre, which Dorsey in large part was responsible for creating, that he was able to express both his renewed faith and his sense of anguish, the latter of which was provoked by his psychological proclivity toward depression above his otherwise difficult circumstances (Harris 1992:91-92).

For Dorsey, the most painful experience and most sublime expression were yet to come. The song which has become emblematic for Black gospel music, "Precious Lord, Take My Hand," was composed by Dorsey following the successive deaths of his wife and newborn son. Dorsey himself described the trauma:

> Next night, I was working in a revival, and I received a telegram: Your wife just died. Come home. Some fellows volunteered to drive me to Chicago, and when I got home the next day, I had the body moved. I had a bouncing boy baby. But that night, the baby died. That was double trouble. I felt like going back on God. He had mistreated me, I felt. About a week later, after we had put the baby and the wife away in the same casket, I was sitting with the late Theodore Frye, just drowsing. Just like water dropping from the crevice of a rock, the words dropped into the music, 'Take My Hand, Precious Lord'. (Horstman 1975:57-58)

His articulation of faith in light of immeasurable grief constituted a watershed for gospel music, since it successfully melded the styles of sorrow songs, spirituals, jubilee, and camp meeting songs into what has since been referred to as the "gospel blues."[9] What Dorsey had introduced was something new (Darden 2004:172).

A few noteworthy observations regarding the emergence of gospel music should be pointed out. First, gospel music has been from the outset a sublime and heartfelt expression of existential anguish and grief. Although "Precious Lord," for example, springs from Dorsey's personal encounter with tragedy, it conveys a universal heart-cry that relates to the human predicament and condition. As Harris explains, the song itself allowed Dorsey to "purge," rather than "soothe" his grief (Harris 1992:239). This suggests that the essence of gospel music is cathartic, and that a major part of its appeal is the ability to address angst.

Second, the music at its root emphasizes affectivity rather than cognition. Gospel music is likely misunderstood when it is judged according to the theological content of the texts. When comparing gospel music texts to many traditional hymns, for example, it is clear that the texts themselves are not by their nature designed to elevate theological articulation, but rather to deal with emotions. This is a key to gospel music's transcendent quality, especially as one begins to speculate about its diffusion across all manners of culture boundaries.

Third, the early patriarchs and matriarchs of gospel had to deal with much opposition. Dorsey himself encountered much rejection early in his gospel music career, especially as he tried to earn a living selling his sheet music. He recounted once that he was "Thrown out of some of the best churches in Chicago" (Harris 1992a:179). This caused him for a time to revert back to playing in secular venues. In terms of the adopter categories of Everett Rogers, it becomes clear that the innovators of gospel music had to endure the "crucible" posed by the criticisms of late adopters and laggards (cf. Rogers 2003:270).[10] The growth and diffusion of early gospel music in the face of staunch opposition has portended the repetition of similar conflicts in connection with gospel music's cross-cultural diffusion.

The rapid spread of gospel music in the U.S. American context following Dorsey's initial impact reveals both the continuum of African-American consciousness and the seeds of intercultural adoptability. In large part due to the innovations of James Cleveland, gospel music took on a more contemporary sound and became indelibly linked to mass choirs (Darden 2004:269-270). Gospel choirs have been a trademark of many African-American churches, but the concept has been pivotal in the mobilization of gospel music participants in Europe and beyond. Gospel singing groups, such as the Dixie Hummingbirds have ventured to take the music and its ethnic heritage beyond its indigenous roots to audiences throughout the European continent (Darden 2004:238). Divas, such as Mahalia Jackson,[11] achieved stardom internationally, which likewise instilled a climate conducive to gospel music's burgeoning popularity (Goines 2005).

It was around the release of the 1969 Edwin Hawkins hit, "O Happy Day," that Black gospel music experienced a global renaissance. Just as Dorsey and "Precious Lord" had signaled the breakthrough of a new music genre, "O Happy Day" now symbolizes the innovation in gospel music which would transfer it from urban African-American churches to the world stage. This innovation is categorized by scholars as "contemporary gospel" (Eschew 2001:183). For the first time, a gospel song began to receive massive airplay on radio stations, which attracted, among others, white audiences throughout Europe and North America.[12]

Other breakout artists, such as Andrae Crouch, continued to bridge gaps between white and black audiences by taking the music out of the Black church context and making it accessible to the mainstream (Darden 2004:278). The fact that Crouch was criticized for doing so places him in good company, with the likes of Dorsey, Cleveland, Rosetta Tharpe, and all others who ventured to innovate and transform the music beyond the established boundaries. The irony, of course, is that the innovators of contemporary gospel music are often judged for "secularizing" the genre and failing to live up to the standards set by the vanguards of traditional gospel music, even though the vanguards themselves were all criticized similarly in their own day. Nevertheless, names such as Kirk Franklin, John P. Kee, Ricky Grundy, the Winans', Fred Hammond, Richard Smallwood, and many other innovators of the contemporary gospel sound and ethos are forging new paths, which are constructing the foundation for Black gospel music's movemental status on a global scale.

Gospel Music as Contextual Theology

In his book, *The Gospel Sound*, Tony Heilbut articulates the irrepressible and broad influence of gospel music:

> All rock's most resilient features, the beat, the drama, the group vibrations derive from gospel. From the rock symphonies to detergent commercials, from Aretha Franklin's proto technique to the Beatle's harmonies, gospel has simply reformed all our listening expectations. The very tension between beats, the climax we anticipate almost subliminally is straight out of the church. The dance steps that ushered in a new physical freedom were copied from the shout, the holy dance of 'victory'. The sit-ins soothed by hymns, the freedom marches powered by shouts, the 'brother and sister' fraternity of revolution: the gospel church gave us all of these. (1969:10-11)

If Heilbut's assessment is true, then the style, sound, and aesthetic of gospel music have caused it to become one of the most diffused music genres in the Western world.

Yet gospel music likewise contains a message. According to numerous accounts, it is a collective message that emphasizes hope and joy – themes which are shared by those who assemble in choirs, congregations, and audiences where this music is featured. A matter of intense discussion revolves around the values and theology that likewise are propelled into the mainstream as part of gospel music's widespread diffusion. Is Christian faith primary, peripheral, or non-essential to gospel music? Is gospel music primarily a theological expression or merely a matter of culture, aesthetics and performance? Is the music first and foremost a symbol of African-American ethnicity, or is it rightfully understood as a vehicle in promoting the Christian faith across ethnic and cultural boundaries? And as gospel music transcends these boundaries, what is the relationship of "form" and "meaning," and to what extent are the actual meanings girding the music transported into the different contexts? These and other questions relate not only to the nature of cross-cultural transference, but also to the missiological enterprise of intercultural Christian communication in general.

Of course, apprehending gospel music as it breaches cultural barriers is contingent upon understanding it within its original context. Theologically speaking, gospel music arguably conveys a clear Christian message of hope and liberation within the African-American context. In the preface to the hymnal, *Songs of Zion*, William McClain frames gospel music theologically:

> The gospel song expresses theology. Not the theology of the academy or the university, not formalistic theology or the theology of the seminary, but a theology of experience – the theology of a God who sends the sunshine and the rain, the theology of a God who is very much alive and active and who has not forsaken those who are poor and oppressed and unemployed. It is a theology of imagination – it grew out of fire shut up in the bones, of words painted in the canvas of the mind. Fear is turned to hope in the sanctuaries and storefronts and bursts forth in songs of celebration. It is a theology of grace that allows the faithful to see the sunshine of His face – even through the tears. Even the words of an ex-slave trader became a song of liberation and an expression of God's amazing grace. It is a theology of survival that allows a people to celebrate the ability to continue the journey in spite of the insidious tentacles of

racism and oppression and to sing, 'It's another day's journey, and I'm glad about it! (McClain 1981:x)

Although the Christian content of Black gospel music can readily be understood and co-opted within various contexts, the theology of gospel music is, among African Americans, indeed contextual. As Walker states it, "[gospel] is an individual expression of a collective predicament in a religious context" (1979:127). It is, in itself, a "social statement" (1979:144). Thus gospel music is, in its original context, an articulation of theology that is inseparable from the socio-political conditions from which it emerges and to which it speaks. If one were to classify gospel music in the African-American context as a mode of contextual theology, it could be argued that it shares, to a degree, an affinity with what Stephen Bevans refers to as the *praxis model* (Bevans 2002:70).[13] The praxis model presupposes that theology is less a matter of intellectual ascent than of responsible doing, as well as assuming that the socio-cultural condition is unjust and necessitates change (Bevans 2002:73-74). In a sense, the gospel music ethos represents the antithesis of an excessively academic approach to theology which is divorced from action/praxis, denies emotions, and neglects the importance of the social location in terms of theological response. While at least tacitly promoting solidarity with the poor and oppressed, gospel music theology defies the normal constructs of Western assumptions, thus constituting an "epistemological discontinuity" (Frostin 1985) with theological expression that does not share liberation as the primary task. Thus, "praxis" is an important element in understanding gospel music's importance in the African-American context.

However, the contextual model that seems to describe the essence of gospel music most completely is the *counter-cultural model* (Bevans 2002:117). In his book, *Protest and Praise*, Jon Michael Spencer applies H. Richard Niebuhr's categories from his classic book, *Christ and Culture*, and argues that gospel music presents an example of the "Christ against culture" paradigm. While comparing the overarching theology to each of Niebuhr's typologies, including "the Christ of culture," "Christ above culture," "Christ and culture in paradox," and "Christ as transformer of culture," Spencer contends that gospel music is radically anticultural (Spencer 1990:205). While noting the contributions of other significant contributors to gospel lore, such as Walker, Louis Charles Harvey, Irene Jackson, Charles B. Copher, and William T. Dargan, Spenser categorizes gospel within the "praise music" genre, which focuses more profoundly on spiritual renewal and rejuvenation rather than transformation of the world. In delineating some of the predominant themes in gospel music, such as "power," "praise," "salvation," and "struggle," he discerns a distinct anticulturalism intrinsic to the theological interpretations within each motif (1990:200).

Niebuhr himself notes that representatives of the "Christ against culture" typology throughout Christian history have been characterized by a rejection of "the world," often due to the harsh treatment of Christians in certain geographical areas and historical epochs. This has caused Christians to reject the dominant culture and resist assimilation, while remaining a faithful remnant in light of overwhelming pagan influence, i.e., oppression (Niebuhr 2001:45-82). Bevans would point out that his particular model is not necessarily anticultural, since the *counter*-cultural approach functions to challenge the human context without sanctioning a retreat from one's cultural context (Bevans 2002:119).

It is not clear whether or not Spencer would be interested in nuancing his categorization of gospel music in light of Bevans' emphasis on "contrast" rather than "rejection" of culture. What cannot be lost in the assessment of gospel music theology is the backdrop of oppression and the eschatological longing for liberation. Spencer states it in this way: "Gospel music is the creation of a people who exist amid the absurdity of American race conventions and is thus a music that constantly raises questions about the relationship of faith and culture or society" (Spencer 1990:204).

The response to this questioning of society is not about achieving victory over the world or in some sense overturning the balance of injustice, which is perhaps the subliminal message in many of the spirituals; rather, gospel music advocates not loving the things of the world and remaining true to Christian conviction. It is about singing praises to God, even when the surrounding world is excessively hostile (1990:204). Although the message of the "goodness of Jesus" and the "badness of the world" is an integral part of many gospel texts, it is still debatable whether or not this overriding theme continues to form gospel music in its more contemporary expressions. As one begins to assess the value of the ethnohistorical perspective in relation to cross-cultural diffusion, it becomes a matter of intense interest whether or not the anticulturalism inherent in African-American gospel music theology has any relevance to gospel music in diffused forms.[14] Yet before delving into issues of meaning construction, we now turn to the actual process of diffusion and its relevance as a theoretical framework to the spread of Black gospel music in Denmark.

Notes

1. "A Celebration of Gospel" was aired on BET (Black Entertainment Television) on February 24, 2005. The two-hour special featured a number of gospel artists, mostly contemporary, and highlighted some of the compositional and stylistic transformations that have taken place in gospel music during the past few decades.

2. I am not at all implying that all African-American churches are or have been univocal in worship style, culture, etc. There has been diversity in African-American church life since its inception, often determined by social factors such as educational standard, economic status, geography, and the like. The churches I am generally referring to are those that have not been particularly influenced by white Christian culture and are considered the vanguards of gospel music.

3. In a sense, the African continent is too geographically massive and culturally diverse to draw blanket generalizations. The use of the name "Africa" in this context refers primarily to the sub-Saharan and western regions, where the slave-trade had greatest impact, and where music and dance styles have been determined by some ethnomusicologists to be somewhat homogenous (Darden 2004:13).

4. Studies in symbolic interactionism point out, at the very least, that meanings attached to various symbols are often multifarious given subjective determinates, as well

as individual and social variables. The point will be made in chapter seven that postmodernism is in part characterized by a plurality of meanings attached to common symbols, which is highly relevant to the discussion of gospel music in postmodern contexts.

5. Secondary orality refers to the notion that rapidly changing forms of communication characteristic of the global era are moving print literacy cultures toward something a bit more attuned to oral transmission.

6. Darden refers to studies, particularly those of early collector of spirituals, Henry Krehbiel, who determined that most spirituals are sung in a major key despite the perception among untrained musicians that they are minor. Many (though not a majority) use a five-note pentatonic scale, while a few are majors without fourths, majors with flatted sevenths, minors without sixths, minors with raised sevenths, and so on.

7. Darden deduces that the Jubilee Singers tempered their repertoire to suit general audiences, which otherwise might have found the more "untamed" melodies of folk spirituals offensive (cf. Darden 2004:119).

8. Chicago has been a primary breeding ground for Black gospel since the time of Dorsey. My thanks to gospel leader and Chicagoan, Gerome Bell, who made this unmistakably clear to me in a 2005 interview.

9. Dorsey's music has often been labeled "gospel blues" because of the blues and jazz elements he infused into the music. This is one of the main features which distinguish his music from that of his predecessors, such as Tindley.

10. The adopter categories in Everett Rogers' *Diffusion of Innovation* are dealt with extensively in Chapter Four. "Late Adopters" and "Laggards" comprise categories describing people who, to varying degrees, are resistant to change or slow to adopt certain innovations, even when the majority of a particular group has accepted them.

11. Mahalia Jackson, who is recognized as one of the all-time leading voices in gospel music, began her career with Thomas Dorsey.

12. The symbolic impact of Edwin Hawkins' breakthrough song is revealed in a 2004 Danish film entitled, "O Happy Day." The film, which was shown in cinemas across the country, is unique and revealing in that it uses gospel music as an essential backdrop in the telling of a fictitious story. This suggests that gospel music is already becoming a part of the mainstream cultural consciousness.

13. In his book, *Models of Contextual Theology*, Bevans categorizes six models, including: the translation model, the anthropological model, the praxis model, the synthetic model, the transcendental model, and the counter-cultural model. A matter of consideration is whether or not gospel music, in the process of cultural diffusion, actually becomes an expression of a model other than the one which it embodies in its original context.

14. The relevance of gospel music theology to belief patterns among the gospel music constituency outside of the African-American context will be illuminated more thoroughly in Chapter Five. This chapter will make reference to the content of interviews and conversations. Chapter Eight is devoted to the subject of meaning construction in the gospel music context.

Chapter 4

The Diffusion and Adoption of Gospel Music in Denmark

The disengagement of gospel music from its ethnic and religious origins raises general questions about authenticity and the nature of meaning. As has been noted, the diffusion of gospel music cross-culturally incites a degree of tension between purists (i.e., those who maintain that the only "valid and true" expression comes from the people and context of origin) and pluralists (those who have taken the forms, symbols, and expressions of the music and attached meanings that are not necessarily congruous with the original). Although issues of authenticity can and should be debated, the pragmatic reality is that gospel music, in all of its multifaceted manifestations, has been and is being disseminated globally at a rapid rate. The Danish gospel scene constitutes a vibrant example, since, as has been mentioned, what was once a scant presence before 1990 has now become recognized for its widespread proliferation. The emergence of workshops, festivals, concerts, worship services, and other gospel events that also have become popular within that timeframe begins to paint a picture of a growing movement that is impacting the cultural landscape.

Contemporary Gospel on Foreign Soil: An Australian Case Study

Before moving on to the specific topic of gospel music diffusion, spirituality, and choir proliferation in Denmark, one would be remiss not to incorporate into the conversation a significant contribution to the cross-cultural gospel music phenomenon provided by E. Patrick Johnson. In his book, entitled, *Appropriating Blackness: Performance and the Politics of Authenticity*, Johnson offers a noteworthy scholarly "roadmap" on the transplantation of Black gospel music in a foreign context. Although his book deals with a number of topics revolving around African-American identity politics and the appropriation of black culture, especially in the area of performance, a critical section deals with his research experiences among an Australian gospel choir, named, *The Café of the Gate of Salvation*. As an African-American music performer and professor at

Northwestern University, he relates his insights as both ethnographer and guest performing artist among an *a cappella* choir comprised predominantly of white Australians. Having been reared on gospel music in a black Southern Baptist Church, his journey began with a tinge of skepticism, especially since the subject of his research was a non-church affiliated "white" gospel choir singing Black gospel music. The references to his own ecclesiological background are helpful since they reveal his sensitivity to the religious suppositions of gospel music as well as his capacity to understand the religious irony of gospel music being enthusiastically adapted by, among others, secularists/atheists. Although his primary agenda involves the cooptation of African-American ethnicity and art forms by white culture, his analysis elicits a number of parallels with my own.

According to a number of Johnson's interviews, Christian faith is not the prevailing spirituality of the choir members; in fact, he notes that those whose religious/spiritual identity is consciously not formed around Christian faith make a "mental flip" in their minds, particularly when singing in a language that conveys the specificity of Christian proclamation (2003:166). For choir adherents who are Jewish, atheist, New Age, or Buddhist, for example, the name "Jesus" (or, as the leader of the choir terms it, "the J-word") becomes a metaphor for "my highest good" or "my highest welfare" (2003:166). References to the "Holy Spirit" are interpreted as "the spirit within" or "inner peace/joy" (2003:169). He likewise speculates about what gospel lyrics with the emphasis on such themes as "freedom from suffering" and "good news in bad times" could mean in a context of "privileged whites" (2003:170). His provisional conclusion seems to point toward syncretism, as Christian symbols are employed and then reinterpreted in ways that do not contravene the belief systems of those who do not share the predetermined meanings attached with those symbols. Though it can be labeled as syncretistic to attach self-constructed meanings to Christian symbols, including song texts and musical expressions, the intriguing thing about gospel music according to Johnson's analysis is that the participants are not uncomfortable working with the inherited Christian language. In an interview with the choir's founder, Tony Backhouse, Jesus is recognized as "Our culture's prevailing metaphor for spiritual excellence," and despite the often debased associations that many choir members have with the Christian religion and the church, Jesus as representative of "nonviolence, non-sexism, and non-racism" is held in high esteem. As Backhouse states, "I feel comfortable working with the Christian metaphor" (2003:170).

Johnson furthermore notes the irony that while the choir members "eschew religious dogma," they nevertheless maintain a Christian ethos. This is demonstrated through gifts of charity and acts of caring, both inwardly (toward fellow choir members) and outwardly (in support of missional and humanitarian causes) (2003:176-177). It would seem that the choir members in Australia, similar to those in Denmark, have created a sense of "church" through expressions of communality and stewardship while gospel music, complete with undiminished references to the content of Christian faith, serves as the magnet that draws them together. In spite of the serious misgivings about the nature and function of the church, the Australian choir constitutes a meeting ground where multiple identities – that is, people representing various religious convictions, different sexual orientation, and diverging subcultures – converge (2003:166).[1] The fact that unity can be created out of such diversity demonstrates that gospel choirs in general elicit traits of the kind of *ecclesia* that many churches could only dream about. It is noteworthy that a general trend among members of *The Café of the Gate of Salvation* seems to be a discontentment with the institutional church or as Johnson deems it, "the stodginess of Anglican worship" (2003:174). This is an especially astute insight since, according to my own analysis based on interviews and conversations, the Scandinavian Lutheranism that has shaped the religious perceptions of most Danish gospel choir adherents is regarded as no less "stodgy;" in fact, it is often implicated as a major culprit in common attitudes pertaining to Christianity's irrelevance among the gospel constituency. This may suggest that singing gospel, in Australia, Denmark, or wherever, may actually provide a means of re-imaging (or re-imagining) Christianity outside of allegiance to a compromised ecclesiological system and within a social context that is ultimately non-judgmental (2003:174). Whether or not gospel music constitutes the subjugation of Christian meaning in some sort of syncretistic blend, it is in some cases using Christian expressions to deconstruct the traditional dogmatic, institutional, and excessively conceptual perception of Christianity that is normative for many gospel choir adherents.

In addition to the disenchantment with organized religion often expressed by gospel choir participants, there are a couple of other broad comparisons between gospel choirs in Australia and Denmark. First, one should acknowledge the fact that while members may distance themselves from personal Christian confession, the cultural "soil" which they have inherited in both contexts has been plowed and fertilized by Christendom. This means that references to Christian symbols, such as biblical images and themes, are not totally foreign, no matter how secular the participants are. Although Cultural Christianity paradoxically can serve as a deterrent to Christian faith, it also creates a common culture where Christian concepts are ingrained on some level. The degree of Christian memory likely varies widely from person to person in a context where Christian faith is historically deep-seated. In some cases it perhaps has mutated far beyond the parameters of traditional Christian faith (cf. Davie 2000); nevertheless, Christian heritage provides common ground that gospel choir members somehow are benefiting from as they utilize texts that, in spite of all else, have a familiar "ring" about them.

Another area of broad comparison involves the shifting of focus between *openness* and *boundaries*. A recurring statement in Johnson's interviews (and my own) is an appreciation for the open, "come-as-you-are" attitude fostered within gospel music contexts. In fact, this is often cited as a primary factor in the appeal of gospel choirs. Interestingly, one particular choir in Denmark has adopted the name, CAYA – an acronym for "Come as You Are" (cf. www.comeasyouare.dk), thus capturing a defining element in the gospel ethos. Unlike the stereotypical perception of the church as culturally and religiously exclusive, choirs are regarded as places where people can converge, no matter what their identity may happen to be outside of the choir. The fact that one does not have to be a Christian, let alone share a "narrowly" defined religious belief system in order to be part of the group, gives the impression that gospel music eradicates the lines of demarcation often associated with Christian faith. The belief that gospel imposes no demands on the participants presents a further breach in perception between gospel choirs and the traditional church.

However, the notion that boundaries do not exist in gospel choirs is an inadequate characterization. Lines are drawn, but merely do not demarcate the dividing points that choir members often associate with the church. Borrowing from the "set theory" of Paul Hiebert, in which categories such as "church" or "gospel choir" often are defined in terms of the boundaries which they impose, one cannot assume that choirs are completely free of restrictions (Hiebert 1994:112-113; cf. Hiebert et al. 1999:235-236). This point was highlighted in one of my own interviews, when a non-Christian gospel singer was asked if he feels that choir participation allows him to "come as you are." His response was, "Fortunately no." The thought behind the response is that one must conform to the musical, performance, and social expectations involved with participation. The idea that Hiebert proposes in terms of a "centered set" – that is, defining a category in terms of its relationship to the "center" or "reference point" rather than focusing on the boundaries – is somewhat true of gospel choirs in the sense that issues of dogma and belief are not used to create distinction or division (Hiebert 1994:113-114). Yet a centered set still has borders. In the case of gospel choirs, one must be able to sing, for example, and the level of talent is determined by each choir individually. Although it is proper to characterize gospel choirs as "open," as many of the interviewees (in Australia and Denmark) strongly suggest, there are indeed limitations that on some level become points of contention for some members in all gospel choir contexts.

One must point out that Johnson's analysis has a few potential shortcomings, which can relate in general to the questionable validity of drawing general conclusions based on analysis of an isolated (sub-) culture or case study. First, Johnson focuses on the peculiarities of Australian history and culture as a way of explaining gospel music's appeal in that context. The analysis relates to their history as descendents of exiled convicts while hypothesizing that it gives them a special affinity with the experience of the descendents of Black American slaves. Johnson proposes that the "catharsis" of gospel singing as a means of expressing repressed sorrow or grief as well as the latent feelings of illegitimacy stemming from criminal ancestry provide a unique segue between Black gospel music and Australian culture (Johnson 2003:181-182). The hypothesis is indeed interesting; however, the assumed proclivity toward receptivity of gospel music as a result of certain historical eccentricities does not offer a clue to gospel's popularity in Denmark, Poland, Japan, or anywhere else, unless, of course, one is referring to the common thread of feeling excluded, marginalized, and oppressed. The notion of "catharsis" is a relevant issue in understanding the appeal of the gospel music experience, but funneling it strictly through the Australian mindset in association with their cultural heritage as a nation of "convicts" does not really shed light on the diffusion of gospel music in countries that do not share this cultural and historical idiosyncrasy.

Another analytical foray in Johnson's work deals with his assertion that singing gospel is indicative of the romanticization of Black American culture (2003:182). This is, of course, an important observation which Johnson is uniquely positioned to make. The Australian choir shows many signs of idealizing the culture and ethnicity from which Black gospel music emerges, even though many choir members do not share the same religious convictions. This is demonstrated in many subtle ways, including perhaps the tolerance or acceptance of Christian expression in gospel music as somehow legitimated by African-American culture. The fact that the choir attempts to do more than merely mimic the music, but to truly understand the source (2003:189) is concurrently a form of flattery and typecasting, since "blackness" becomes commodified and assumed to be something that it is not. The notion of romanticization is not without irony, especially when considering how the appropriation of the music of an oppressed people by a people of privilege occurs while ignoring the oppression directed toward the Aborigines. While endeavoring to relate to the African-American struggle through participation in one of its aesthetic expressions, the choir members demonstrate a cultural blind spot by failing "to acknowledge the ways in which they participate in the subjugation of 'the blacks' (i.e., the Aborigines) of their own country" (2003:182).

However, the specific attitudes toward African-American culture engendered by Johnson's Australian case study is likely not indicative of all, or even most gospel choirs. My own interviews reveal a generally strong appreciation (if not romanticization) of American blacks and African American culture, but the importance of mimicking and appropriating the "blackness" of gospel does not exist in all cases. Leaders of gospel choirs in Denmark are close to univocal in their approbation of the source of gospel music, but are in sharp disagreement regarding the continued influence of the black church in its ongoing development. As gospel music becomes contextualized in foreign locations, it is not certain that even an acknowledgement of gospel music's origin will have any relevance to its future proliferation. This has indeed been the case for some time with jazz, blues, and other art/music forms originating in the African-American context, and there is no reason to think that gospel one day will be regarded differently. It is often true within European gospel music contexts, just like in Australia, that blacks are viewed as a kind of "exotic Other," which in itself is dehumanizing and therefore inadvertently racist.[2] Yet since cultural diffusion involves selectivity and eventual integration of a foreign innovation until it becomes one's own, there is no reason to assume that gospel's culture of origin will play a pivotal role in its future success, which ultimately would render the notion of romanticization moot.

A third potential shortcoming deals with the fact that the subject of Johnson's study is a non-church based gospel choir.[3] Although gospel choirs outside of the African-American church context are generally not church choirs *per se*, there is often a distinction between choirs that meet in churches and those that hold regular rehearsals in schools, gyms, and theaters, for example. The faith-orientation of the leaders is also a telling factor. The difference deals with the likelihood that Christian meaning is integrated with the symbols of gospel music. Trine Berg Nielsen explores the possibilities of "faith-integration" in her Master's thesis, which draws conclusions on the basis of an analysis of the well-known Methodist church-based gospel choir, *Kefas*. (Nielsen 2006). In exploring the effects of church-based gospel activity on Christian faith, the study at least implies that the correlation of Christian meaning and gospel music is more likely to be drawn when the leaders and symbols of the church are present.

Although it is not clear at this point what conclusions can be drawn in regard to the church-based/non-church-based dichotomy, it should nevertheless be noted that the subject of Johnson's choir qualifies as the latter. This would provisionally suggest that the presence of Christian meaning is more likely to be dampened or marginalized than would be the case in Australian gospel choirs that are meeting within a church complex with at least some degree of association with church leaders. Nielsen's research raises the question of a meaning differential on the basis of location and affiliation – a question that did not figure into Johnson's otherwise astute analysis.

Diffusion Theory

The fact that gospel music has successfully traversed many cultural boundaries means that it has been subjected to the process of cultural diffusion. Anthropologist Gary Ferraro defines cultural diffusion as "the spreading of a thing, an idea, or a behavior pattern from one culture to another" (2001:350). Ferraro reminds the reader that only a relatively small percentage of cultural items in any given context are products of their own invention. The development of all societies is contingent upon the adoption of resources and items that hasten growth and spark creativity. This generally takes place according to patterns of diffusion that involve selectivity, reciprocity (between cultures, despite any technological disparity), and modification (2001:350-352). Like a tree that is transplanted from one soil to another, the steps involved in the diffusion process are of necessity complex in order to facilitate the chances of survival in a context foreign to the original one. Thus understanding observable patterns and trends inherent in the cross-cultural dissemination of products in general is germane to the study of gospel music's multi-contextual viability.

The most definitive summary into research regarding diffusion of innovation theory is propounded in Everett Rogers' authoritative work, *Diffusion of Innovations*. As a social change analysis predicated on social systems theory, Rogers' thesis regarding how innovations in actuality become diffused and adopted in different contexts provides useful categories in understanding the successful adoption of Black gospel music across cultural boundaries. The primary focus of Rogers' work deals with how the inception of a "perceived" new idea, that is, an innovation, becomes diffused among people, thus changing their habits, customs, ideas, practices, and so forth. The four elements entailed in the diffusion of innovations include: 1- the innovation itself, 2- the communication channels that facilitate the spread of an idea, 3- the rate of time involved from the innovation to the decision to adopt or reject, and 4- the social systems/structures that are featured in the process (Rogers 2003:11).

One of the many issues raised pertains to the relationship between an innovation and the felt need for change or adoption. Although marketing strategies are sometimes capable of creating the perception of need for a certain innovation, change likely occurs when the need or desire is genuine, or when the perceived new idea, metaphorically speaking, is able to "scratch where it itches." This relates to the first prominent characteristic of innovations: *relative advantage* (Rogers 2003:15). Other key characteristics of innovations according to Rogers' analysis include: *compatibility* with existing values, experiences, and needs; surmountable *complexity* (or relative simplicity); *trialability* (or testability); and *observability* (or visibility to others) (2003:15-16). Innovations that engender these characteristics are thus disseminated/diffused through communication channels and diffusion networks, most notably by way of opinion leaders and *heterophilous* contacts (i.e. persons from differing cultural, educational, and social backgrounds who interact), which enable an idea to transcend the barriers of culture, social class, etc. (2003:18-19). This does not preclude the presence of *homophily*, which acknowledges the diffusion of innovations among persons who are homogeneous in regard to background characteristics, such as education, social class, experience, etc.

A significant facet of Rogers' research entails the entire time-oriented process from innovation to the decision on behalf of the consumer to accept or reject the product. The "innovation-decision process" begins with *knowledge* of the innovation, which is initiated by need or an awareness of the idea. A complex issue arises when one attempts to diffuse knowledge of an innovation where there is no immediate perceived need. This leads to the second phase, namely *persuasion*, which is based on the ability to affect the overall attitude toward the concept/product. The next step involves the eventual *decision* whether to adopt or reject the idea – the latter consisting of both active rejection (rejection based on consideration of the idea) and passive rejection (non-consideration of the innovation). If the innovation is accepted, then it becomes *implemented* via some form of modification or re-invention, as the original concept is changed to fit the context. Finally, the innovation is reinforced in the *confirmation* stage, lest it eventually becomes discontinued either due to replacement, disenchantment, or in a few cases, forced discontinuance (Rogers 2003:20-21).

The telling aspect of the innovation-decision process is that the length of time required to pass through these sequenced stages varies greatly among persons. The rate of diffusion is contingent upon the varying ways individuals tend to respond to innovations, which Rogers has neatly divided into "adopter categories." *Innovators*, for example, tend to be "venturesome" risk-takers who dare to forge new paths without relying on majority opinion. They are visionary, though are often misunderstood and risk rejection by those who have not caught on to the nature of their idea (2003:282-283). *Early adopters* tend to be innovators themselves, as well as opinion leaders who perceive the advantage of the innovation while possessing the social skills needed to persuade others to follow. According to Rogers, innovators are often reliant upon early adopters since they are respected socially, and since their commitment to and implementation of an idea give the innovation credibility and integrity in the minds of others (2003:283). Therefore, early adopters tend to be the most potent *change agents* since they possess a certain ethos that catalyzes and facilitates diffusion in ways that radical innovators themselves can not. The *early majority* tend to be more deliberate and initially resistant to change, at least until the idea has been tried out and the element of uncertainty has been partially mitigated (2003:283-284). The *late majority* and *laggards* are the most resistant to change; the laggard's point of reference in refusing to adopt is the past, thus implying that they are ensconced in traditionalism (2003:284-285).

According to Rogers' analysis, the innovation movement from ideation to utilization generally follows a developmental pattern that, graphically speaking, resembles an S-shaped curve. Although there is variation in the slope of the "S" in accordance with the rapidity of adoption, there remains an identifiable pattern in the general diffusion process. This means that an innovation goes through a period of non-recognition before it gains momentum, followed by recognition and acceptance, and finally the point where the curve reaches its asymptote, marking the tapering off and completion of the process (Rogers 2003:23). As has already been noted in the case of gospel music', the process from non-recognition and non-acceptance to adoption can be painful for the innovators themselves, at least until other change agents among the early adopter category become involved.

A final element of diffusion according to Rogers' analysis involves the social system(s) within which a particular innovation becomes diffused. This is an important component since the system constitutes the boundaries within which the innovation is applied, and thereby defined and understood (Rogers 2003:24). Marketing strategists might refer to a particular system as a "target group," denoting the demographic or interest group that is perceived to be most likely to adopt a specific innovation, although the notion of "systems" takes on a much more abstract connotation in accordance with the philosophy of structuralism (Culler 1998:174, Gutting 1998:596). According to Rogers, the structures within a system, or the "patterned arrangements of the units within a system," promote predictability, thereby assisting the change agent in facilitating or enhancing the innovation-decision process (Rogers 2003:24). This means that understanding those structures within a social system becomes a crucial element in the overall communication and diffusion of an idea, practice, or behavior, even though variables within each system often make it difficult to discern structural patterns. As will be explored in a subsequent section, the diffusion of Black gospel music in countries like Denmark is likely ameliorated by cultural affects and traits that cause the music and participation in choirs to be particularly desirable among a diverse constituency. These factors, which include everything from globalization, to religious-cultural scripting, to certain social networking patterns, etc., are all contributing to the systemic favorability for the diffusion of an innovation such as a foreign ethnic and religious musical expression.

Before applying Rogers' theoretical framework to the specific case of Black gospel music diffusion in a northern European context, it is important to recognize a couple of potential flaws in the overall approach. Rogers himself acknowledges a certain pro-innovation bias in diffusion research (Rogers 2003:106). Although this bias is rarely stated explicitly, it is nevertheless present in the sometimes uncritical assumption that innovations are by nature good, and that acceptance of change and progress *de facto* are signs of virtue and intelligence (2003:288). In fairness to Rogers, he does note exceptions to the adoption of innovations, as in the case of the farmer whom he had wrongfully classified as a "laggard" for resisting the use of chemical agents that since have been banned (2003:193-194). However, there are many issues – from genetic engineering, to nuclear proliferation, to pharmaceutical inventions, *ad infinitum* – which imply that the acceptance of an innovation should not be considered in isolation from careful and deliberate ethical and moral consideration. Even certain ecclesiological innovations which may be popular for the time being may one day be exposed as deleterious to the church's witness in the long run by failing to account for how consumerism and the thirst for technological progress, which is incommensurate with society's moral and ethical development, are infiltrating the current ecclesiastical mindset. There is much taking place in the name of innovative church growth strategy, for example, which may be undermining the message and validity of Christian proclamation by filtering it through systems, such as "Big Business" or a particular political party, thus shifting the foundation of Christian faith to something that foundationally is not Christian.

In addition, as a systems approach, diffusion theory demonstrates the tendency to ignore the historical perspective in favor of an almost one-dimensional focus on innovation diffusivity as a coherent system. This relates to a general critique of structuralism[4] by poststructuralists for its lack of a diachronic or historical perspective (Gutting 1998:597). One wonders for example, if tradition plays any significant role in diffusion, besides its association with the resistance end on the adopter categories scale. Although this critique of diffusion theory's structuralist foundation is not entirely germane to the discussion of Black gospel music diffusion, it does point out that other perspectives, such as ethnohistorical analysis and the globalization forces behind meaning deconstruction/ reconstruction, are needed.

Black Gospel Diffusion: The Danish Case

Gospel music has diffused rapidly in Denmark since the early 1990's, as evidenced by the proliferation of gospel choirs, festivals, workshops, and the like. According to data collected and distributed on the Danish "Gospel Factory" website, there were 123 registered gospel choirs throughout the country in the year 2004, including choirs that had split into two groups due to size (Gospel Factory 2005, 2005a). More recent data indicates that by the end of 2006 the number of registered gospel choirs had decreased slightly to 105 (Gospel Factory 2007, 2007a). Whether or not this decrease is indicative of a trend that may signal the onset of saturation is impossible to determine at this point. There are still too many variables, such as the size of choirs (which are in constant fluctuation), the existence of choirs not registered officially, the inevitable ebb and flow throughout the diffusion process, etc., which preclude present conclusions regarding the S-curve trajectory. The fact that at least thirteen new choirs were formed between 2005 and 2006, including a number of children's and youth choirs, indicates that the diffusion process is not in recession.

Of the existing gospel choirs, information has been gathered, via the Gospel Factory website, the homepages of many of the individual groups, and personal contacts, regarding the year of origin of eighty-three choirs. This information is indicated in the following table:

Table 4.1: Year of Origin of Existing Gospel Choirs in Denmark

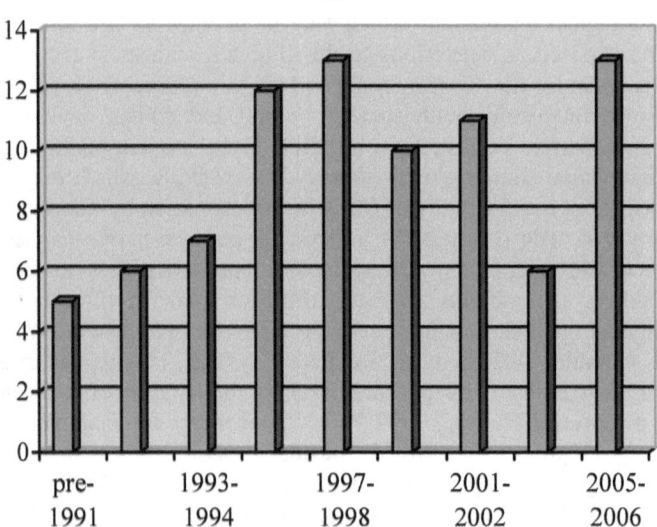

Source: www.gospelnet.dk

One must keep in mind several things: First, the data exists only on *existing* choirs (except for a single choir, *Nardus*, in Odense, that folded and restarted under new leadership a couple of years later), and therefore does not include choirs that were formed and since have disbanded. Second, it is difficult to classify pre-1991 choirs as gospel choirs by the standards and ethos set in this dissertation. A case in point involves the *Lusangi* gospel choir, located in the city of Kolding, in the Vejle area. Although the Danish YMCA/YWCA-affiliated choir itself has existed since 1976, it underwent a transformation in 1998, becoming aligned with the sound and ethos of gospel (Lusagi 2006). One of the oldest existing choirs, *Kefas*, associated with Jerusalem Methodist Church in Copenhagen and directed by Peter Steinvig, went through a similar transition in the early 1990's, although Steinvig maintains the choir has remained somewhat constant from its origin in 1975 to the present (Steinvig 2004).

Third, the historical correlation between the number of gospel choirs and actual membership is unknown. According to current data, interviews, and my own deductions, total gospel choir membership among the registered choirs is around 4,616 participants, plus fourteen choirs for which membership as of yet is unaccounted. Factoring in the number of attenders in unregistered choirs, the choirs whose actual membership is unknown, and other variables, such as those who sing in more than one choir and non-singers who work behind the scenes, one can assume that actual participation runs in the neighborhood of 5,000 persons. It is not clear to what extent membership tallies have fluctuated in recent years. Yet it can once again be surmised that gospel music/choir participation is still on the rise given the continued proliferation of gospel festivals and workshops throughout the country, where the number of actual participants (not including audiences) can sometimes exceed 1,000 (per festival), and the formation and growing popularity of gospel among a relatively new target group: children and youth.

The purpose of the data is not to create the illusion that this study provides an in-depth sociological analysis of gospel choir proliferation in Denmark. As noted, the data is still too incomplete and the timeframe from the advent of the gospel choir concept until the present is, relatively speaking, too short. Nevertheless, the information does paint in broad strokes a significant event that is underway and, as of yet, showing no real signs of atrophy. When considering the fact that what is taking place in Denmark is occurring in a number of other countries, in addition to the reality that the number of gospel choir participants alone would equal in membership one of the larger Danish Free churches, then the data more than legitimates the importance of research into this topic.

The Perceived Attributes of Gospel Music

According to Rogers, the popularity, acceptance and diffusion of innovations are framed by their relative *advantage* over preceding concepts, their *compatibility* with existing values and experiences, the *complexity* (or relative simplicity) involved with their usage, the *trialability* (or testability) of the innovation, and the degree of *observability* of the idea. These criteria provide a means of empirical analysis to determine the nature and extent of innovations as well as their ability to be diffused. In relation to gospel music in Denmark, it can be argued that each criterion is accounted for.

An implied hypothesis of this thesis is that participation in gospel choirs provides an alternate way of expressing Christian faith in a manner that respects those who are not Christians; it also relates to people in a way that is more suitable to those who can aptly be classified as Cultural Christians and postmoderns. Since Europeans in the late-modern/postmodern era have by-and-large relegated religion to the realm of private opinion and do not value tradition in the way it has been upheld in the past, the church is perceived as irrelevant.[5] The distinct advantage of gospel is the "come as you are" approach that allows freedom and latitude among those who attend, over and above a common interest in a particular music form, and the relative ability to sing (unless, of course, one is content supporting the choir in other ways).

Likewise, choirs provide the sort of social networking that often is not found in the Danish Folk Church. This means that conversations are able to take place in an environment where people do not necessarily feel threatened to express convictions that may not mesh with the mainstream theology of the church. Those who come generally feel very comfortable in coming. Further, participation in a gospel choir implies that people come due to a genuine interest in coming. There is very little sense of drudgery in showing up at a church for rehearsal, or attending a worship service where the choir will be singing. Interviewees often express a sense of joy in singing gospel, which is not often experienced when attending a normal church service in Denmark.

The gospel music movement does not constitute a complete break with the worldview assumptions of most Danes, although those who have insight into Danish culture may be somewhat mystified by the burgeoning interest in gospel. A more in depth analysis of Danish culture will be presented in Chapter Six, however a few insights at this point may help to illuminate the irony of gospel music in this context. In some regards, the gospel music genre is considered loud and boisterous, which in itself runs antithetical to a pronounced element of Danish culture. Culturally speaking, Danes value subtlety and irony, which is summed up by the word *Janteloven* (i.e., the "law of Jante"). Similar to the Japanese adage, "the nail that sticks out is the one that gets hit," Janteloven serves to harness individual expression and haughtiness in favor of the collective through use of ridicule and irony. The cultural principle permeates many things, including the value of quaintness, as evident, for example, in the size of their national symbol, "The Little Mermaid." Since gospel music, at least on the surface, entails little subtlety, some would wonder if its appeal signals a decided shift in Danish culture.

On the basis of systems theory and functionalism, it can be surmised that the compatibility of gospel music to Danish society most likely relates to other elements of their culture. First, the church still maintains an established position in society, in spite of its marginalization in terms of day to day life. Since Denmark's cultural undercurrent is and has been Christianity for about a millennium, the church is not a non-entity. This means that people in general are not offended by the thought of entering a church, and though Danes are not exactly enthusiastic about the church, the level of animosity against it is somewhat low. Second, Danish culture is very musical, as evidenced by their rich hymn and folk song traditions. The idea of musical innovations is not difficult to imagine in a country that encourages all forms of artistic expression, and even subsidizes such expressions very generously. Third, postmodernism and globalization are affecting Denmark as dramatically as any other Western country (cf. Chapter Seven), which means that the openness to cultural exchange and implementation of new concepts is at a peak. Fourth, Denmark, in spite of its embracing of socialism in terms of health care and other social issues, is also an individualistic society. Although Danes have a much higher sense of cultural identity than

Americans, for example, many elements of their culture are "fluid" rather than rigid, which makes the espousal or embracing of innovations more likely. These and other cultural features have created a milieu that has enhanced the adoption and spread of gospel music in this Scandinavian Country.

The degree of complexity of gospel music can be analyzed on several different levels. First, one should point out that participation in gospel choirs presupposes a degree of musical talent and interest, in addition to a special affinity for the gospel genre. This will, of course, limit the number of actual participants a great deal. Needless to say, this is likewise true of any musical style or art form. Within the church alone, "praise and worship" choruses, classical hymns/anthems, and Christian folk and children's songs appeal to different segments of people who attend. Since cultures in the West are not monolithic, including smaller countries like Denmark, there is no real possibility that any innovation involving a type of artistic expression will enjoy universal appeal. Having stated the obvious, gospel music has achieved a sort of pop status, which is testimony to its "palatability" and simplicity. A number of advertisements, including television commercials, for example, have utilized gospel music and choirs in some form or another. Two of Peter Steinvig's choirs, for example, including the one based in my former church in Copenhagen, were used in a 2001 television ad promoting a shopping mall in Copenhagen. This may (and perhaps should) be viewed as crass exploitation of gospel music; however, it does indicate how culturally integrated the sound is becoming. The degree of accessibility, however, is best conveyed by the appeal of the rhythms and the simplicity of the texts. Gospel music is relatively easy to sing, and though it is almost always performed in English, the concepts and words are not threatening to those who otherwise do not have a strong background in the language. In addition, the gospel message in the music is image-laden and expressive in ways that do not reflect the conceptual theology engendered by many homilies or traditional hymns. People can sing "Blessed Be the Rock," "Shackles," or "O Happy Day" again and again, and be free to be moved by the message, or simply sing and sway without any real regard for the message.

In terms of trialability, people are allowed to come and go as they please, without immediate pressure to sign up, at least until the trial period expires. Choirs that are more ambitious and maintain high standards of musical excellence are less flexible, but those who pass auditions and are chosen to participate in the elite choirs have usually already passed through a trial stage. A typical scenario in an average choir might begin with a telephone call to the church office (if the choir meets in a church) or the choir leader inquiring about when rehearsals are held. Often, others come as a direct result of an invitation from another choir member. The inquirer will be invited to observe a rehearsal, and if they feel comfortable right away, they may join the others from their voice group and attempt to sing along. During a "coffee break,"[6] there is ample opportunity to ask questions or talk with others. If the person is attracted to the experience, they will usually return the next week. Since some rehearsals begin with Scripture reading and a short devotional geared toward an "eclectic" group, the person will determine if this aspect is acceptable, and then decide whether or not to continue for a trial period. Although some choirs demand tryouts or only allow new members to join during distinct times (August and January, for example), others are open to new members throughout the choir season. Participation in concerts and other events is usually contingent upon familiarity with the material.

Since gospel music has become so common, the degree of observability is very high, especially in urban areas.[7] Concerts and gospel worship services take place in a number of churches, but the music has become so mainstreamed that performances often take place in areas of commerce, business parties, government functions, *ad infinitum*. The fact that gospel music is performed so frequently and by many different groups in various contexts means that there is a substantial degree of visibility.

Communication Channels

The process of communication utilized in diffusing the innovation of gospel music and choirs in Denmark has occurred through both homophilous and heterophilous contacts. The origin and development of *Kefas* provides a case in point. *Kefas* was founded in 1975, and in its nascent phase it was simply a youth choir affiliated with *Betania* Methodist Church in Copenhagen. Under the direction of Steinvig, the choir performed a variety of contemporary Christian folk and rock songs, which were popular in the 1970's. The choir was clearly grafted into the Methodist church, as the participants typically were members of one of the Methodist youth groups in the city. The choir grew, largely through personal contacts and via the internal church network of the Methodist Children's, Youth and Scouts organization (MBUF). The choir evolved over the next fifteen years, and in the process changed their home base to the more central Jerusalem Church, which is the oldest and largest Methodist church in Denmark. However, around 1990, Steinvig shared the vision of revamping the choir, thus changing the style to Black gospel. Since he had learned the style while studying music in the U.S. and had known of gospel music's popularity in other parts of Scandinavia, as well as prior attempts to diffuse the idea in Denmark, he and a task force presented the idea at the choir's annual organizational meeting. The committee consisted of Steinvig, the choir director, and the leaders elected by the choir at their previous meeting. The choir adopted their recommendation and made the commitment to move in that direction. Within a short time, the communication network became heterophilous since the choir moved beyond the relatively obscure Free church (Methodist) and then caught the attention of the music community. Young and talented musicians were then given a chance to perform the style, and *Kefas* had undergone a metamorphosis (Steinvig 2004).

In time, the choir began to network with other choirs, which began to be noticed by segments of the media, thus widening the channels of communication. Articles were written in newspapers and magazines, and larger events received news coverage on Danish television. By the time of the first CGF in 1992, gospel was recognized as a legitimate art/music form in Denmark, as well as an innovative expression of Christian faith. As a result, new choirs were formed to accommodate the burgeoning interest, and contacts were made due to a growing array of communication channels that incorporated both personal and impersonal means.

Today, gospel choirs continue to grow as a result of transfer of information from media to opinion leaders, and from opinion leaders to their followers via interpersonal influence. The problem does not seem to be generating enough interest to start a choir, but rather maintaining enthusiasm once it passes the honeymoon phase. At this point, choirs are dependent upon energetic and talented leadership as well as continued innovation in order to avoid stagnation and decline. Likewise, local choirs sometimes tend to become more homogeneous as choir members establish social relations within the organization and invite likeminded friends and associates to join. Thus diffusion conduits within each individual choir tend to be more homophilous, while choir leaders, who likely are well-trained, connected with larger networks, and enjoy esteemed status in the greater gospel community, draw people from outside the normal social sphere. Churches that offer support to the gospel choirs that are "housed" in their facilities widen the communication process by incorporating their realm of influence, thus attracting other potential participants in addition to increasing the audience at gospel events.

Pastors play a pivotal role as change agents, since their attitude toward gospel music and the choirs influence the attitude of their congregations in the long run. The failure of clergy to support this form of Christian expression can and does lead to the disengagement of choirs from the church, thus mitigating the nexus between gospel choirs and the church. If the choir, for example, is not invited to sing at church functions and the pastor does not interact with the choir in any other way, then choir members often will interpret this as a negative signal. It is not coincidental that gospel music flourishes in churches where the choirs are truly wanted. Thus the continued harmony between gospel choirs and the church is dependent somewhat on favorable promotion by opinion leaders in the church and their sanctioning of the seeker-oriented disposition of those who often comprise a large constituency within each group.

Time-frame from Innovation to Decision

As table 4.1 indicates, the time involved in the rate of adoption from the point of first knowledge to the actual implementation of gospel music can be traced in Denmark from around 1990. Unlike innovations that have emerged with no prior history, such as the internet, gospel has been around, relatively speaking, for a long time. The major question has been whether or not a music genre and all its offshoots could be transformed into an indigenous expression of faith and life in the Danish context. Since gospel music has been unambiguously linked with the ethos of the African-American ethnic and religious experience, Danes often have presupposed that it represents a type of expression that is foreign to Danish culture, no matter whether the initial reaction has been positive or negative. Thus the rate of adoption perhaps was initially impacted by the fact that a great deal of cultural reconfiguration has had to take place before the diffusion of this cultural implant could occur. One particular friend and observer summed it up succinctly when he stated: "We Danes are (historically) peasants. No Dane is too far removed from the farm. Gospel music is just too damned boisterous and happy for many of us!"

According to Rogers, the innovation-decision process involves a series of steps that, conceptually speaking, entail knowledge, persuasion, decision, implementation, and confirmation. The diffusion of gospel music can certainly be traced along these lines. Knowledge of gospel in Denmark began as it did throughout much of Europe: via concert tours from known ambassadors of gospel music and Black spirituals. Records indicate that Mahalia Jackson visited the country in the 1950's, and there was a subsequent visit by gospel artist, Jester Hairston (Nielsen 2005:98). However, the primary innovator and change agent in Denmark's gospel music history is gospel diva, Etta Cameron (1939-present).

Etta Cameron was born in the Bahamas and moved to Miami, Florida, at age nine. She grew up as an African American in a Baptist and musical family, and began to sing in a Methodist church choir at around age ten. She developed into an accomplished jazz singer, and visited Denmark for the first time as a guest artist in the mid-1960's. She moved permanently to the country in 1972. Although the original intention was to stay for only a short period of time, the opportunity to create avenues for her favorite musical genre, gospel music, became too compelling. Cameron was knighted by Queen Margrethe of Denmark in the early 1990's for "outstanding achievement in music," and has become a cultural icon, constantly touring throughout the country (and abroad) as solo artist, as leader of the gospel choir, "Voices of Joy," and as headliner for "The Etta Cameron Jazz Group." As a regular on the popular weekly TV program/talent show, "Scenen er Din" ("The Stage is Yours"), her often quoted ditty, "Du får et stort fem tal af mig" ("You get five big stars from me!") likewise has become imbedded in popular culture. In addition to all her accomplishments, Cameron is also an entrepreneur, owning the "Americana" food and specialty shop in downtown Copenhagen.

According to my November 2006 interview, Cameron revealed that the onset of her gospel career in Denmark was far from easy. When asked how she was received in the late 1960's and early 1970's, she responded, "I was not wanted, especially in the churches! Ministers, organists, and perish clerks rejected me totally at that time" (Cameron 2006). This was painfully ironic, noted Cameron, since she often was invited to sing jazz in churches, in spite of the non-Christian content of the lyrics, while her gospel music received a cold shoulder. It was around the mid- to late 1970's that she began to notice a turnaround. During that time, she was increasingly invited to sing spirituals – first in concert venues, and then in churches – and within time, the ordinarily staid congregations began to clap to the music and applaud. To her knowledge, this had never happened before in a Danish church prior to the late 1970's. She added, "It was a real fight to get to this point."

Cameron's background reveals that early innovators must often bear the brunt of criticism and rejection before a degree of acceptance and early adoption begin to sway public opinion in a favorable direction. In her case, a period of about ten years passed from the time of her initial attempts to sing gospel music before Danish audiences/congregations to the formation of her first gospel choir around 1980 – which Cameron contends was the first truly Black gospel music choir in the country (Cameron 2006). The "X" factor, of course, was the reaction of the Danish Folk Church during this time frame and beyond. The reluctance or unwillingness of the church power structure to embrace Cameron's otherwise very traditional gospel music repertoire reinforces the notion that ecclesiastical institutions are exceedingly slow to adopt (or even adjust) to social movements and innovations, thus conveying the classic characteristics of late-adopters and laggards. The fact that Cameron was persistent in her efforts to form a nexus between gospel music/choirs and the church likely was pivotal in establishing the Danish gospel ethos as a primarily Christian expression, in spite of the early response of many church leaders. Her background as an African American and cross-cultural transplant meant that she has been strategically positioned to facilitate heterophilous communication as bridge-builder between the original (African-American) gospel music context and the new context. However, as a result of her capacity to become culturally assimilated, as well as her tireless efforts to construct a gospel music culture, Cameron has functioned as both primary innovator and change agent, together with the concert promoters and other gospel music visionaries from Denmark.

Although Cameron is widely regarded as the "Queen of Gospel" in Denmark, other musicians were able to pick up the gospel sound and reinvent it for growing Danish audiences. Some, like Cameron, were cultural transplants; however, the Danish gospel movement was garnered by a number of indigenous leaders. One of those, as mentioned, has been Peter Steinvig. As a choir director, pianist and accomplished church organist, Steinvig was immersed in the church music scene, which enabled him to gain access to musical strains from other parts of the globe. During a study sabbatical at Duke University in 1986, he became better acquainted with the gospel style and was able to establish contacts with gospel music directors who were able to foster his vision for Denmark. In addition to *Kefas*, Steinvig leads two other gospel choirs: *Saints and Sinners*, from the now defunct Wesley Methodist church in Gladsaxe, Copenhagen, and *Grace*, which is stationed at the Karlslunde Strand Folk Church.

It was perhaps Steinvig's vision for and implementation of the Copenhagen Gospel Festival that best catalyzed gospel music in the early phase and created a new accessibility within Danish society. Since its inaugural year, CGF has attracted some of the biggest names in gospel music from the U.S., Britain, and elsewhere, who in turn have been instrumental in the diffusion process. A frequent CGF guest leader, Gerome Bell, from Chicago, reflected on the evolution of gospel music interest in Denmark from the time of his first visit in 1992 to his most recent in 2005. In an October 2005 interview, Bell expressed his positive assessment over the development of the talent level, enthusiasm, and authenticity. He added that the sight of "white Europeans" singing Black gospel is no longer, and perhaps never was, an anomaly (Bell 2005). Of course, Bell's association with Steinvig over the years has provided the channel through which this gospel innovator was able to diffuse the music style and message in Denmark.

Since the inception of CGF in 1992, festivals have been established throughout much of the country, including: Aarhus, Southern Jutland, Roskilde, Kolding, Odense, Amager, and elsewhere. Although Steinvig has not directly been integral to the emergence and administration of other festivals, his early innovations have propelled the movement and given rise to new leaders. It has been his ability as a musician, experience as a choir leader, passion for learning gospel from authentic vanguards of the genre, strong Christian faith, and status as bridge-builder between Denmark and the international music scene that have catapulted him, among others, to the acknowledged position of *primus modem* of the movement.

In more recent years, the name Hans Christian Jochimsen has become a staple in gospel music circles. As a choir leader, composer, and primary innovator, Jochimsen began his musical career as a classical pianist. After becoming exposed to the *Oslo Gospel Choir* while working as a piano teacher, Jochimsen began to pick up the style. As he stated, regarding his transition to gospel music, "it just seemed right" (Jochimsen 2006). In 1993, Jochimsen started the *Going Up* choir in Aarhus, which has now grown to over three-hundred singers. Today he leads four choirs, including the *Copenhagen Gospel Voices*, which is home-base for over six-hundred singers. In addition to leading choirs and countless workshops, he is the primary administrator of the *Gospel Factory* network, which, among other things, has both monitored and promoted the Danish gospel movement. Several other well-known gospel arrangements, including *Summer Gospel* and festivals in Århus and Copenhagen can be attributed to his leadership. Like Steinvig, Jochimsen maintains a strong connection between the content of Christian faith and the form of Black gospel music. His choirs are open to people of all religious or non-religious persuasion, who come to experience the Christian message in ways that promote joy in a non-judgmental environment.

There are many other important innovators and leaders of the gospel music movement in Denmark whom have, in their own right, shaped gospel choirs with their own innovations. Names such as Carsten Morsbøl, Lars Jochimsen, Lene Matthiesen Nørrelykke, Claes Wegner, Albert Campos, Bob Bailey, Janne Wind, among a host of others, are associated with significant contributions to the diffusion and contextualization process in Denmark. The leaders also bring diverse perspectives in regard to the position of Christian faith in the overall gospel-mix. In addition to their leadership, they have all had a persuasive effect (cf. Rogers 2003:174-177). Other agents of persuasion in the early stages have been interested pastors, laypersons, gospel concert promoters, as well as the musicians and leaders themselves. The success of *Kefas*, for example, was enhanced greatly when the pastor of the Jerusalem congregation, Christian Alsted, legitimated the choir as an outreach focus in the eyes of the otherwise tradition-based congregation. He accomplished this through personal involvement, including contact with the members, and leadership on the CGF planning committee. By making the choir part of his work schedule, the relationship has been reciprocal since the members have not had to second-guess the interest of the church in them due to the weekly presence of the pastor, as well as the scheduling of events such as concerts and Sunday evening gospel worship services in the church. The gospel services in particular, which take place once a month except during the summer, usually are better attended than the principal Sunday morning service. Of course, the involvement of key laypersons is necessary for the eventual integration of choir members into the church, which is an ongoing challenge in the Danish context.

Leadership is likewise making a significant impact on newer innovations in relation to gospel music diffusion, such as the formation of gospel churches. As mentioned, the idea of forming an ecclesial structure centering on involvement with a gospel choir and interest in attending gospel events is in a nascent stage, but the vision is beginning to be tested. A potential model is emerging in connection with the Copenhagen Free Church, under the leadership of Pastor Jørgen Mortensen and Julie Lindell. The notion was conceived with direction from Hans Christian Jochimsen, who had contacted Mortensen about the possibility of using the church facilities to house one of his fast-growing choirs, *The Copenhagen Gospel Voices*. Catalyzed by the *Summer Gospel* camp,[8] the choir grew to around two-hundred and fifty singers. Since many of the members were recognized as "soul-searching," Jochimsen recommended the initiation of gospel worship services, which were held monthly over a period of time. Mortensen admitted that tensions mounted because respect for the gospel ethos of "come-as-you-are" and "unconditional acceptance" contravened his driving impulse to "evangelize" the choir. Jochimsen's intentions, which precluded overt evangelism, came in conflict with Mortensen's own evangelistic impulses. Mortensen likewise experienced reticence on behalf of his own congregation to accept the gospel constituency on their own terms.

After working through these conflicts, a new choir of around fifty participants was formed under the direction of Lindell. This became the foundation for a new congregation. On the basis of questionnaires and personal contacts, the gospel worship service concept was expanded to include communion, liturgy, and other rituals, and began to meet more frequently. As Mortensen stated it, "The gatherings developed a life of their own." As a result, a new congregation which propagates the Christian message and sacraments through the medium of gospel music was started in 2006, meeting twice a month in the Copenhagen Free Church facility, and growing primarily through first time confessions of Christian faith (Mortensen 2007).

Mortensen's own journey into gospel leadership reveals not only the importance of visionary leadership, but the necessity of leaders to adapt the gospel ethos, even when it comes in conflict with one's own style and theological conviction. Presiding over communion services, for example, where many of the communicants were not confessing Christians constituted a barrier that Mortensen admittedly had to overcome. This meant a sort of "conversion" on his own part had to take place in order to facilitate and shape the communication of Christian truth in the inherited context. In true missiological fashion, Mortensen and many others like him have demonstrated that effective leadership entails a combination of persuasive ability and contextual understanding – factors that are integral to gospel choir (and gospel church) proliferation.

Besides the role of leadership, the emphasis on talent and professionalism constitutes another persuasive element. A number of choirs, such as *Sound of Gospel* in Copenhagen, *Kefas,* and Jochimsen's *Opstand*, have ambitiously maintained a high level of ability, as evidenced by recordings and high-profile concerts. The insistence on ability, however, can necessitate that the choir implement a policy of exclusion. My current choir, *Noiz*, is a middle-tiered choir, but nevertheless demands an audition before membership can be accepted. Occasionally, willing participants are turned away because they cannot pass the audition, or are invited to support the choir in ways other than singing.[9] Some leaders, including Steinvig and Jochimsen, have started gospel choirs which have compromised the talent level for the sake of inclusion. On the other hand, the emphasis on professionalism has served to weed out potential over-adoption or involvement by those who otherwise are not capable of adopting the innovation of gospel, such as (in extreme cases) the tone-deaf. When choirs serve a more decided social/communal function, or some other purpose besides the music itself, then the weeding out process becomes much more complex.

Professionalism has fostered the appreciation of gospel by a more critical group, which has opened the door to heterophilous contacts. Because of the overall presentation, the more "serious" choirs have come across as much more than the effort of a provincial or local group; they work as instruments of persuasion, particularly by appealing to those outside the immediate contact circles of the participants. Choirs that are not as performance-oriented persuade in other ways, notably through the benefits of friendships, closer contact with a church (which is not a given in a State/Folk Church driven context), and the accessibility of gospel to those who are not among the musical elite. The involvement of some talented performers often is needed in order to facilitate the rate of adoption, since the ability to emulate the style and learn the music is an exceedingly slow process without internal leaders.

The decision stage takes place in various ways. Most commonly, interested persons are invited to attend during a trial period before being asked to commit. In my former choir, *Saints & Sinners*, the trial stage could last up to a month, during which time the person involved would have an opportunity to talk with other choir members, get familiar with the songs, learn about the level of involvement and commitment demanded of the choir, make judgments about whether the Christian content is acceptable or not, and make general assessments regarding one's own desire to continue. In certain cases, each visitor is greeted very warmly at the beginning of the rehearsal through words of welcome and a hearty applause by the choir members in attendance, and the visit has no strings attached. When the trial phase ends, the person is expected to join the choir. This involves paying membership dues for each season (spring and fall), and purchasing a choir shirt (or other regalia) to be used during performances. Membership costs about fifty dollars per season, and is used to offset administrative expenses, compensate the leaders and musicians (when an honorarium is appropriate), pay for registration in the Methodist church's MBUF, provide funds for trips, and compensate the local church or meeting place proprietor for heating expenses. Sometimes, people choose to discontinue involvement, usually due to other time commitments, but sometimes because of structural or philosophical disagreements. Those who continue become officially registered with the choir and are encouraged to remain faithful to their decision by attending rehearsals on a regular basis and support the choir at all other functions.

The implementation of gospel music relates directly to participation in rehearsals, concerts, worship services, and other occasions for gathering. Since the turnover rate is at times fairly rapid, there is a need to keep old material fresh and constantly hold newer members informed regarding the structure, process and content.

The style of music employed by gospel constitutes an intriguing area of study. Etta Cameron's repertoire, for example, is strictly traditional; in fact, it could sometimes be classified more as "spirituals" than gospel. As a result of newer innovations in gospel, including the infusion of Hip Hop, R & B, and other influences, many choirs are constantly challenged to revamp their repertoire in order to stay up-to-date. Some choir leaders choose to maintain a more traditional base, which means resisting some of the more contemporary directions in the musical genre. As a result, choirs tend to be somewhat segmented in terms of age differential, as younger pop-influenced participants tend to be attracted to the more energetic and "funky" rhythms characteristic of the Hip-Hop influenced style, which is also infusing Rap. Kirk Franklin is a name in gospel that often resonates with a younger gospel audience. However, many other choirs adhere more closely to the roots of gospel while introducing variations on occasion. My current choir actually utilizes a number of songs classified as "Scandinavian Gospel," which are written by gospel composers in Sweden, Norway, and Denmark, and are on occasion written in the indigenous language. The emphasis in all cases remains on vocal harmonies and employment of gospel ballads, in addition to the more frenetic songs typically associated with gospel music. At any rate, gospel music in any style up to this point has only rarely compromised the distinctly Christian content of its message, and most of the choir leaders that I have contacted remain steadfast about either holding regular devotionals or promoting conversation in an effort to preserve the connection with Christian faith.

The confirmation step is likely the most revealing in terms of the overall acceptance and impact of the movement. As stated before, the turnover rate is rather high, which means that the fluctuation between those coming in and those moving on is constant, depending on the circumstances. It is the general understanding that most choirs demand a commitment, in spite of the "come as you are" attitude, which varies according to the level of performance and the number of engagements. As a result, those who adopt totally tend to be very loyal, on the level of anyone steadfastly committed to a local church. In my current choir, *Noiz*, only a few of the core members have participated since their inception in 1992. Over the past sixteen years, the average membership has fluctuated from fifteen to around fifty, and is currently (2008) around forty-five; eight persons have been with the choir since the first couple of years, most of those being members of the host Methodist church. Most of those tend to be committed

Christians, who perceive gospel as something larger than music and performance.

Every season, in every choir, new faces come, and others disappear. The biggest reason for the failure to reconfirm or the tendency to reverse one's decision has to do with some sort of life change. Switching jobs, moving further out of the city, getting married or having children, physical or psychological illness, or some other commitment that involves time and energy have been known to enervate one's level of participation, thus causing the person to drop out, either temporarily or permanently. Another common reason for reversing the prior decision deals with a festering disenchantment with the structure of the choir, including leadership changes or conflicts. If one, for example, is more interested in a higher level of performance and less socializing during breaks, then *Saints & Sinners* would be much less preferable than *Kefas*. If one grows weary of the song selection, or the laborious attention given to learning new songs, then this might affect the overall attitude.

Leadership often comes into play after one's decision to commit to the innovation. If a participant, for example, realizes in time that the style of leadership constitutes a hindrance to one's own expectations, then conflicts can arise which will lead to withdrawal. Several choirs which have disbanded in recent years did so because of either lack of leadership or conflict with leadership style. Steinvig's leadership mode, at least when he is conducting the middle-tiered *Saints & Sinners*, tends to appeal to "Type B" personalities, meaning rehearsals are more loosely structured in order to accommodate impulsiveness, laughter, and interaction. Those who are "Type A" and expect more rigidity and structure often are disappointed. My current choir has been, until recently, led democratically by three females, all different in style and approach. This solution was an ongoing source of both contentment and frustration. Stylistic differences may be difficult to detect in the beginning, but over time may create problems.

Another phenomenon relates to the sort of clientele that are attracted to gospel. Gospel choirs often cater to those with a "seekers" disposition. They can be young or old, as evidenced by the fact that members of my current choir range in age from sixteen to seventy. The eternal dilemma in "truth-seeking" is that after a period of time, the initial commitment becomes drudgery, thus promoting the need to move on. The essence is in seeking and not finding, which may be descriptive of many postmodern people in general. On occasion, the Christian foundation of gospel choirs winds up being an insurmountable impediment. One particular interviewee, a caregiver for several physically handicapped persons, was led to a choir by one of his patients. He was initially attracted to the warm and open atmosphere, and quickly assimilated the gospel style. However, he was a staunch adherent of New Age religion and philosophy, and often was very outspoken about his convictions. Since a number of gospel singers in Denmark have had some extent of involvement in the New Age milieu, it is not often regarded as a bone of contention (cf. M. Lewis 2004). In typical postmodern fashion, people often react to New Age apologetes the same way that they react to Christian evangelists – by remarking, "That's interesting," or, "That's your opinion." Yet, he felt that the prevalence of the Christian message in the devotionals, the music itself, the apologetic approach espoused by evangelical Christian choir members, and the number of performances in church contexts was too imposing for his taste, and he felt more and more like an outcast. After about a year, he opted for discontinuance. His story is perhaps a bit unusual since many who find Christianity thoroughly offensive or unpalatable never adopt in the first place.

An issue that demands careful attention and scrutiny in regard to continued confirmation deals with the fact that the innovation of gospel music in Denmark no longer is a new idea. As choirs become older and gospel becomes more passé, the need for reinventing (or re-implementing) and re-contextualizing becomes stronger, especially in a culture that is exposed to change occurring with unprecedented rapidity. As other forms of artistic expression gain precedence, it is questionable whether or not gospel in Denmark can be transferred by generations. A number of churches or gospel leaders have piloted youth gospel choirs in recent years, which seem to be gaining momentum in light of the sheer number of choirs started for children and youth, and the emergence of at least one youth gospel festival. It should be noted that many adherents are older teenagers and young adults, suggesting that confirmation and routinization are not just occurring with a particular age-based demographic. However, given the fact that musical styles tend to change very rapidly, it is still difficult to assess the staying power of a genre that has only enjoyed prominence in society for around two decades. Likewise, since gospel encompasses much more than music, but also relates to social networking and a "non-judgmental, acceptance-oriented" form of Christian witness, assessments should keep in mind the holistic appeal of the movement. The confirmation step must be monitored carefully, and attention must be given to the degree of continued commitment and rate of discontinuance, and how they reflect the ongoing development, or eventual stagnation, of the innovation.

According to Rogers, innovations generally follow developmental patterns that, graphically speaking, resemble an S-shaped curve. His research concludes that the diffusion of any idea eventually will reach a point of saturation, where the innovation begins to stagnate or decline before picking up momentum again, which in turn invariably leads to another ebb. As stated, it may be too early to chart the overall course of the gospel movement in Denmark. Assessment of indications and tendencies might entail a degree of subjectivity, such as grading changes in the overall atmosphere or determining the general "feeling" toward gospel in all of its manifestations. Based on enthusiasm toward and participation in festivals and workshops, as well as the continued formation of new choirs, there has not been a significant lull from 1990 to the present, except in the number of choirs started in the years 2003-2004 (cf. table 4.1). Although CGF concert attendance seems to have decreased a bit in recent years, other events have emerged to more than pick up the slack. It is never a problem attracting the biggest names in gospel worldwide to all of the major events. An anomaly occurred during the 10th Anniversary of *CGF* in 2001. In light of the global situation following September 11, many of the artists, particularly from the U.S., opted at the last minute to cancel their trip, creating an air of uncertainty. The festival carried on as Etta Cameron filled in as a last minute replacement, and was received very warmly. As the U.S. began its invasion of Afghanistan, the Festival continued, although the effects of the global crisis were acknowledged and felt.

The ebb and flow of the gospel movement perhaps can best be traced by following the development of the choirs themselves. When looking at each constituted gospel choir individually, it is clear that the path has been far from linear. Groups have come and gone, which alone indicates that there has not been unilateral success. The story of *Saints & Sinners* provides some insights into the growth and dissemination of the innovation. The choir was formed in 1994 by Steinvig, who was interested in giving the newly relocated Gladsaxe Methodist Church (formerly Betania and Golgata Methodist churches in downtown Copenhagen) a boost in their outreach potential. Some members of *Kefas* were encouraged to join in order to give the newly formed choir a talent base and additional leadership. After about a year, the choir grew from about twenty-five to around forty (unofficially), and continued to increase steadily through the next several years. Official records were kept beginning in 1998 with the formation of their constitution and the adoption of their name. Membership topped out in the year 2000 at sixty-six, and has since averaged between forty and fifty participants.

Reasons for the slight downswing relate to several factors, including the loss of some of the core members due to personal matters. However, at the time of my departure in July 2002, there were slight murmurings about the waning enthusiasm in the choir. A planned trip to the U.S. originally did not materialize as expected, and the fact that the capable leader of the choir also was leading two other gospel choirs in addition to his full-time position as church organist and musician contributed to the plateau in membership and enthusiasm. A U.S. tour did finally come to fruition in 2004, which I helped to arrange while studying in the U.S., together with Steinvig and a planning group. This led to a new level in both commitment and enthusiasm, as well as a noticeable improvement in the choir's overall performance.

After that time, Steinvig took a one-year sabbatical from all choir engagement, which led to a period of stagnation until his eventual return in January 2006. More recently (October 2006), the Methodist church in Gladsaxe folded and fused together with the larger Jerusalem church, creating renewed uncertainty regarding the location of the choir and its ability to continue. *Saints & Sinners* is just one story out of many, but the trends probably relate very favorably to other choirs that deal with waning excitement following the initial growth stage, subsequent challenges to rekindle enthusiasm and commitment by finding new ways to implement the concept for old and new members alike, and the capacity to overcome structural and leadership problems, in addition to unforeseen circumstances.

Adopter Categories

It is somewhat difficult to assess the rate of adoption of gospel music according to adopter categories. One of the reasons is that acceptance of gospel music constitutes a subjective opinion, which can rise or diminish almost from day to day. In other words, someone who is enamored with gospel at one moment may find the next concert unappealing and therefore change from adopter to critic. My own documentation verifies this, as several "enthusiastic" interviewees within the past two years have dropped out of their respective choirs, citing "burnout." Unlike adopting a farming innovation or something else that is measured in concrete results, the acceptance of gospel is measured also in terms of "attitudes" and "feelings," in addition to actual numbers of people joining choirs and attending concerts.

Since the gospel music movement originally sprang from the church, one possible way of employing the adopter categories method is to analyze the diffusion of gospel among congregations that were not integral to the innovation. Once again, *Saints & Sinners* and their affiliate church in Gladsaxe provide relevant case study material. When I first arrived as pastor of the congregation in August, 1996, the choir had existed for almost two years, although they had not yet become officially organized. During my inaugural Sunday, the choir sang several songs, at my request. Though the general tone of the worship service was very upbeat and celebratory, the mood changed as the choir began to sing. As the fifteen or so singers were "belting out" high-energy tunes to the rhythmic and accomplished piano playing of Steinvig, the majority of the congregation sat glum-faced and unresponsive. A couple of people actually walked out of the sanctuary while the choir was performing, claiming later that the "decibel level crossed the pain threshold" for them. It was clear to me from the beginning that many in my new congregation had not embraced the gospel choir. After the worship service, as all in attendance entered the fellowship hall and sat around tables while enjoying refreshments and conversation (a tradition in most Northern European Free churches), the people were segregated. Almost no interaction took place between choir members and members of the congregation, except for the three members of the congregation who sang in the gospel choir.

On another occasion, I had an opportunity to question members from the church about their response to gospel music. According to many of the elderly/senior members, their music was "obstreperous, unrefined, and foreign." They sang exclusively in English, which was a huge impediment for those who either could not understand the texts or believed that church music should be sung in their native language. Some complained that some choir members were not trained in proper church etiquette, which created awkward situations. The fact that a large percentage of the choir members at the time were smokers, for example, and were uninhibited about smoking in the foyer immediately prior to entering the sanctuary, was interpreted as insolence.

Some of the young adults in the congregation, who were no strangers to adolescent rebellion and counter-cultural lifestyles, nevertheless did not embrace the choir either. They claimed the music was "superficial" and "too simplistic."

They were accustomed to different genres, such as Christian folk songs/melodies and more rock-influenced music, as well as traditional hymns. They were suspicious of texts that they considered "lacked content," and were especially critical of a related Christian genre, *Praise and Worship* music. Gospel was still too foreign for them, even though they understood the language and respected African-American culture. Subsequent interviews and conversations with pastors who similarly serve churches that house gospel choirs across the denominational spectrum have given uncannily similar accounts.

As a result of my observations and the negative feedback from a large constituency within the congregation, I committed myself during my six year tenure at the church to building a bridge between the gospel choir and the congregation. Thus I assumed the role of culture broker and opinion leader. I became active in the choir, which met in the church building on Thursday evenings from 7:30 – 9:30 p.m., and filled in regularly at concerts as bass guitarist. Eventually, as I got to know the choir members and gained their trust, I fielded as many questions and concerns from the choir about the church as I did from the church about the choir. I did not act alone. Several of the early adopters were likewise participating in the choir and were attempting to influence and shape attitudes. There were several other influential persons in the congregation who were outspoken in their support of the choir, and used every opportunity to confront those who were not. The primary innovator, Steinvig, was also raised in a Methodist parsonage family, and was likewise influential as an opinion leader. However, his primary concern was the promotion of gospel and the training of his three choirs, not the opinions of those who did not adopt. The early adopters who also sang in the choir all had leadership positions in the church and were likely candidates to facilitate a change of heart among the early and late majority.

As the choir was asked to participate more regularly at our worship services, attitudes began to soften gradually yet noticeably. The key issue was missional, not personal preference in church music. Once the early and late majority realized that the choir constituted a constituency of unreached people who were suddenly in contact with "our" church, an interest was kindled. By their mere presence in the sanctuary during times of worship, the participation of the choir offered insights into how to reach people for the Gospel who ordinarily are closed to traditional forms of church and Christian outreach – that is, by allowing them to take part (or "belong") without requiring that they first "believe." As familiarity developed and relationships were formed, the choir became more than a group of "performers" to church members, and church members were gradually perceived as more hospitable by the choir. The fact that choir members in general are only rarely integrated into church membership continues to be a source of misunderstanding for many congregations, which indicates that gospel choirs constitute, at least in the minds of Christians who are non-church attenders, an alternative to the institutional church.

Conversations and confrontations with late adopters and laggards continued for years. To them, gospel music was not the "Gospel." The uninhibited style of the music, the "unrefined" behavior of certain people, the "swinging, swaying, and hand-clapping," and a number of other intangibles presented "roadblocks" for those who otherwise were not inclined to accept. However, early adopters, including opinion leaders, used every opportunity to defend the choir and gospel music as a legitimate Christian expression, even in a traditional church setting. When I left the congregation in 2002 after six years of ministry there, the choir was generally well-received by the church members, but was not really an integrated part of the church's overall ministry. My successor likewise participated in the choir and received a couple of choir members into the church on confession of faith, but this did not amount to a significant trend. The unwillingness of choir participants to join established churches is not unusual, although some churches experience more moderate success at surmounting barriers between choirs and the host congregations. The Methodist church in Odense is providing such an example, as a gospel choir (*Emmau*s) has recently been formed from their existing choir (*Nardus*) and beyond for the purpose of Sunday worship involvement. However, similar attempts by many other churches have not been successful.

According to the rate of adoption of gospel music and the choir itself by the Gladsaxe congregation, a pattern emerged along the lines that Rogers predicts. Since early adopters were few in the beginning, the acceptance of the innovation was a slow process, taking at least a couple of years before improvement could be observed. However, the unwavering commitment of key leaders, such as the choir leader, the pastor, and outspoken lay persons, gave the phenomenon credibility in the minds of those who were not prepared to embrace gospel with their hearts. In time, the early and late majority "got on board" as they realized that the issue was not just about music, but involved deeper matters of Christian faith, such as outreach, hospitality, community, and love for neighbor. The fact that gospel concerts could draw more people to the church than regular worship services caused many to realize that the choir itself is an effective instrument in Christian outreach. Thus, after about three to four years, *Saints & Sinners* no longer stirred controversy and was accepted by most in the congregation. A few laggards remained, but their voices on the issue increasingly were regarded as insignificant. On the whole, the instance of the diffusion of gospel music within a particular local context seemed to illustrate ideally the S-shaped model of adoption and normalcy, that is, the process from knowledge to implementation, as well as the varying rate of acceptance among members of my former constituency.

The Consequences of Gospel as an Innovation

According to Rogers, *consequences* are "the changes that occur to an individual or to a social system as a result of the adoption or rejection of an innovation" (2003:30-31). They can, of course, be desirable or undesirable, or more to the point with gospel choirs in Denmark, "anticipated or unanticipated." The latter categories are perhaps most relevant since it would be hard to imagine before the early 1990's that the gospel music movement would create such a splash in a part of the world that some analysts would term "post-Christian."

The fact that so many people would be attracted to a form of music that glorifies God with such transparent expression, despite the fact that many who sing would not classify themselves as "believers," was clearly unanticipated and unexpected. Many who are integrally involved in the movement claim unabatedly that God is using gospel to bring renewal to the church, as well as to a previously unreached segment of the population at large. Those who have experienced traditional worship services, especially in the Danish Folk Church, often attach the descriptors "boring," "unengaging," or "irrelevant" to the experience. As stated previously, worship in a Northern European context is geared almost solely to the cognitive dimension of faith. Liturgies tend to be long and routine; prayers are often read from a prayer manual; sermons often use (Lutheran) theological constructs and (Reformation) church history as primary reference points, while neglecting entirely contemporary human experience and contextual references; hymns reflect a musical style and textual formulations that seem anachronistic to many except the few who adhere to this high-church cultural manifestation; and variation in the services is virtually non-existent.

What gospel has done is to appeal to a different dimension – the affective side of faith and spirituality. While cognitive-based worshippers are complaining that the texts offer poor theology, those who are engulfed in the "spirit" of the sounds and rhythms are oblivious to the critique. The important thing for them is the "warm feeling," the powerful emotions and the almost primordial appeal of the repetitive verses, the constant swaying, and the "melding of body and soul" that occurs when one becomes absorbed in the entire ambiance of gospel. The fact that gospel music is a "foreign" invention is an advantage in places like Denmark, at least for now, since the language is unencumbered with negative associations, which would invariably occur if the songs were translated. Gospel in essence has legitimated a degree of church involvement among followers who have been distant from the church, as long as gospel music is on the program. More importantly, it is challenging at least a segment of the arbiters of church tradition to reconsider issues of contextualization of the Good News. The impact of gospel music is undeniable, and even late adopters in the church now realize that the genre has widespread appeal, in addition to unusual missiological potential.

Notes

1. In analyzing the blending and unifying of multiple identities in a gospel choir context, Johnson uses the work of Victor Turner as a theoretical framework. The employment of terms such as "liminality," "betwixt and between," "separation," and "reintegration" show a connection between ritual studies and gospel choir analysis. I have not delved into this nexus more at this point since it constitutes an important issue to be dealt with in Chapter Nine.

2. The idea of a black American gospel singer being viewed as an "exotic Other" is unwittingly portrayed in the popular Danish movie, "O Happy Day." In the movie, an African-American gospel choir director appears "out of nowhere" in a Danish village and proceeds to "miraculously" resurrect a gospel choir. In the course of the film, the "myste-

rious" black man becomes the subject of great adulation, especially by one of the doting female singers, thus leading to an adulterous encounter. The movie is quaint, but seen from a different cultural perspective it seems to rely on romanticized typecasting of an African American, which can be indicative of racial stereotyping, though this was apparently not the intent.

3. The distinction between church and non-church affiliated gospel choirs has not been thoroughly explored, although the issue was given light in Trine Berg Nielsen's Masters' thesis, "What Can Church-Based Gospel Activity Do in Terms of In-Reach Mission to its Danish Participants – and What Can it Not Do." Her work focuses exclusively on a church-based choir, which means that the Christian ethos is *de facto* present in terms of leadership, location, and a number of performance venues. Christian faith is no more required in church-based choirs than non-church ones; however, the tangible Christian associations would hypothetically give church-based gospel activity an advantage in terms of Christian missionary activity.

4. Structuralism refers to the idea that structures are defined synchronically in accordance with their relationship to and differences from other similar systems, as well as the interrelatedness of 'signs,' the 'signified' concept, and the concrete 'signifier' of the concept. A brief discussion on structuralism and its relation to poststructuralism will be taken up in Chapter Eight.

5. Statements regarding the irrelevance or inadequacy of the institutional church were common in a great number of my interviews. See Chapter Six for a more in depth analysis of the Danish Folk Church and prevailing attitudes toward it.

6. A typical choir rehearsal begins with a short devotional or time of fellowship, about fifteen minutes of vocal warm-ups, an hour or so of rehearsal, followed by a fifteen-twenty minute coffee/tea break. The break provides an opportunity for socializing, as well as giving smokers a chance to "feed" their habit. Following the break, the rehearsal continues for another forty-five minutes. There are, of course, many variations to this model. My current choir in Rønne, for example, serves refreshments and provides time for fellowship and a short devotional after the rehearsal.

7. Information from the "Gospel Factory" website demonstrates that the overwhelming majority of gospel choirs are located in the larger urban areas of Copenhagen and Århus. This pertains to gospel festivals as well.

8. Summer Gospel has become an annual event, meeting over a three week period in the town of Slagelse. It offers varying modules under the direction of respected gospel leaders and musicians. The camp was initiated under the leadership of Hans Christian Jochimsen.

9. Choirs are often assisted by people who perform practical functions, such as making coffee, serving as treasurer, helping with sound equipment, providing technical services, and the like.

Chapter 5

Meaning and Identity through Gospel Music Participation

The purpose of this chapter is to develop the conclusions on gospel music diffusion as reported in Chapter Four. This will be done by conveying the meaning of gospel choir involvement from the viewpoint of the leaders and participants of the gospel music culture. As stated, my own involvement with gospel choirs in Denmark has spanned over a decade, and has included such roles as chaplain, musician, culture broker between choirs and congregations, and speaker/lecturer. During that span, I have had an opportunity to talk with or interview approximately two-hundred choir members, attendees at various gospel events, and other aficionados, and have interviewed a number of the key leaders. Many of these interviews and conversations represent the findings accounted for in the preceding section on gospel music diffusion. As an integral member of two choirs, it has been particularly meaningful not only to interview participants as a detached observer, but also to witness the impact of gospel involvement on individuals over time. Hence the most significant role I have served (for the purposes of this study) has been that of participant observer. In this position it has been possible to ascertain the construction of meaning in connection with the movement, as well as to observe changes in meaning formation and faith among individuals.

In conversations with gospel participants, I often asked a number of questions revolving around the perception of gospel music, what it means, and the relationship to Christian faith. When interviewees responded that they were not adherents of the Christian faith, which comprised about one-fourth of my conversations and interviews, I often asked a separate set of questions involving their particular attitudes toward the Christian content of the music and how they are able to reconcile the religious ethos with their own convictions (or non-convictions). Christians were generally asked whether or not their gospel involvement has had any impact on their faith, and how so. Musicians and leaders, who were primary targets of more formal interviews, were asked some additional questions regarding their overall perception from their particular vantage point. The primary innovators, as well as those who have engaged in serious reflection were asked an additional set of questions, which allowed them to share their insights into the current state and perceived future of the gospel movement and culture.

One of my primary concerns as a participant observer has been the potential tainting effect that my role as pastor/chaplain would have on those who had grown accustomed to seeing me in that role. Since members of the choirs that I have served have witnessed me time and again as worship leader, preacher, and as general ambassador of the Christian faith, there has been on occasion a slight suspicion that some members had difficulty distinguishing between my roles. The extent to which this has influenced some of their responses, especially to questions of faith, cannot be known for certain. However, I have also discovered that my status as guitarist and bass guitarist has given certain credibility in the minds of some choir participants who otherwise might be leery of, or overly reactionary to, my vocation as Christian Minister.

The greatest advantage of the participant observer in my experience has been the ability to *overhear* many conversations that have taken place in the gospel milieu.[1] Some of the most revealing insights have come when I was not directly involved in the conversation, but rather was in a position to eavesdrop. Judith Hansen's research has proved to be a helpful guide in that the researcher is also a kind of "voyeur," that is, one who watches and studies others, even friends and acquaintances, without them realizing that they are being watched and studied (Hansen 1976). In many situations – whether around coffee tables in a fellowship hall, before or after concerts, touring with a choir, mingling during a gospel festival, or socializing in some other context – gospel members often could be overheard sharing their opinions and feelings in ways that seemed less inhibited than in interview settings. Matters of faith in particular, such as attitudes toward God and the church, involvement in Christian and non-Christian spirituality, and choir members' internal conversations and debates have revealed not only their personal confessions, but also the role that gospel music is playing in facilitating these conversations.

A particular experience highlighted the importance of "overhearing" others in order to ascertain the authenticity of others' meaning construction and meaning associations in the gospel culture. On several occasions, I had an opportunity to converse with Lene A. about what gospel music and choir involvement has meant to her. During our talks, she gave the impression that Christian faith was a central component of her gospel experience. However, her conversations with others while not aware that I was present exposed her heavy involvement in New Age religiosity, including "healing" and "crystals." On another occasion, she was seen discretely hanging a flier announcing a New Age festival on a message board in the church's foyer. In this case, the interviewee evidently was compelled to conceal certain information from me and perhaps other members of the choir that eventually came out in more natural interaction with select others.

The Meaning of Gospel: Responses to Interviews and Conversations

In conversations and interviews, I often asked choir participants how they became involved with gospel music and what it was that drew them to it. The questions and ensuing conversations revealed central components dealing with the diffusion of gospel music, which likewise was reflective of each individual's meaning construction. The answers were quite diverse. A number of respondents cited the influence of gospel festivals as a key factor in gospel music involvement. In my former gospel choir, *Saints and Sinners*, for example, a stream of new participants would discover the choir following their exposure to CGF, which is held each year in early October. It has been reported that the same phenomenon occurs with many choirs ensuing various festivals and workshops. One interviewee cited the effect of a workshop with a well-known gospel artist, Ricky Grundy, as pivotal in her gospel music formation. It is significant that my current choir, *Noiz*, experienced a roughly ten percent increase in membership following a March 2007 workshop with known Danish Methodist gospel artist, Lene Nørlykke. This sort of increase in local membership following a publicized gospel event is not at all unusual. Of the most potent catalyzing agents in attracting people to gospel choirs in Denmark, festivals and workshops are by far the most influential.

Other factors can be briefly noted. Several interviewees have recounted the impact of high schools and boarding schools, where gospel music is either part of the curriculum or gospel events are staged. Others have cited the importance of newspaper and church newsletter advertisements. A few were drawn to gospel music through recordings of gospel choirs or gospel artists that they have heard, ranging from Mahalia Jackson to Aretha Franklin to Kirk Franklin. Several conversations noted the influence of African-American pop music and artists, such as Stevie Wonder, in attracting them to a gospel choir. Not surprisingly, many conversations have borne out that personal invitations by friends who already were involved in some way with gospel music have been a primary factor. Neils, a high school physics teacher, credits a simple invitation by a friend and member of the host church for his contact with a nearby choir. After hearing a choir performance, he decided to audition and later joined – a decision he likely would not have considered without an invitation from a personal contact. Kristine represents a number of interviewees who understated the importance of personal invitation in conversation, while observations and conversations with acquaintances belied her direct account. Although she did not state it overtly, instead citing a gospel festival as pivotal in her decision to join a choir, her choir friends suggested that it was their urging to register for the gospel festival in the first place that introduced her to gospel music. The existence of friendships and cliques in choirs which preceded actual choir involvement suggests that personal connections are a key to gospel diffusion.

It is one thing to ascertain what was initially responsible for drawing individuals to gospel choir involvement and something different to determine what entices them to maintain their connection. Conversations often incorporated questions regarding what participants often liked best about gospel, what "feelings" they associated with the experience, whether or not the texts had any significance, and what they perceived to be most important about gospel. Again, responses were quite varied. Many respondents indicated that they come for the fellowship. Choirs that tend to prioritize social networks higher than performance generally attract participants that come for the camaraderie and friendships established in this context. My past and present choirs fit succinctly into this categorization and therefore many of my contacts and observations are shaped by the assumption that fellowship is a key driving component in continued gospel choir involvement. In fact, several participants in *Saints and Sinners* who likewise sang in the more musically advanced *Kefas* choir often remarked that they enjoyed rehearsing more with the former due to the emphasis on socializing, which they sorely missed in the latter. A key aspect of "fellowship" is the degree of acceptance adopters experience as a result of their participation. As explained in Chapter Four, the "come-as-you-are" aspect of gospel is a huge factor, as revealed in interviews and conversations. Inversely, the attraction wanes for those, such as Inge, who in a conversation acknowledged that she did not feel the same degree of personal acceptance. In her case, she opted for discontinuance after several years of involvement.

When asked what they like best about gospel, respondents referred overwhelmingly to how it makes them "feel." Neils characterized the majority when he stated, "It is uplifting to sing gospel. It recharges the batteries, especially after a hard day at work." A number of others cited "alleviation of stress" from the routines of school and work as an attractive element. Mikkel described singing gospel as a "rush," comparing it to being "high on drugs" without the side-effects. Helle B. expressed the feeling as a "warm sensation." Although she is outspokenly skeptical about the church and Christianity, the feeling she receives from singing the music temporarily suspends her critical feelings about the faith to which the music refers. In addition to the fellowship, Ole and Helle S. both referred to gospel as "life-affirming" and "faith-affirming." As active Christians, they conveyed the importance of the music and choir involvement to their faith, but stated that the overall experience is not in any way limited to those who associate the feelings with religious beliefs.

An almost univocal response to the most attractive element in gospel music, among Christians and non-Christians, was the feeling of "joy" that one experiences. What joy actually means to those who named it as important to the gospel experience is exceedingly diverse. Many respondents implied that "it makes them feel good (or happy)," without any deeper reflection or notion as to what the source of "the good feeling" for them actually may be. In fact, it was not uncommon to hear people say, sometimes with tears in their eyes, that they could not articulate or "find the words" to describe the feeling of joy they experienced. In these cases, joy is the word they use because no other words come to mind, or no other word seems adequate enough.[2]

However, some respondents attempted to elaborate. For Christians, like Eva, the music evokes a sense of gratitude which reminds her of life's foundation in God. In an interview, she states: "The sensation of singing out what one believes in a large and energetic choir often moves me to tears and gives my life a sense of meaning." For atheists, like Henning, on the other hand, it relates to the overwhelming sensation of being connected to something greater, even if that "something greater" cannot be named. He stated: "It does not relate to the specific Christian message; it is something that involves a combination of the rhythm and energy which causes such powerful emotions." Trine A., a gospel choir soloist echoes Henning's sentiment by relating the feeling of joy to something outside the confines of Christian faith. For her, singing gospel evokes thoughts and feelings which she associates with the things she holds most dear, such as her "boyfriend." In such cases, joy may be something akin to the feeling of sentimentality, or even sensuality.

Some gospel choir leaders point out that the feeling of joy is only part of the story. Lene Nørlykke, for example, affirms that the beauty of gospel is that it covers the entire gamut of emotions and feelings: "You can express anything in gospel – grief, joy, discouragement – the entire emotional register. That is a big part of its appeal" (Nørlykke 2006). As a national celebrity due to her winning performance on a televised singing contest, as well as a highlighter of numerous festivals and workshops across Denmark, she also associates these feelings with her own Christian faith. For her, it also involves a deep sense of "freedom" that comes when singing the music that expresses what one believes.

Primary gospel music innovator, Hans Christian Jochimsen, states it similarly when he asserts that it is not correct to assume that gospel is "happy" music. "It is better to say that it gives the possibility to express the self in a way that goes to where it hurts. It's O.K., for example, to question God in the music. Gospel is a tool that gives expression to all feelings, even doubt" (Jochimsen 2006). In these and similar accounts, gospel music is acknowledged for its cathartic affect in that it constitutes a conduit through which one's innermost feelings are expressed, which in turn allows for a kind of "cleansing of the soul" (as one interviewee stated). Nørlykke and Jochimsen, among many others, draw a personal nexus between gospel music expression and Christian faith; however, they are quick to add that the impact of gospel on the emotions, whether it is a feeling of joy, expression of grief, etc., does not or even need not involve Christian faith for many participants. Helle S. contends that the depth of emotion experienced in gospel music by non-Christians is no less intense than those who confess Christian faith.

Regarding the most important thing about gospel, responses were again diverse. Those who are professing Christians tended to cite "faith" as the primary answer. Eva confessed that her gospel choir is her main source of faith. Since she does not often attend church services yet strongly maintains that she is a Christian, it is the Christian message in gospel music, including the "texts, feelings, joy, and inspiration" that provide her primary connection to the Christian message and fellowship. She added that her gospel involvement has helped her through personal trials, including mental illness.

Another interviewee, Helene, recounts that association with a gospel choir actually led her to confess Christian faith for the first time. She described herself as a "truth-seeker" during her youth and into young adulthood. As a talented singer and now noted soloist, she was attracted to the "good voices" of the gospel artists that she first heard while in high school, in addition to the fascination regarding gospel's connection to the church. It was the combination of music and faith that helped her to draw a connection between the content of Christianity and the gospel music medium, which would eventually enable her to find her own voice. As a result, she was baptized and became an active member of a local church, in addition to her involvement in two gospel choirs and her congregation's *Praise and Worship* group.

Helene's story is not rare among the gospel constituency in that a number of participants have expressed some sort of transition to Christian faith as a result of their involvement. However, joining a local church after becoming involved with a choir is not the norm. Many interviewees concur with Eva's statement in that gospel music has a positive impact on their faith, or is the catalyst in their newfound faith, but does not necessarily translate into regular church attendance, unless gospel music is part of the agenda. Michael stated very succinctly what other people of faith within the gospel movement also have expressed: "Gospel is my church." As a "not too active church-going Christian," he purports: "Gospel music involvement takes care of my spiritual needs. I can hitch a ride in the music."

For others, such as Evan, gospel music and involvement in a choir has provided the strength to fight the plague of alcohol addiction. He recalls a time when he hit "rock bottom" after being hospitalized for alcohol poisoning: "When I was asked by the hospital staff where I could turn for support after being discharged, I told them it was my choir." With the help of a local Alcoholics Anonymous chapter and submission to the "twelve-step program," Evan recounted how gospel participation also factored into his discovery of religious faith, due to the music and the social network he found in his choir. This is quite interesting since gospel choirs, like AA, are able to express unconditional support for "lapsed" Christians and others in a similar state – in contrast to the way traditional churches often are perceived.

Many of those responding to what was most important about gospel were not as confessional in nature. It is common to hear people refer to the overall experience of singing and performing in a large group as most appealing. Often, words like "energy," "rhythm," "beauty," and "quality" are applied to the experience, in addition to comments about the message and content. In many ways, general attitudes toward the importance of gospel from a more secular perspective are summarized in the following flyer, announcing a gospel workshop sponsored by a high school in the town of Hasle:

Gospel Makes You Glad:
- A unique key to positive energy and personal development
- A powerful means to stress management
- A path to joy, deliverance, and contact
- A fellowship with like-minded persons, where you can influence the content and benefit

If you wish to ...
- develop your singing and speaking voice with the help of a team of professional experts
- take time to work on your personal potential in a creative space
- optimize your breathing technique and increase your capacity to keep your body and voice healthy and harmonious
- experiment with your solo voice and individual performance expression

... then 'Gospel Makes You Glad' is the right place for you (my translation)[3]

Some of the expressions in the flyer, such as "positive energy," "stress-management," and other factors dealing with some sort of personal benefit are indicative of how gospel music often is perceived and employed in contexts where the religious affiliation is either mitigated or truncated. This underscores the fact that while gospel music's foundation is unequivocally imbedded in the Christian thought-world, the meanings often attached to the experience of singing gospel can easily be construed in other ways. This is equally true of those who adhere to or show leanings toward alternative spiritualities, such as New Age movements. "Positive energy" is an especially common expression among those who find a certain satisfaction in gospel music participation while cultivating spiritualities that may be incompatible with traditional evangelical Christian faith. What seems evident, among those whose worldview is formed by either secularism or some other non-Christian spirituality is that the formation of meaning constitutes a kind of syncretism, which becomes particularly exposed in attitudes toward song texts.

Song Texts

When asked about the importance of the song texts in gospel music, the responses varied substantially. As stated, gospel music is sung almost exclusively in English, which creates a special situation for those who sing gospel and are not well versed in the English language. Children and youth choirs, for example, can be heard "mimicking" the texts without really understanding what they are singing about. Katja provides a good example. When she started singing in a gospel choir at the age of ten, she was not yet proficient in English. Since English is typically taught in schools beginning around the third or fourth grade, the words in gospel songs are usually hard for children to follow. Part of the appeal is the opportunity to learn the language through the music. Katja, who is now a young adult and choir leader/soloist, asserted that it was not until she became older that the texts became meaningful. Some adults find themselves in a similar situation. Tom, for example, is a confessing Christian and active church member, but admittedly at times has trouble with song contents due to the language barrier. For him, the texts are not so important; it is the "spirit" behind the music that really matters.

Vibeke represents another kind of Christian for whom the texts are unimportant, but for different reasons. As a trained classical singer and former church singer[4] in one of the Folk churches, the texts generally do not measure up to the high-church theological standards to which she has become accustomed. The appeal of gospel music for her involves things other than the words of the songs. Vibeke's attitude is somewhat typical of many late-adopters who are more or less ensconced in traditional Danish religiosity, but the primary difference is her choice to remain affiliated with gospel music. Following a gospel festival, a group conversation with, among others, Danish pastors, revealed their disdain for several of the texts that were used during the event. Although the consensus was that the festival was a "success," it was not, in their opinion, due to the content of the songs. Like Vibeke, they pointed to the overall "experience" as foundational to gospel's appeal to them, rather than any one specific thing, such as the texts.

However, gospel texts are, at least on the surface, considered somewhat important to many gospel participants. Tina Buchholtz, a freelance gospel singer/songwriter, has poured much thought and contemplation into her texts, and has received much positive feedback from workshop choirs and audiences at her gospel events. A September 2007 gospel workshop in Rønne (of which I was a musician/participant), revealed the impact of certain song texts, particularly her title song: "Where Do I Go, But to the Lord." Conversations with members of the makeshift choir and audience participants suggest that the song, which very simply expresses seeking a relationship to God under all of life's circumstances, struck a general chord with many in attendance.

Ole represents the constituency of theologically sophisticated singers who find Christian meaning in the words that are sung. As an Ordained Minister, he asserts that the songs express our relationship to God, which is central to the gospel movement. The language may be easily accessible and simple to learn, but that does not undermine its value as a Christian expression. Many other interviewees concur. When asked the simple question: "Are gospel texts important to you?" more than half responded affirmatively, if only "half-heartedly." Very few, however, could name a specific song text that was especially meaningful. Michael stated it succinctly when he said: "The texts and the music are one. You cannot separate them." In his view, the message in the words alone is not an adequate reflection of gospel music. One becomes "awe-struck" when the message in the music names the "power" that one feels when singing or listening. Michael and others agree that "not all lyrics are created equally," meaning that some texts cannot be accepted uncritically.

An example was provided in a song that has been frequently used during festivals/workshops and adopted by several choirs, but nevertheless contains biblical references that Michael, among many others, found repugnant. The song, entitled, "Bless Me," is based on the prayer of Jabez in I Chronicles 4:10, where the descendent of Judah implores God: "Bless me! Enlarge my territory!" Unless the song is understood completely in its context, which it usually is not, then it appears to discerning individuals to be a selfish prayer for affluence. Nevertheless, the song remains popular, primarily due to its overall musicality. This seems to underscore that texts in general are considered significant when viewed in the larger context of the music and performance, and are generally (but not always) appreciated by those who maintain a personal affinity with the Christian religion.

An intriguing phenomenon with gospel music revolves around the attitude of non-Christian respondents to the decidedly Christian element in the song texts. As Patrick Johnson articulated it in reference to his association with the Australian gospel choir, many members make a "mental flip" when singing about concepts that they either do not believe in or do not understand (2003:166). There is clearly a type of "disconnect" that occurs for those who distance themselves from Christian proclamation, and yet the gospel movement continues to be noted for its appeal to people of all faith and non-faith perspectives. According to my conversations and observations, it appears that religion simply does not play a significant role in the lives of many gospel singers. For those who fall in this category, the content of the songs makes no difference. For members such as Connie and Heidi, singing praises to Jesus is neither offensive nor interesting. "I come because it's fun to sing and I love the rhythm," responded one of them. "The texts don't matter." Though it is difficult for the Christian constituency in general to grasp, a fairly large group of those who sing gospel appear simply indifferent to what they are singing about. Again, the important thing is how the music and the overall experience make them feel. The approach is not conceptual; it is affective. Though it may sound cynical to some, the ability for many to sing about matters that do not fit into one's belief patterns is merely to not reflect on it or think about it. This was often reflected in the "blank stares" I sometimes received when asking questions pertaining to faith in interviews or conversations. "Not really" was a more than occasional response to the question: "Do you have any religious convictions?"

Other respondents were more articulate in their "indifference" toward gospel song texts. Neils, for example, made it clear that it is neither the religious element in the music nor the texts themselves that appeal to him. Although his views toward Christianity and the church are admittedly scripted by his cultural background, as evidenced in occasional church attendance and his preference for the singing of the benediction at gospel events, he does not profess to be a Christian. He furthermore states that the texts in general hold no real meaning for him. His real joy in gospel comes by merely singing "from the bottom of your soul" and through the experience of interaction with audiences during performances. "If I can sing and make others happy by doing it, then it is my duty to sing," was his response. Like many others who sing gospel without professing the tenets of Christian faith, Neils believes it is a religion or spirituality with strong ethics, which makes the foundation of the music palatable. He makes it clear that he does not personally sing "to the glory of God," though he in no way objects to those who do. In the end, he made a confession that perhaps articulates what others in his religious category might want to say: "When it comes to the matter of faith and the meaning behind the texts, I don't think so much about it. If I did, I'd have to quit."

It is noteworthy that most Danish gospel choir participants I have been in contact with can be classified as nominal Cultural Christians. Neils represents those whose knowledge of Christianity and relationship to it are part of the cultural scripting of Christendom while consciously rejecting it as a personal confession. Most Danish gospel choir members share the same cultural heritage as Neils; however, others maintain that they, in some way are Christians. The gospel constituency reflects the population at large in that most are baptized and confirmed members of the Danish Folk Church. This often means that the level of hostility toward Christianity and the church is generally low; however, the degree of commitment to it on a personal level is also low. Henny's words are indicative of how many interviewees think and feel: "Of course I am a Christian; I was born in Denmark." Yet there often exists an inability to articulate the meaning of faith, which in turn is reflected in the attitude among many to the content of the songs employed in gospel music.

However, another segment of participants comprises those who distance themselves even more so from religious/Christian suppositions than Neils, while exhibiting the ability to articulate their (anti-religious) thoughts thoroughly. Their relationship to gospel texts by admission involves their own meaning constructions. Henning, for example, views Christian faith as a mere social construct with no basis in any transcendence. Yet for him, Christian metaphors often have a universal relevance that goes beyond dogmatic assertions. He admittedly prefers texts that omit direct references to the particularities of Christianity. The pop song and gospel arrangement, "Lean On Me," provides such an example. Since he has studied the Bible from a secular educational perspective and shares a common cultural Christian heritage, the concepts are not foreign to him, although he is repulsed by texts that seem (for him) too imposing. During gospel events that take place in churches, he admittedly "tunes out" parts of the program, such as the reciting of the Lord's Prayer. Nevertheless, his justification for singing texts that contradict his personal convictions is his capacity to interpret them as referring to themes that are more general to human experience, such as love, joy, fear, liberation, etc. This enables him not only to sing the texts, but also to write gospel songs that are on occasion performed by his gospel choir.

Trine A., who associates feelings of joy in gospel with the things she holds dearly, such as her boyfriend, provides an example of the kind of active meaning appropriation that takes place among at least part of the gospel constituency. The ability to associate other meaning-constructs to words generally reserved for Christian use, such as "God," "Jesus," "Lord," "Cross," "praise (God)," and the like, is common for those who embrace gospel music while remaining indifferent or antagonistic toward the Christian content in the music. The overwhelming majority of respondents, of both faith and non-faith persuasions, contend in some manner of speaking that the brilliance of gospel music is that it allows the freedom to do this. Again, part of the "come-as-you-are" ethos in gospel is that it permits the kind of syncretism or "blending" that is evident in the reconstruction of meanings attached to known symbols (words).

Why in English?

One of the more interesting conversations revolved around why gospel participants believe the music is, or should be, sung almost exclusively in English. Quite often, respondents referred to the background of the music as emerging from the English speaking part of the world. A number of leaders, such as Steinvig and Nørlykke, suggest that it is important for the music to sound authentic, and this could not be done if it is translated into Danish. Steinvig remarked on stage at the opening of a gospel festival that the Danish language lacks a certain finesse or elegance that is necessary to truly capture the spirit of gospel music. There is, for example, a significant difference between singing in English: "Make a joyful noise unto the Lord," and then trying to sing the Danish translation: *"Bryd ud i fryderåb for Herren."* As Steinvig asserted, "it just doesn't sound right, even for many Danes." The issue of authenticity was more than occasionally mentioned as a justification for singing gospel music in English rather than Danish. Helene mentioned the origin of gospel music and the importance of remaining as true as possible to its African-American heritage. Ole stated matter-of-factly: "That is where it comes from." Helle S. and a host of others simply responded: "It seems more natural."

It is interesting to note that while discontents of gospel music in Denmark often cite the failure to translate the texts into their indigenous language as their most prominent criticism, gospel singers themselves, even those who struggle with the English language usually could not envision it being sung in any other way. To do so would be perceived as changing the entire nature of the music. In an effort to appease certain members of the audience, some choirs have routinely printed out rough translations of song titles with a short summary of the song content, to be distributed before each performance.

Yet the issue of authenticity is not the only reason why Danish gospel adherents prefer singing in English. In observations and interviews, one of the primary responses involved the desire for "distance," which is created when songs are performed in a different language. Nørlykke has observed that many of her choir members that are not confessing Christians would have difficulty performing if a direct equivalent of the texts were sung in their own Danish language. As she noted, singing, "I love you, Lord," is much more palatable for non-religious people than singing in Danish, *"Herre, jeg elsker dig."* The issue is not whether or not people understand English, but rather what people generally associate with words when the words are too familiar. According to Nørlykke, it is the insistence that gospel music be sung in English that constitutes one of the major differences from the *praise and worship* genre. Since many praise songs are translated into the indigenous language, the music is too imposing for non-Christians (Nørlykke 2006).

Carsten Morsbøl concurs with Nørlykke's observation regarding the difference between gospel and praise and worship music. Reflecting on his own observations as founder of several choirs and author of a book on gospel music spirituality, Morsbøl has noted that many of his gospel associates are notably "suspicious" of the related music genre because of a degree of ambiguity regarding its background and intent. The issue of language is considered a primary factor in the reticence among the gospel constituency to embrace praise and worship music with the same degree of enthusiasm.

It is interesting that the concern for maintaining "distance" from the imposition of indigenous religious constructs by singing gospel in a "foreign" language is expressed by confessing Christians as well as non-Christians. Eva suggests that singing gospel in Danish would be "invasive," and that the distance created by the foreignness of the language is a precondition for its popularity. Helene stated that the music would sound too "pious" if it was sung in her everyday language. Even though, as a Christian, she appreciates the Christian element, she recognizes that non-Christians singing the music would tend to feel alienated if it got "too close." Nina suggests that even Christians can be "overwhelmed" when the songs become too personal, which can be the case when music is sung in the heart-language. "When it's not too personal, there is room to think and feel in different ways," she responded. In fact, gospel participants commonly pointed out that religious language in Danish is laden with associations that can cause a feeling of "bondage" rather than liberation. Rasmus, a young convert to Christianity through musical involvement, stated bluntly that "typical Danish Christianity" does not speak to him at all. "The sound of a church organ sometimes makes me nauseous," he asserted, and added that hearing sermons in Danish (rather than English) often conjured feelings of boredom. Rasmus is equally critical of what he and others refer to as "Scandinavian gospel," that is, gospel music that is composed by Scandinavians with texts that sometimes are sung in the Nordic languages of Danish, Swedish, and Norwegian. Although many Danish gospel singers would disagree, he appropriately raises the issue of authenticity in the language and the importance of singing and performing without reverting to "lesser" imitations.

Michael suggests another reason for safeguarding English as the language of gospel music. Noting that many people who are attracted to the music and choirs are "stricken with church-phobia," he contends that singing in English helps to ameliorate feelings towards the church. It is a common attitude among a large part of the gospel constituency that the Lutheran Folk Church is "stuffy," "boring," and "irrelevant." When gospel choirs and performances are connected with a church, a different perspective emerges. For singers such as Michael, the English language is one of several identifying features of gospel music that "help people feel better about going to church."

For Jochimsen, the perception of those outside Christian confession is a major concern and a rationale for perpetuating gospel music in English. As he stated: "[Gospel] gets too close when it is sung in Danish. Christians are used to singing and worshipping in Danish, but non-Christians can sing without having their boundaries invaded; it by-passes barriers. The God language is not 'dangerous' when it is in English." Although he stresses the importance of the Christian content of the music and overall gospel experience among his choirs, as evidenced in his insistence on connecting devotionals and prayers to rehearsals and frequent involvement in gospel worship services, he stresses that "gospel evangelism" is not an intellectual approach. "It deals primarily in changing people's hearts before it seeks to change their minds" (Jochimsen 2006).

Those who embrace gospel while rejecting Christianity have similar reasons for insisting on employing the English language. In most instances, the issue of "distance" has profound significance. Peter R. compared singing gospel in English to being an actor: "When I sing [in English], I feel like I'm performing a role. It's not really me; I'm just performing the lines that are part of my script." Signe thinks that the language makes the experience more "exotic," while several others mentioned that the English language makes one feel like part of the world at large, rather than singing in the native language, which some perceive as too "provincial" for a musical expression that is sung worldwide. In each case, participating in a style that has a strong religious foundation while remaining personally detached from the actual content involves imitating what one sees and hears, much as an actor might perform while wearing a certain "mask." The words are then appropriated according to each individual's meaning construction. Once again, the adoption of a foreign language facilitates the process by allowing the mental flexibility to attach the feelings, images, and thoughts that one chooses.

Gospel Music Roots

In terms of authenticity, many gospel singers agree that the music's background in African-American religion and ethnicity is a highly significant factor. The purpose for raising this issue in interviews and conversations was to determine the extent to which gospel music's origin plays a constitutive role in the framing of the gospel ethos in a foreign context. As one might suspect, leaders in particular have usually affirmed that consciousness of the socio-political realities of gospel origins is important to understanding gospel, even in Denmark. Morsbøl is perhaps one of the more emphatic proponents of maintaining the connection to the African-American struggle for survival as the music is imported to foreign soil (Morsbøl 2003:12). Steinvig, Jochimsen, Nørlykke, and a number of other leaders are in agreement that while gospel music belongs to people of all cultures and races, the background of the music and the movement itself is an integral part of its popularity and credibility.

American gospel leader and frequent guest CGF artist, Gerome Bell, has made a conscious effort to incorporate the roots of gospel into his overall message, as was exemplified in a medley performed at the 2005 CGF in which he paid tribute to Clara Ward, Mahalia Jackson, and others. For him, the primary emphasis has been the effective communication of the Christian message, which is integral to its historical expression. Since the overwhelming majority of guest leaders and artists at workshops and festivals come from African-American gospel churches, the roots of gospel music have been effectively parlayed into the mainstream by those, who by virtue of their heritage and talent, are considered to be the authentic ambassadors of gospel. Indigenous Danish gospel leaders are nearly univocal in their expression not only of indebtedness to the prodigious representatives of U.S. gospel, but also committed to sustaining its ethos in their own context, including its spirituality.

British gospel constitutes a slight exception. Festival highlighters from England, Solomon Casey and David Elevique, have appropriately pointed out that gospel music in their context has been heavily influenced by music from the West Indies and from the African continent, in addition to the U.S., and thereby does not look solely to the African-American story involving oppressive segregation and racism in constituting their own story (Casey and Elevique 2005). It is clear that the gospel culture among certain primarily black churches in England has made a pronounced impact on the culture at large. However, the Danish gospel experience in general recognizes indebtedness to gospel music emerging from the U.S. black church experience within its own gospel framework.

While there is consensus, especially among gospel leaders, that the high degree of respect for African-American history and ethnicity afforded by their constituencies has given the music and its spirituality certain credibility, there is disagreement regarding the continued relationship between gospel's origins in the U.S. and development in places like Denmark. It seems apparent that some leaders and participants maintain a romanticized view of African Americans in general; however, Jochimsen, among others, disparages the notion of an unbroken continuum existing between the roots of gospel and its subsequent foreign manifestations. It is the functional nature of gospel music in the context of the American black church, as well as the foundation of Christian faith that cannot be replicated in contexts that do not share the same cultural scripting. As a result, one might anticipate that the influence of American gospel will not be as formational in the future as it has been in the past.

Preliminary Conclusions Regarding Meaning Formation

Although a full-blown discussion of meaning construction, semiology, and music aesthetics in association with gospel music participation will comprise the content of Chapter Eight, some precursory remarks relating to interviews and observations are in order. Based exclusively on the accounts provided by gospel affiliates – including leaders, singers, musicians, and audience participants – the meaning constructs in relation to the inherited Christian forms are far from uniform. In many cases, participants have expressed a deepened faith as a direct result of exposure to choirs, festivals, camps, and the like. In a number of instances, gospel involvement has precipitated first time confessions of Christian faith. In these cases, a combination of the music, texts, performance experiences, community-formation, and overall absorption of the Christian meanings that the gospel culture engenders has facilitated either a personal acceptance or a positive mental/emotional movement in favor of the content of Christian faith. In relation to Hiebert's centered-set theory, one can note that gospel music involvement often provides the impetus for experiencing Christian faith in a more positive light, no matter how far the individual participants may be from actual conversion or conformity, even in the most generic sense, to Christian meanings, practices, and lifestyle.

Due to Denmark's extensive program of Christian enculturation – which relates to religio-cultural factors – the capacity to measure actual conversions or first time confessions as a result of gospel exposure is exceedingly difficult to quantify. Since choir participants, for example, are typically Danish Cultural Christians, Christian faith on some level arguably is often pre-existent. What interviews, conversations, and observations often reveal is that the participants who are open to Christian content often discover a new or different interpretation of Christianity than the "Christianity" of cultural inheritance. This re-imaging of faith is generally perceived as "fresh" and "life-affirming," thus giving Christianity a new relevance, at least for those who have chosen to adopt it, or adapt to the Christian elements in gospel music.

On the other hand, the construction of meanings in relation to gospel symbols can veer off into directions that generally are not compatible with the particularities of Christian faith. Since words that are common to gospel music and Christian faith in general – such as "Jesus," "God," and "salvation" can be construed to mean something relating, for example, to "good feelings," there is a sense that traditional Christianity is not the overriding factor that unifies the gospel music constituency in places like Denmark. In fact, it is likely that the inability of traditional ecclesiological structures to incorporate gospel choirs into existing congregations relates to the reality that the gospel culture does not share the same constitutive foundation as the traditional church. Although the nondiscursive symbols are generally the same, the connotations attached to those symbols are in distinct variance. The church in general does not encourage such latitude in meaning-associations; to the contrary, one of the profound purposes of the church is to be – in the words of Lesslie Newbigin – the "hermeneutic of the Gospel" (Newbigin 1989:227). This means that the church's function is to interpret meaning in accordance with the distinct revelation of Jesus Christ, and to draw distinctions between faith in Christ and its absence. Gospel music semiology is taken from the traditional church, but the scope for many participants circumvents the boundaries of historic Christianity. Rather than establishing the parameters for conceptually-based meaning associations, the gospel culture facilitates an ethos based on openness and an exploration of affectivity. In such a context, Christian faith is part of the mix and thus becomes a distinct possibility for many participants, but it is not the driving or unifying force. In this distinct case, Christian symbols are used to construct a collective identity that either mitigates Christian particularity or transcends the kind of Christianity of which most gospel constituents are aware.

Interviews, conversations, and observations reveal that the gospel milieu constitutes a marketplace of beliefs and a convergence of variant identities. Since gospel music origins and content are not religiously neutral, Christianity maintains a distinct advantage. However, it is the capacity to create an environment that is essentially non-judgmental toward those who do not adopt the prescribed meaning-associations that makes the gospel music culture, missiologically speaking, both interesting and challenging. Since proactive and overt evangelism runs antithetical to the very elements that gospel adherents find so appealing, efforts to Christianize members and associates by propagating Christian meanings in relation to the extant signs and symbols should proceed only with great respect for the context and culture. Part of that respect is forged by an understanding of the general cultural scripting that shapes and influences most of the gospel music constituency in the Danish context. Exegeting that culture and realizing the wider mega-trends that are reconstituting the social context are the foci of the following two chapters.

Notes

1. The idea of "overhearing" is articulated most profoundly in Fred B. Craddock's book, *Overhearing the Gospel* (1978).
2. It is my contention that this unarticulated feeling relates to something deeper which gospel music elicits – namely the "sublime." The experience of the sublime is discussed in Chapter Eight.
3. The quote was cited in a flyer announcing a gospel workshop in the town of Hasle, in August 2007.
4. Church singers in Denmark are often paid professionals in the Folk churches.

Chapter 6

The Cultural Christian Heritage of Denmark and Implications for Religious Life and Faith

Thus far, I have suggested that the ability of the gospel music genre to traverse boundaries of culture, ethnicity, and religious persuasion is related to the universal themes and motifs emanating from the African-American gospel context, the process outlined by diffusion theory, and the capacity for participants to (re)construct their own meanings. These factors promote both the adoption and appropriation of gospel music cross-culturally.

However, the actual deconstruction/reconstruction process involved in transplanting a foreign aesthetic expression with strong religious and spiritual overtones raises parallel issues and questions about the cultural variables that have created this high degree of diffusion favorability. As mentioned from the outset, gospel music has become widespread and gospel choirs have become prolific in a number of countries. What is not entirely clear, though, is the extent to which each separate context has helped to create a unique environment for the fostering of meaning-formation. This chapter will exegete the cultural conditioning engendered by the specificity of the Danish context, while the following chapter will examine "macro" trends, which are superimposed on Denmark from global currents, and are created in large part by transmigration and communication technology. These chapters together will hopefully shed light on the cultural and transcultural factors which constitute the soil and the arena in which diffused gospel music expressions are emerging.

The Particularities of Danish Culture in Relation to Gospel Diffusion

Denmark is a part of Western and Northern Europe, and for that reason is often viewed by outsiders as part of the larger European context, as well as the geo-regional Scandinavian context. However, Europe is not a unity. Even the Scandinavian countries in closest cultural, geographical, and linguistic proximity – Denmark, Sweden, and Norway – have differences. In spite of the enormous strides made by the European Union in recent years, each European country remains unique and possesses cultural traits that are its own. Danish culture is no exception, and understanding some of the foundational cultural and worldview elements can shed some light on why widespread gospel music participation is perceived as being somewhat peculiar.

The work of Edward T. and Mildred Hall is useful at this point. As experts in cross-cultural communication, they have developed categories, referred to as *primary message systems*, which are designed to assess the values, habits, and trends within each context. They posit that the world of communication, including words, material things, and behavior, is shaped and determined by different cultural suppositions. Some of the major categories for understanding culture are *context*, which can be "high"/assumed context, or "low"/explicit context; *space/territory*, which implies both physical and invisible boundaries; and *temporality*, which includes monochronic and polychronic time (Hall 1990:6-17). The primary implication is that awareness of how culture can affect dispositions toward context, space, and time not only can increase awareness of fundamental differences in perception, but likewise enhance the possibility of analyzing and overcoming traditional barriers in cross-cultural communication. Other categories can also be employed, such as how each culture structures familial relationships, society, religious faith, relates to nature and the cosmos, etc., all of which can enhance understanding of particular cultural characteristics. The point is that Danes in general function according to certain distinguishable cultural patterns, which are evident to those who are immersed in them, thus providing the framework within which all of Danish life – including Danish gospel choirs – is tempered.

A key principle of cultural anthropology is the fact that people's behavior is not haphazard, but somehow connected into a coherent worldview (Nida 1997:52). However, discerning the patterns is sometimes a long and arduous process in a cross-cultural situation, and when we bring our own cultural assumptions to the new context, the difficulty of discerning and adopting becomes greatly exacerbated. Some of the differences are more superficial in nature, and thus easier to assimilate. For example, the fact that many Danes use bicycles instead of cars, and bike paths are built parallel to most streets means that a motorist making a right-hand turn must be much more cautious than in many other countries. There are naturally countless examples of such banal observations, which any observant tourist could pick up on and adjust to in a short period of time. Yet a thorough analysis of culture reveals that even seemingly superficial patterns of behavior often have some basis in deeper aspects of meaning within the culture. Many Danes ride bicycles, for example, for a number of reasons: cars are expensive due to heavy taxes, and families only rarely have more than one vehicle; a driver's license is not permitted until age eighteen, and costs around $1,500; gasoline was recently close to four times more expensive than in the U.S. (at least until U.S. prices started skyrocketing in 2008); the terrain is generally flat, and more ideal for biking; cars are not status symbols to the extent they often are in the U.S.; distances are relatively short; and bike paths are highly developed and a visible part of the infrastructure. Sometimes reasons themselves are based on deeper layers of meaning and truth, such as the fact that the high taxes on vehicles help to fund Denmark's first rate universal health care system. Perhaps the biking culture in Denmark is likewise related to the acute need among especially smaller countries to maintain careful stewardship over their environment and natural resources.

The foundational elements of a culture, of course, go far beyond modes of transportation and environmental leanings. One of the primary observations made when actually learning a new culture is whether, or to what extent it is essentially individualistic or communal in orientation. One might assume that Denmark, on the whole, is shaped by the same individualistic ontology evident in (U.S.) American culture. In some respects, this assumption is true, though some nuancing is required. Denmark is a free and democratic society – in some ways, among the freest of Western Europe. Danes seem relatively unencumbered by the rigid mores indicative of other cultures. Beer and wine are served freely at most social events and when visiting other families. Even many evangelical Free churches, known for more rigid piety, generally have no qualms about serving light beer, if not more, at church events. Dress codes are generally casual. Ties for men are not common, except for businessmen. Tops for women are optional on beaches. The American perception would almost automatically associate this latter behavior with sex or vulgarity; but the Danish worldview is not shaped by Victorian attitudes toward nudity; instead, they view it in the context of their own relaxed, "live and let live" individualistic culture. Residents and visitors to the cities can receive regular doses of Danish individuality in terms of creativity through the arts, including drama, music, and every other art form imaginable. Individuality is expressed in the fact that Danes are free-thinkers when it comes to matters of religion and morality. Anti-smoking campaigns, for example, have been attempted for years with very little impact, at least until recently. Even still, as no-smoking ordinances are enacted in public buildings and restaurants, it is questionable whether years of presenting smoking as a health and moral issue has resulted in a significant reduction of smokers. Danes often stubbornly contend that they will make up their own minds.

Marriage invites another means of self-expression in Danish society. Many young (and even older) couples choose to live together, rather than bother with the marriage ceremony and ritual. Quite often, the couples seem to be as committed to the relationship as those who have taken the nuptial vows. Sexual promiscuity is scorned, but pregnancy before marriage is not stigmatized (Levinson 1992:89). Thus cohabitation is sometimes regarded as a form of covenantal living arrangement, and though the church does not look favorably upon it, living together in Denmark does not really violate societal taboos surrounding marriage and sexuality.

A particular incident helped me to gain insight into the nature of individuality as expressed in the context of marriage and family. Shortly after arriving as pastor of a Methodist congregation in a Copenhagen suburb, a leading layperson and his live-in companion (both doctors and both close friends for many years) decided that they wanted to "make it official." The decision to marry was made nineteen years and three children after they began to live together. The event was greeted with great jubilation throughout much of Danish Methodism, and general quips, such as: "It's about time!" or, "You should know each other well enough by now!" were commonly heard. However, there was no hint of anyone frowning on the event or indications that the couple had been "living in sin." Their relationship was actually considered a sort of model of consistency and Christian commitment. The general attitude was that a document with the church's stamp does not guarantee a Christian union. It might even be suggested that Danish individualism, in such cases, is linked to anti-authoritarianism.

It is safe to say that in Danish culture, one of the gravest abominations is hypocrisy. As "individualists," the Danish attitude is more congruent with Shakespeare's adage, "To thine own self be true" – or better still, more in keeping with their own national storyteller, Hans Christian Andersen, who mocked hypocrisy and pretentiousness in fairy tales such as "The Emperor's New Clothes." Moral standards are matters of individual assertion, but this does not imply that Danes are amoral. Morality is simply not to be confused with conformity to culturally determined forms of decorum or allegiance to traditional symbols of authority. In Denmark, "police" and "politicians" are the butts of many jokes, and a minister's opinion, even about God and spiritual matters, is deemed no better or worse than anyone else's. During the recent (2005) uproar regarding the Muhammad drawings published in one of Denmark's leading newspapers, the phrase "freedom of speech" was recited with the frequency of a religious incantation, and was vituperatively defended by government spokespersons and laypeople alike, in spite of the ensuing conflict with Muslim leaders.[1] When it comes to conversations regarding faith, many Danes, if not most, will respond by saying, "I have my own beliefs." Of course, this can be excessively frustrating for ministers who gauge success in terms of church attendance, since Danes in general will only attend a worship service if they have a good reason for going, such as a baptism, confirmation, some other rite of passage event, or a major religious holiday, namely Christmas Eve.

Yet for all the many examples of individuality, Denmark is at heart a tribal culture (Iversen 1999:6). Many Danes might be insulted to hear it expressed in this way, but the fact remains that Danes are keenly aware of and united by their unique cultural identity and heritage. Since Denmark has never consisted of multiple people and language groups to any great extent, it can be classified as a homogeneous culture. This would explain the ambivalence that many "foreigners" feel when they settle in the country. As individualists, Denmark is very "rights" conscious and thus has until the early part of this decade had one of the most liberal immigration policies in Western Europe. However, as "members of the tribe," Danes tend to keep foreigners at a distance; hence the difficulty for refugees and immigrants to become fully integrated into society, at least until they take the time and make the effort to become culturally and linguistically assimilated.

Anthropologist Judith Friedman Hansen made some interesting observations a number of years ago while living short-term in Denmark. After noting the ambiguity she felt as both "participant-friend" and "detached-observer," her research pointed out how Danes are not likely to become intimate friends over a short period of time. Acquaintances are not confused with friends, and those that often are referred to as "friends" are those that one has known since childhood or youth (Hansen 1976:129). This cultural insight is revealing, and explains why Danes in general, despite being notably hospitable, have difficulty in establishing community with strangers, or those outside of one's immediate circle of kinship/friendship. It likewise means that assimilation by outsiders usually takes a great deal of time and effort.

Since Danes in general share a similar cultural scripting, a primary advantage is a prevailing sense of safety and security. Parents do not live with the general fear that their children may be abducted, and people are generally not afraid of getting mugged if they go out at night. A particular case made the Danish headlines in the mid- 1990's, involving a Danish woman visiting New York with her infant child. While eating in a restaurant, the woman left her sleeping child in her baby carriage outside the restaurant – which is a common practice in Denmark. She was, of course, promptly arrested and charged with child neglect. The incident serves to point out basic cultural differences involving the issue of safety, which relate to the deeper issues of cultural homogeneity versus heterogeneity, and communal ontology versus individualism.

The Danish language constitutes another major barrier for many outsiders. Linguists have rated Danish as one of the most difficult languages to learn in the world, primarily because of the inordinately high number of vowel sounds (which are sometimes indistinguishable to the ears of outsiders, and yet make a world of difference to Danes), the frequency of sounds which have few parallels in other languages, and the number of grammatical exceptions[2] – and Danes often seem proud of this fact. (Outsiders and Danes alike sarcastically quip that Danish is not a language; it's a throat disease!). Most foreigners can recall a type of "hazing" or rite of passage in Danish culture, where a group of Danes will jokingly ask them to pronounce "*rød grød med fløde*" ("red porridge with cream" – a common dessert, which is much easier to digest than pronounce), after which they will proceed to laugh and giggle. They might then add, "It is only when you can pronounce this without an accent that you can be invited to a Swede-free party" (Iversen 1999:7).

The Danish tribal identity is enhanced by their very rich song tradition, as the content of many hymns and folk songs laud and romanticize Denmark's nature (beech tree forests, beaches, and sunrises, for example), and sing of other characteristics unique to their culture and history. They are likewise acutely aware of their history and mythology, which is likewise perpetuated in songs and storytelling. Danes are proud descendents of the conquering Vikings and Norsemen (which is a bit ironic now, since Denmark is one of the most peaceful countries in the world), and can recite on cue how their national flag, *Dannebro*, descended directly from heaven on June 15, 1219 A.D. (Mortensen 2005:12). The importance of the red and white cross-shaped flag is underscored by the fact that it is illegal in Denmark to fly another flag, unless it is flown lower than and is not larger than *Dannebro*. Danes might exert their individuality on the surface, but when their soccer team is competing in the European or World Cup, their true tribal nature is uniformly revealed beneath a sea of flags, face-paintings, and the chant: "We are red, we are white; we are Danish dynamite."

Despite being a somewhat typical high-tech Western and Scandinavian society, Denmark at times constitutes a relatively high-context culture, which is a direct result of their underlying cultural homogeneity. Although Hall rightfully classifies the Scandinavian countries as low-context due to the tendency to compartmentalize human relationships in work and day-to-day life (Hall 1990:7), there are exceptions. Everyday life in the country can be frustrating to the outsider because so many of the rules are implicit and assumed. Traveling on the intra-city rail system, for example, can be strange since Danes usually know how many tickets or "clips" from a clip-card are needed, and though ticket controllers are not frequently spotted on the trains, almost everyone seems to respect the honor system. The lack of well-defined and easy-to-read street signs can also be frustrating to the outsider, which suggests that city planners assume they are not needed since everyone more or less knows how to get where they want to go, or at least have on hand a publication of city street maps known as a *Kraks kort*.

Denmark has its share of national heroes and other cultural icons, which serve to strengthen the Danish identity. Hans Christian Andersen, author Karen Blixen, astronomer Tycho Brahe, physicist Niels Bohr, Søren Kierkegaard, and N.F.S. Grundtvig (the patriarch of Denmark's educational system, theologian, and hymnodist) among others, are more than historical Danes who have made great contributions to the world in various fields; they are archetypes who somehow embody the essence of the Danish identity.

The strong sense of national and cultural identity is observed in other events. In 2000, the strong feeling of Danish particularity was exemplified in voting booths, as Danes narrowly rejected a proposal to join other European nations in accepting a common currency – the Euro. The result of the vote occurred in spite of pleas from political parties on differing ends of the spectrum, as well as pressure from other participating European Union countries to demonstrate solidarity with their European neighbors, which at the time included other Scandinavian countries. There are strong indications that the cultural fabric is in transition. After electing a conservative government in 2001 running on a political platform of tougher immigration laws and greater individual prosperity, many insiders and outsiders began to detect changing trends in favor of greater individualism. However, the perceived threat of unchecked immigration, which remained an issue in the most recent 2007 election, merely underscores the desire to maintain their distinct identity, and oppose with "venom" any forces that seek to undermine it, including excessive foreign influence.

Even certain foods symbolize Danish identity, namely open-faced sandwiches on dark rye bread, covered with mackerel, herring, Danish salami, and a liver paste called *leverpostej*. (The fact that I could never cultivate a taste for this "cornerstone" of Danish cuisine has been an ongoing source of many jokes among Danish friends and associates). Of course, the sort of "ribbing" I received when I simply could not digest everything that was offered to me presented another hallmark of tribal Danish culture: its sense of humor. Danes tend to share a common humor, which is based on irony and subtle sarcasm. They tend to be masters of the "understated." If someone from Denmark wants to say that they like you, for example, it would be most common to say, "You're not so bad after all," or, "You could be worse." Again, Danes generally are keenly aware of their own special brand of humor.

The Principle of *Janteloven*

After living in Denmark for a while, one becomes acquainted with the cultural principle of *Janteloven*. As previously stated, "the law of Jante" is a mythical construct which serves as a cultural corrective to haughtiness and pride, instead promoting egalitarianism and humility. The Danish author, Axel Sandemose, gave expression to this cultural phenomenon in his publication, *An Immigrant Crosses the Line*. Herein he lists the basic laws of Jante: "Don't believe you're anything special; don't think you're better than anyone else; don't think you're smarter than anyone else; don't believe your accomplishments are better than anyone else's; don't believe that what you do really makes a difference..." and so on.[3] This basic attitude, which is usually unbeknownst to tourists and other casual acquaintances of Danish life and culture, operates as the unwritten law of the land, and explains why Danes and other likeminded Europeans are sarcastically critical of Americans and American culture. Such Americanisms as "bigger is better" and "I am the greatest" constitute the antithesis of a culture that values quaintness, subtlety, equality, and fairness. Tourists in Copenhagen, upon first viewing the most famous national symbol, "The Little Mermaid," will invariably be surprised by how small it is. Yet to Danes, the size conveys an important statement about their culture. Visitors to Northern Europe's oldest amusement park, "Tivoli Gardens," are sometimes disappointed to discover that it's not Disneyland. Yet the beauty and popularity of the park is expressed in the Danish virtues of understatedness and quaintness, not size, speed, and power.

Regarding issues of size and space, Danish culture underscores "compactness." This is, of course, not unlike most of Europe, since the development of this cultural attitude is related to issues of geography and urban development throughout European history (cf. J. Rifkin 2004:93-103). An American who is accustomed to wide-open areas and roominess will likely find Danish homes and architecture in general very confining. Grocery stores and other shops can at times be frustrating to those who are accustomed to mega-sized supermarkets, since aisle space may too closely resemble a cattle stall, and any store or building that is more spacious and grandiose is summarily dismissed as "American-style." Cars in general are much smaller, though the gap is diminishing. Refrigerators and other appliances seem compact to those who are accustomed to size rather than economy. This means that certain products, such as gallon size milk cartons sold in the U.S. could never be marketable since they would be difficult to store in the average Danish-size cooler. Of course, use of space constitutes an area of study within every culture, and in Denmark, the preference for compactness fits well in a country that associates mansions and skyscrapers with haughtiness and effrontery while romanticizing the thatched-roof village tavern.

The principle of *Janteloven*, which is a culturally constructed expression of socialism, is subliminally taught in Danish grade schools, which emphasize cooperation more than competition. Although individual expression is encouraged, children learn to work together at an early age. School children and youth, for example, are assigned projects as a group, and are graded as a group, no matter the differential within the group in terms of ability and effort. The principle applies equally to traditionally high status positions, such as doctors, surgeons, and other skilled medical professionals, who generally do not receive the same financial compensation that would be expected in the U.S. As a minister in a Free church, my salary is uniformly equitable with all my other colleagues, regardless of experience, talent, size of congregation, political connections, or any other standard of measurement that is familiar to the salary system of the same denomination in the U.S. In Denmark, a District Superintendent earns the same as the neophyte fresh out of seminary. This is a visible result of the ubiquity of an invisible principle.

The disparity between rich and poor in Denmark is decidedly minimal, as a result of socialization and the accompanying high taxes, which are well-suited to a *Janteloven*-based (socialistic) culture. In fact, one study affirms that Denmark is one of the most egalitarian countries in the world, since the richest ten percent have only 2.8 percent more available monetary funds than the poorest ten percent (Iversen 2006:6). It could and should be argued that egalitarianism, which aids the poor and marginalized in society, has been supported by Denmark's Christian cultural heritage, which is a result of integrating the primary social ethics of the Bible into the very fabric of the culture. The extent to which *Janteloven* correlates with Christian humility and love for neighbor is a matter for debate. At any rate, the "law of Jante" is evident in the fact that people of means are in no way exempt from the strident tax laws; there are no loopholes for the wealthy. Although private healthcare is gaining some momentum, Denmark remains a primary example to the world of a country that provides equal and non-discriminatory health benefits to all legal residents. As further evidence of the function of *Janteloven*, even members of the Danish royal family can be spotted doing their own grocery shopping from time to time, which implies that even Queen Marguerite herself is not exempt from the intangible yet dominant forces of culture.

As a direct or at least partial result of their tribal culture and *Janteloven*, Danes often are perceived by outsiders as reserved, although they are more outgoing than their Scandinavian neighbors in Norway and Sweden (Iversen 2006:5). Riding public transportation can be a "chilling" experience for those who are accustomed to more casual interaction among strangers. On buses and trains, as well as strolling on the walking streets of the inner cities, people rarely make eye contact. To do so would often be interpreted as "staring." Inversely, Danes who have traveled to certain parts of the U.S., for example, often are struck by the "friendliness" and "openness" of strangers or casual acquaintances they encounter along the way. Though they may be intrigued and enchanted by the more transparent style of contact, numerous interviews and conversations with Danes reveal that many believe casual friendliness to be "superficial." Thus the Jante-influenced and tribal cultural dynamic is decidedly introverted.

Another Danish word equally captures the Danish identity: *hygge* (meaning "cozy," or "laid back"). In association with the love of quaintness, Danes, in spite of their outwardly reserved nature, are well-known as fun-loving and relaxed. During nice sunny weather (which can never be taken for granted in Denmark), small gatherings consisting of family and close friends often assemble in the backyard around picnic tables, eating food from the grill, and sipping red wine, Danish beer, club soda, or cola. During the dark winter months it is more customary to gather indoors around a coffee table, with lots of candles, pastries, and strong coffee. (Decaf is unacceptable). Even worship services, especially in the Free churches, would be inconceivable without "*hygge*-time" afterwards in the fellowship hall, where people convene around cakes, cookies, coffee, hot tea, and conversation. The language itself reflects the fact that *hygge* is a concept that continues to develop in Danish culture. In the past twenty-five years or so, the second person singular pronoun "*De*," which connotes formality (similar to the German "*Sie*") has almost disappeared from usage, except in purely business transactions. Instead, the more informal "*du*" is used almost exclusively, except among some of the elderly.

Cultural Analysis in Relation to Gospel Music Popularity

Although these "smatterings" of experiences and insights into the peculiarities of Danish culture may or may not enable the reader to better understand some of the nuances and idiosyncrasies of life in this Scandinavian country, it does imply that the adherents of the gospel music movement in Denmark also are shaped by a particular cultural scripting. The striking thing is that traditional Danish culture is not always in sync with the gospel ethos. The fact that honest critics as well as late adopters and laggards have complained that gospel music is "boisterous" and the singers are too "self-promoting" suggests that at least in some areas, the gospel ethos is a counter-cultural expression in Denmark. For those who are accustomed to seeing the world through the lens of "Janteloven," "quaintness," and "understatedness," gospel singing, especially by other Danes, can appear like outright histrionic behavior.

Yet the expression of catharsis that is central to the ultimate meaning of gospel music, both in the African-American and Danish contexts, suggests that gospel music is symbolically helping to "liberate" many participants from aspects of their culture that are increasingly faulted as imposing and oppressive.[4] Gospel music popularity may signal, among many other things, cultural transition – an observation that is common among sociologists and casual observers alike (cf. Højsgaard 2005:13).

A contemporary gospel song that is commonly used by many choirs is called "Shackles." The chorus states:

> Take the shackles off my feet so I can dance,
> I just want to praise ya, I just want to praise ya.
> You broke the chains, now I can lift my hands,
> I just want to praise ya, I just want to praise ya.

There is likely little doubt what the text alludes to in an African-American context. However, in the Danish context (and perhaps many other foreign cultures as well), the lyrics symbolize a desire to break free from life's debilitating constraints – constraints that include elements of culture that no longer seem to ameliorate life in contemporary society. It would seem that as the society becomes more individualistic in its ontological orientation, there is an increasing urge to displace classical cultural characteristics, such as "the law of Jante." The fact that gospel music in Denmark is not translated into the indigenous language suggests that some Danes are conceding that even their own language is inadequate to voice the desire for catharsis and liberation from oppressive cultural elements. At this point, it can be noted that the traditional cultural scripting of Danes and the general ethos promulgated by gospel music participation often are at odds, which concurrently adds to the curiousness of its popularity and suggests a growing discontentment with certain facets of Danish identity, at least among the gospel constituency.

Danish Religiosity and the Problem of Cross-Cultural Analysis

Perhaps the greatest and most subtle cultural difference between Denmark and the United States revolves around the church and religion in general. Harkening once again the principles of symbolic interactionism, it is sometimes easy to ignore the fact that the same words or linguistic constructs can be construed in profoundly diverse, even diametrically opposite ways. It is interesting to discover that common Christian words, such as "God," "church," "worship," "baptism," "Christendom," and the like, are more than theological expressions that are uniformly understood within the Christian "universe;" they are essentially "forms" laden with "meanings" that are social constructs associated with the particularities of each context and the thought-patterns of each person. Hence there is a need, when examining religion from the vantage-point of cross-cultural analysis, to not assume the meanings attached to the symbols.

There is an important place for cross-cultural analysis. In his book, *Foolishness to the Greeks: The Gospel in Western Culture*, Lesslie Newbigin employs an often quoted Chinese proverb: "If you want a definition of water, don't ask a fish" (1986:21). The meaning of the proverb, of course, implies that true self-understanding, whether it deals with the individual or the collective culture, is difficult to attain apart from the insights of those from the outside. The outside, or etic, perspective brings a degree of objectivity, as well as analogical awareness that sometimes eludes those on the "inside," that is, those who are too closely related to something to see it for what it is in relation to the world outside. In other words, if someone has been swimming in a polluted stream for too long, the person may actually forget, or not realize altogether, that the stream is polluted. Hence there is an important function for those outside the "stream."

Although the Chinese proverb often makes common sense, it does not completely capture the dilemma of cross-cultural analysis. When endeavoring to assess the reality and value of another system, it cannot be forgotten that the "outsider" also brings culturally determined biases, mindsets, and expectations into the mix. Emic and etic interplay are indeed indispensable components in attaining understanding of the indigenous culture, yet the ethnographer/observer must also be critically aware of how one's own perception is framed more or less by the cultural, temperamental, and experiential "lenses" that invariably influence any assessment.

The unwitting imposition of analytical myopia is widespread, and can be discerned even in advanced scholarship. It is, for example, the temptation to universalize a sociological method or perspective that in actuality is culturally biased, and then employed in critiquing another culture which may be the potential bane in Rodney Stark's assessment of European religion. Stark's contributions to the field of sociology of religion are formidable, and have attracted the attention of scholars everywhere – not least of all in Denmark.[5] The world of religious sociology is indeed indebted to Stark for standing as a consistent voice in promoting religion as a viable and important research topic in Western society – which is a perspective that should not be taken lightly given the secularization theorists contention that religion is (or soon will be) a spent force. His book, *The Rise of Christianity*, in particular presents a perspicacious look at primordial Christianity as it existed before morphing into the Constantinian layout, which has dominated European Christianity for more than 1,500 years. In light of Christianity's rapid and auspicious expansion in the Roman world, Stark theorizes about the causes of this growth, which led him to the conclusion that multiple factors - including social attachment, social outreach, and courageous witness – were involved (Stark 1997).

However, his assessment of the development of Christian missions throughout much of the European enterprise turns particularly bleak in his article, "Efforts to Christianize Europe, 400-2000." In other writings, including a book co-written with Roger Fincke entitled, *The Churching of America: Winners and Losers in Our Religious Economy*, Stark lays out the premise that religion in any society will always be in demand, and that religious organizations should therefore be equipped to provide the supply (Fincke and Stark 1992). Stark's article on "Efforts to Christianize Europe" perpetuates this premise, which is commonly referred to as "Rational Choice Theory" (Davie 2002:41), by using the structure of free market capitalism as a theoretical "springboard" for critically engaging state church sponsored and socialized religion. He laments the absence of competition, choice, and "passion," which assumably could invigorate churches in the monopolistic state/folk church

European context (2001:117-118). The fallacy is that it ignores the fact that the combination of religion and "passion" are not valued in Europe the way they are in the U.S. On a continent where centuries of religious wars – generally due to religious passion gone awry – are part of the heritage, the proliferation of religious movements is often regarded with natural suspicion. Stark is partially correct in propounding that religious participation has not been high in modern times, thus debunking the notion that there has been a dramatic "secularizing" decline in recent decades (2001:105). Although he may be underestimating the impact of European secularization, he rightfully points out that participation was simply not high to begin with. However, the history behind the pacification of religious sentiment cannot be segmented from the history of religious wars, persecutions, inquisitions, crusades, forced conversions, incomplete conversions, and the invariable backlash against the overly pietistic and moralistic Christian expressions that have dominated their past.

Danish chief editor and journalist, Erik Bjerager, has appropriately captured a primary difference in church/state relations between the U.S. and Europe: whereas in the U.S., religion is protected from the state, the European condition has arguably necessitated that the state be protected from religion (Bjerager 2006:170). Detailed accounts of European Christian history, such as Richard Fletcher's *The Barbarian Conversion: From Paganism to Christianity* (1999), usually portray all that is "good, bad, and ugly" from the contours of Europe's past, and the affects in the present cannot be ignored. The unfortunate thing about European history is that the church, while serving as a primary power-broker, has sometimes behaved very badly. This is a well-known fact and cannot easily be erased from the collective European consciousness. However, the blanket assertion that Europe was never really Christianized (Stark 2001:105) or to draw sharp conclusions on the rhetorical title of Anton Wessels' book, *Europe: Was it Ever Really Christian?* (1994), is polemical. It is entirely possible that the emergence of national and state churches throughout the continent were at least in part predicated on the pathology that has plagued their religious history, thus serving a "self-monitoring" purpose in society. It is certain that pre-Constantinian Christianity, which Stark recognizes as the better paradigm, has not been normative in Europe for many centuries; in fact, Constantinian Christianity is essentially the only model that countries like Denmark have to any large extent ever known (Mortensen 2005:19). However, to leap to the assertion that Christianization has never taken place seems to discard the fact that Christianity has diffused in accordance with the historical circumstances and process of contextualization unique to each culture.

Current assessments of contemporary religious life in Europe cannot unreservedly hold churches to standards that do not share or understand the affects of that past. The contextualization of Christianity in Europe has of necessity taken into account the pathology that is part of the past. As stated from the outset, the emergence of the gospel music movement may be drawing attention to the need for recontextualization of Christianity in a part of the world where it has been thoroughly contextualized – and with a less than satisfactory result. But Stark's call for a free market base which instills competition as a driving force, quite simply, runs antithetical to European church culture, as evidenced in Denmark by the relative paucity of Free churches, despite one-hundred and fifty years of evangelistic efforts (Iversen 2006:7). In the end, Stark's indictment against the (European) church for not facilitating revitalization according to the principles of the free market are much like blaming someone with a crippled leg for not running faster. The development of the gospel music movement throughout Europe in some small way circumvents the program of Christian contextualization by re-imaging Christian faith apart from the pacification of religion imposed as a result of a broken past. Issues of context must be respected, however, lest one wind up employing systems of measurement that negate the uniqueness of the cultural context.

Though lacking a certain phenomenological perspective, analyses such as those offered by Stark nevertheless constitute an important facet of an ongoing dialogue about the state of the church and religion in Europe. The likelihood that Europe constitutes, in the words of Grace Davie, "an exceptional case" (Davie 2002) is substantial, in spite of recent challenges by Philip Jenkins (2007:19);[6] however, the likelihood that Danish or European religious studies can account for the gospel music movement is, at best, uncertain. Therefore, in reference to the Chinese proverb, indigenous, expatriate, and foreign perspectives are needed to create the categories that might facilitate the understanding of a phenomenon that does not neatly fit into extant typologies or systems.

Danish Christianity: An Exceptional Case?

On the surface, Denmark can legitimately stake her claim as an old Christian country. From the first visit of Willibrord to the Viking Danes around 700 AD, to the missionary efforts of Ansgar over a hundred years later, to the impact of King Harald Bluetooth who Christianized Denmark over one-thousand years ago,[7] the Danes gradually embraced the Christian Gospel, if only lukewarmly (Schwarz Lausten 2002:5-12). King Harald in particular is recognized as the one primarily responsible for the transition of Denmark to a Christian country – a transition that would take several centuries (Mortensen 2005:14). Although there are theories proposing that many Danes were converted as a result of Celtic influences, the primary factor in conversion was likely royal decree – a move that not only altered the religious orientation of the earlier pagan Danes, but was a savvy political maneuver which averted a potential crusade against Denmark by the German emperor (Mortensen 2005:11).

The likelihood that the conversion of Denmark to the Christian Gospel involved a complex mixture of spiritual and political motives probably established the tone which has shaped the nature of Christianity in the country ever since. Even the Reformation and the spread of Lutheranism, which is often thought to have been a grass-roots folk movement, was implemented in Denmark in 1536 as part of King Christian III's agenda for religious change (Mortensen 2005:20). The king himself was a confessing Christian and a strong Lutheran; however, in keeping with the method of the times, the dissemination of Christianity throughout Scandinavia was a "top-down" affair, coming as a result of political decisions rather than cross-cultural missionary encounters. This means that Reformation Christianity in Denmark, in spite of the many positive aspects that one might associate with the emergence of Protestantism, has never really been conceived apart from Danish culture and politics. Of course, one could argue equally, in light of the ubiquity of Christian symbols that exist to the present, that Danish culture has been forged by Christianity (Mortensen 2005:11). Nevertheless, the kind of Christianity "constructed" in the Nordic country is integrally related to the political realities that have forged Denmark into the nation that it is today.

The affects of Denmark's Christian heritage, for good and ill, are very much part of the present. Today, around eighty-five percent of all Danes are baptized members of the Evangelical Lutheran Church (The Danish National/Folk Church) and willingly pay their church taxes – and the statistics have declined only moderately in the past twenty years (from ninety-one percent in 1984) (Mortensen 2005:88). In spite of high membership, regular church attendance is around two to three percent of the population; and except during baptisms, confirmations, weddings, funerals, and Christmas Eve services, the church seems largely unimportant to the lives of ordinary Danes.

Confirmation rituals in themselves provide interesting insights into the program of Christian enculturation, which is part of Denmark's cultural heritage. Each year in September, boys and girls in the seventh or eighth grade begin meeting once a week with a local priest or minister. The period of confirmation "preparation" usually runs until April, during which time the confirmands are taught the "essentials" of Christian faith, including Bible content, the Apostle's Creed, the Lord's Prayer, a few hymns, church history, worship rituals and sacraments, and the like. Although the process can indeed be a meaningful time of learning and growth, it is difficult to determine its religious impact because it has been thoroughly coopted. Many confirmands will admit, after the fact, that the process is really all about "the gifts and the parties" that are part and parcel of the overall experience. Since youth and their families in increasing numbers are opting out of confirmation but still want some sort of non-religious celebration, it is not uncommon to hear of "non-firmation" parties and gatherings.

Apart from the rite of passage experiences, it is clear that religious conviction constitutes the primary sphere in life where individualism reigns supreme – and faith remains a fiercely private affair (Lüchau 2005:55). It is perplexing to outsiders why Danes maintain membership in an institution they do not attend and generally find irrelevant. The reasons again relate to their cultural identity. As a tribal culture, rites of passage have a special significance in Denmark, and the church is the primary institution sanctioned by society to safeguard these life-cycle rites – not necessarily in promoting Christianity on its own terms, but in strengthening the Danish national identity.[8] As Iversen points out, like it or not, there is no other viable alternative when it comes to the performance of these rites (Iversen 2006:5). The parish churches in Denmark still serve a state function by keeping records and issuing certificates for baptisms, weddings, deaths, and name changes.[9] Yet besides these and other tangible functions, the church exists for the majority, not as a visible community, but as a sort of "archetype," appealing to the Danish collective unconscious, and invoking the image of a "silhouette" blending into the skyline at dusk (Jensen 1996:7) – in other words, distant and peripheral, yet not wholly disestablished.[10]

Some theologians have argued that the Danish Folk Church is a monopolistic ecclesiology for a culture that deep down does not really want a church (Iversen 1999:12). This statement may be somewhat unrefined. As Hans Raun Iversen restates it: "The Danish Folk Church is respected and used by its members in the same way as public hospitals" (Iversen 2006:7). This coincides with the analysis of Grace Davie, who surmises that the general European mentality looks upon the church similarly to "public utilities" (Davie 2002:43-44). In each case, the church is not recognized as anything that the populace gets excited about; just like the gas and electric company, it's nice to know that it's there when it's needed. As Iversen furthermore notes, this would also suggest, in the context of the debate regarding "believing and belonging," that Danes tend to belong without believing (Iversen 2006:8). This runs contrary to Davie's conclusion about the religious condition of Brits (and Europeans in general), whom she characterizes as "believing without belonging" (Davie 1994).

It should be noted that a primary hypothesis regarding the emergence of the gospel choir movement is that it provides a forum where adherents can safely "belong without believing," though one might strongly suspect that the relationship is much different than what Iversen is proposing about the Folk Church. In fact, he goes further in stating that Danes more correctly can be labeled as "belonging without even believing in belonging" (Iversen 2006:8). This only augments the enigma of having a "monopolistic" church, to which the overwhelming majority maintains membership, but only a miniscule percent attend with any regularity.

In spite of the church's high profile and arguably low status position in society, the vanguards of the Danish Folk Church do not seem inclined to initiate transformation of the church in order to make it more culturally relevant. Reflective of low church-attendance (the lowest in Western Europe, according to the 1999/2000 European Values Study – cf. Davie 2002:6), worship services often are characterized as dull and monotonous. Some pastors and congregations have implemented innovations in order to make Christianity more contextually relevant, including the implementation and housing of gospel choirs, but churches generally remain domesticated within the larger context of Denmark's rite of passage church culture. This means that, in the context of the church/state arrangement in Denmark, it is the state that sets the church's agenda – just as Hauerwas and Willimon generally asserted (1993). It also means that pastors spend an inordinate amount of time tending life-cycle rites such as baptisms, confirmations, weddings, and funerals, which in many cases consume the better part of an entire work week.

It has been suggested in recent times that the alliance between the church and state should be loosened, but some of the more articulate apologetes of Folk Church religiosity have warned that the severance of this bond will lead to the altogether displacement of the church from society. Bishop Jan Lindhardt, for example, rhetorically contends that "if the state divorces itself from the church, it will quickly find another mistress" (Lindhardt 2005:117). The argument continues that, separated from its role in society as a legitimating factor in the larger culture, Christianity will become further privatized and the process of secularization will be hastened (Bjerager 2006:210).

The unfortunate aspect of the argument against church/state separation, at least seen through non-European or even European Free church eyes, is that it fails to envision the church and Christianity apart from the Constantinian church model. The synthesis between state and church enacted by Emperor Constantine in 313 AD when Christianity was declared the official religion of the Roman Empire has been the primary model for State and Folk churches throughout much of European church history. The question that only occasionally gets asked is whether or not this alliance in some sense represented a fulfillment of Christian mission, or signaled a catastrophic deviation from which large sectors of Christianity have not yet recovered. This is an important consideration since the possibility that the latter proposition may be true casts grave aspersions on a church whose primary function is to legitimate and perpetuate the culture of the nation/state, rather than the authenticity of Christian witness in the world at large for the sake of God's kingdom. While outspoken voices of Folk Church advocacy, such as Lindhardt and Bjerager, perceive that erosion of the state/church alliance will lead to the altogether dissolution of church and Christian influence, one wonders if their position is the equivalent to what psychologists would call "co-dependency." Since Christian worship participation is already exceedingly low, and the church will not really be able to resume her apostolic function while remaining subordinate to the state, it is hard to imagine how the situation could deteriorate much more than it already has. While Stark and company may not fully understand and appreciate the uniqueness of European religion, pathology and all, European State and Folk Church advocates, such as Bjerager and Lindhardt, may be under the impression that the "pathology" they have inherited is not just normative, but preferable.

The primary defenders of the Folk Church would likewise emphasize that the church is not irrelevant. While "pessimists" point out that church attendance is exceedingly low, "optimists" remind them that church membership is exceedingly high (Bjerager 2006:155-156). This defense cuts to the heart of the dilemma regarding the very essence of the church: Is the church's purpose to be the guardian of the culture of the baptized masses, or is it representative of the visible, gathered congregation? To Christians coming from outside Europe, the idea of the Body of Christ serving primarily as a legitimizer of national culture rather than a sign or portend of God's universal kingdom is largely incomprehensible. It is often suggested that the church in Danish society exists, at least subconsciously, as an "inoculation program" – that is, it provides a "vaccination," which ironically pacifies people from the true content of an active and participatory faith in Jesus Christ. The rationale behind the pacification of religion can elicit a number of explanations, perhaps entailing aforementioned aspects of a European history riddled by religious wars, inquisitions and crusades – matters that cannot be lightly ignored. The pragmatic truth of the matter is that Danes are notoriously afraid of too much religion – a fact which resurfaced in light of the national crisis stirred by the controversial Muhammad caricatures in 2005, and which has been exploited by politicians who zealously endeavor to eradicate religion from the realm of public discourse (Iversen 2005:27, 2006:7-8; cf. Bjerager 2006:87-114). The extent to which the church is an unwitting accomplice by 1) allowing the "dual kingdoms" Lutheran construct to be domesticated by dominant cultural forces that seek to pigeonhole faith within the "spiritual" realm, or 2) by serving as a proactive guardian of the state in the effort to protect the populace from religious pathology remains fodder for ongoing debate.

Altogether, the reasons, theories, and speculations regarding the unique character of the Danish Folk Church are plentiful, but the simple truth remains that no group in large and significant numbers seems to be or is able to object to its arrangement within Danish society. Of course, Free churches, which include all other Protestant denominations, Catholics, and other state sanctioned sects, provide the most notable exceptions. The role of Free churches in Danish religious life has likely been understated in many reports. After all, of the two to three percent of Danes that are active church attenders, about one-third choose to attend a Free church, which is significant considering that non-Lutheran church members comprise only around two percent of the Danish population (Løbner 2006:6; cf. Harbsmeier 1995:34). Certainly the proliferation of gospel choirs, for example, would hardly be imaginable without the vision, resources, and support of other denominations, particularly the Apostolic, Baptist, and Methodist churches. However, the fact remains that their numbers in comparison to the population at large remain dwarfed by the Danish Folk Church (Iversen 1999:12). This does not preclude the possibility for non-Evangelical Lutheran churches to make a significant contribution to religious dialogue and agenda in Denmark; the reality is that most people within the country are either unaware of or indifferent toward the Christian alternatives to Folk church religiosity that actually exist.

As Iversen points out, the ability of the Folk Church to integrate religion and culture in Danish life, even if that religion constitutes a pacification or inoculation against evangelical Christianity, has cast a pall of suspicion over Free churches as "sectarian" and "un-Danish" to the extent that it has hindered their development (2006:7). Christianity as defined by the Danish Folk Church remains an integral part of the culture. Thus any phenomenological understanding of both the religious mentality of Danes as well as the institution they call church necessitates a suspension of some of the basic tenets of what can be called "American-style" or "management-oriented" evangelical Christianity.

In deference to the Danish theological and cultural perspective, the church in the U.S. is viewed with equal suspicion due to the perceived proclivity to become so "needs and consumer-oriented" that it jettisons historical Christian theology. This alludes to another aspect of Davie's analysis. In purporting that the European religious mentality treats the church as public utilities, the

American church is viewed as an extension of a society forged on the tenets of free market capitalism – that is, "competing firms" (Davie 2002:44). Painting in broad strokes according to the language of rhetoric, it could be said that the Folk Church of Denmark and European State churches in general, apart from their role as legitimizing national culture, focus almost exclusively on the *logos* of Christian proclamation, to the neglect of the general *pathos* of public perception, while the "competing firms" church paradigm of (U.S.) American churches accommodates the *pathos* of the "consumer" so thoroughly that it compromises or excessively reconfigures its *logos*. In both cases, the *ethos* or integrity of the church is or can be severely compromised.[11] The analogy admittedly draws upon stereotypes emanating from both sides of the North Atlantic. At any rate, the church in general would do well to heed the wisdom of Lesslie Newbigin, who exhorts the church to navigate between the dual hazards of "Scylla" and "Charybdis," that is, the extremes of cultural accommodation on the one hand, and cultural irrelevance on the other (Newbigin 1994:67).

Individualization of Religious Faith

In light of the onslaught of secularism and postmodernism, which are in full force in Denmark, as well as the influx of New Age movements, Islam, and the rise of neo-pagan sects, the established churches may very well be facing their own identity crisis. To some extent, this constitutes the backdrop of a recent and thoroughgoing study on Danish religious life entitled, *Gudstro i Danmark* (*Danish Faith in God*). In the book's opening article, entitled, "Faith in God - with Reservation," Højsgaard and Iversen deduce that actual belief in God (or lack thereof) among the Danes is not the main problem. An empirical study shows that it has not fallen dramatically in the last thirty-five years, although a significant drop off was measured between 1948 and 1970 (Lüchau 2005:35).[12] This coincides with Stark's assertion regarding European Christianity in general, which to some would suggest that secularization is an inadequate theory since religious belief has not been in a perpetual freefall (cf. Stark and Bainbridge 1984). The issue is not "faith," but rather, "what kind of faith."

Perhaps in keeping with the spirit of the postmodern cultural and religious transition, Danish faith in God is something that individuals proactively shape and determine, not reject outright (Højsgaard and Iversen 2005:25). This coincides with the research of Lüchau, who states that Danes have an increasing aversion to the word "religion," (an aversion that evangelical Christians have shared for a long time) thus precluding largely the acceptance of any "prepackaged" theological constructs and traditional formulations. Since church attendance is at the lowest end of the trans-European spectrum, one could surmise that the doctrinal positions of the church regarding the Supreme Being are either not adequately communicated, not widely accepted, or both. Religion is passé; spirituality is the new catch-word. The assertion that Danes in general are not abandoning faith suggests, according to Lüchau, that secularization is not the concept that adequately portrays the religious situation. Following up on the research of Stark and Bainbridge (1984), Lüchau confirms that secularization is a largely self-limiting process since those who discontinue one faith often either opt for another, or construct a private faith (2005:34). There are, of course, differing definitions and opinions as to what secularization actually means – the gradual decline and eventual disappearance of religion, and the retreat of religious influence from the public sphere being the two most prominent (Lüchau 2005:34). The latter description seems to reflect Lüchau's premise, but since belief in God has not dissipated in the past few decades, a different indicator or conceptual framework is called for.

Instead of secularization, Lüchau proposes the term *individualization* as the more appropriate model of explanation in regard to Danish religiosity. According to his analysis based on quantitative data, religious belief has become far less traditional, but it nevertheless remains (2005:55). The difference is that individuals no longer feel obligated to espouse church dogma, which also accounts for rising beliefs in concepts such as reincarnation. The point is that determining what belief in God means is perceived as a matter for each individual to decide (Lüchau 2005:55).

The idea that individualization can be understood as a category that is juxtaposed to, but not coterminous with, secularization can be placed within a larger religious framework, such as the one presented by church historian Hugh McLeod. In noting the general decline of Christendom throughout modernity, McLeod is well aware of the theorists who forged the "dechristianization" or "secularization" conclusion, based initially on studies in France in relation to changing attitudes toward death (McLeod 2003:7). The theory has dominated religious studies in Europe throughout much of modernity, and should not be casually dismissed. In Western society, generations in the past century have experienced the dislocation of religion and culture as a consequence of economic development, rapid material progress, and intellectual forces which have instilled a combative attitude toward religion and the church (Christopher Dawson in Russello 1998:173). As a result, the Christian foundationalism that has unified Europe since the late middle ages has been undermined.

However, secularization theory seems to be lacking when it comes to the fact that in many European countries, including Denmark, identification with the Christian religion among the populace remains high. In light of the fact that this association with Christianity often is nominal, the questions and doubts it raises regarding secularization hardly leads to the opposite conclusion. The likelihood exists that secularization and individualization theories are concurrently valid in that they speak to different aspects of a common reality. Christendom is clearly in decline in terms of influence in society, and can no longer be regarded as the *lingua franca* among those outside the boundaries of actively professing Christians (McLeod 2003:11). On the other hand, Stark's opposition to secularization theory has been duly noted; his "supply side" argument regarding the need for the church to change by providing the religious needs that people innately are seeking to fulfill is likewise recognized by McLeod as a coherent "American" assertion – an assertion that the fate of Christianity is not necessarily determined by forces beyond its control (McLeod 2003:15). This idea, however, seems dwarfed in light of forces that have greatly enervated Christian influence, such as urbanization and socialization (McLeod 2003:16, Iversen 1982). Though the kind of pluralism and competition that Stark, Finke, and Bainbridge applaud may be a consequence of city life, and even though opportunities for mission and evangelism among urban populations do present themselves, it is difficult to deny that urbanization and socialization have undermined religious interest, at least in terms of participation in religious community.

While McLeod presents the "tapestry" of perspectives in relation to the decline of Christian influence in European society, especially in the public spectrum, while offering a nuanced secularization approach, Lüchau's analysis seems to support the hypothesis of Grace Davie, which contends that Europe constitutes "an exceptional case." An exceptional case, of course, necessitates categorizations that do not merely recapitulate those that already are in use. Instead, religious studies and missiological approaches in Europe should spring from a phenomenological starting point. Davie's unique contribution to the field of sociology of religion is the reminder that an object of study must be understood for what it is on its own terms, rather than settling for analytical tools, such as secularization theory or rational choice / supply-side theory, that impose categories which do not appropriately match the culture and context. Phenomenology, of course, is only a step, albeit an important one, in the overall process which Hiebert calls "critical contextualization" (Hiebert, Shaw, and Tiénou 1999:21-29). Nevertheless, agendas of change agency that endeavor to facilitate revitalization in Denmark (and elsewhere) should begin with an understanding of the exceptional nature of the people, their culture, and relevant history, in addition to the interplay of Christian faith within that context.

Lüchau's usage of individualization as a construct for interpreting religious life in Denmark raises a number of questions, not least of all including how a "nebulous" belief in God could qualify as a "religious" response, let alone an indicator in the presence of Christian meaning. An article by Peter la Cour provides a more critical assessment of the phenomenon of individualization in faith, particularly in the concept of God. Referring to the diminishing belief in a god that can be understood concretely and with clear "mythological structures," la Cour laments this development from a therapeutic perspective. Without a cognitive belief structure, the ability to interpret the world from a religious point of view, including instances where individuals are beset with crisis, is lost (la Cour 2005:77-78). The article furthermore notes that Denmark is among the lowest Western nations when it comes to faith in the classical or Christian God, which is the reason why la Cour appropriately entitles his analysis, "The God of the Danes in Crisis." One should recognize that it is unfair to measure Christian faith according to what it allegedly can or cannot do for the individual; as important as each individual is in accordance with the central Christian precept of God's love, it may also be wise to remain cautious about the effects of the prevailing consumer mindset on the perception and application of faith. However, la Cour does temper, correctly I believe, the "individualization" construct by arguing that it, too, does not indicate the emergence of a stable and vibrant faith, which is capable of ameliorating life and culture among the Danes (2005:78).

A final noteworthy contribution to the understanding of religious faith in Denmark from the *Gudstro i Danmark* project comes from Hans Raun Iversen. In a revealing article, Iversen employs the metaphor of a "park" as a way of suggesting that all religious innovations in Denmark take place within the distinct parameters of the Danish historical-cultural framework. Even though religious pluralism or a plurality of faiths does exist, they are all formed within the structure of the religious "park." Other studies often tend to support a more linear progression in terms of religion and meaning formation – from modernity to secularization, or from postmodernity to globalization, for example – but the "park" metaphor maintains that the cultural-historical uniqueness of the Danish context provides the cauldron or "arena" within which religious meanings are constructed (Iversen 2005:104). Just like a city park, there is a great deal of latitude in terms of activity, interest, and so forth. In like manner, the religious park is individualistic in the sense that people are welcome to construct whatever meanings they choose, as well as to visit the park whenever and as frequently as they want. The only constraint is that these individualistic constructs are devised and rooted within the larger framework, wherein Iversen locates seven dominant motifs that characterize the parameters of Danish religious thought. These are translated and illustrated in the following table:

Table 5.1: Seven Motifs that Characterize Danish Religious Thought

Religious Form	God-image	Moral/Ethic	Primary Belief
Implied religion/ Natural religion	Encounter with the "Other"	Moral "Guideposts"	Luck and Good Fortune
Folk Religion	God as Creator	Virtue	Immortality
New Age Religion/ Spirituality	Micro-Macro Cosmology	Karma / Cosmic Cause and Effect	Rebirth to a Higher Level
Church Christianity	The Trinity	Love for Neighbor	Resurrection of the Body
Cultural Christianity	God as Partner	Do what is Good	Need for Perspective and Good Advice
Civil Religion	God as Overseer	Good Citizenship	Peace, Welfare, and Stability
Islam	Allah	Shari'a Law	Allah's Will

Source: Iversen 2005:117

Iversen's characterization, which is admittedly indebted to Robert Bellah's classic, *Habits of the Heart*, is helpful in that it illustrates the significance of cultural context in faith/religious-formation, as well as implies the difficulty of importing a spirituality that cannot easily be domesticated within the parameters of extant mental constructs. Of the seven religious forms, Islam is the only one that has been transplanted on Danish soil. The Islamic Diaspora, that is, the influx of Muslim immigrants throughout much of Europe has had some effect, though the suggestion that Islam shares rootedness in the Judeo-Christian thought world has been cited as a possible reason why it is able to survive as a cross-cultural transplant (Iversen 2005:116). The primary question regarding the "park" metaphor in the Danish or Scandinavian context is the extent to which Folk Church Lutheranism has dominated religious perceptions. Iversen acknowledges this (2005:117), but one wonders if Lutheranism as conveyed through the Folk Church conduit is still more hegemonic than this analysis may indicate. As the guardian and legitimating religious force in Denmark, the monopolistic Folk Church must surely be seen as the most formidable controlling agency in the construction of religious meaning, including the "paradoxical effect" syndrome of those who define their religious life/beliefs in contrast to the hegemonic church. Even though interest in the church, at least in terms of actual participation, is low, Danish Lutheranism is likely not only part of the religious park, but its primary proprietor.

Another factor that has not yet received adequate attention is the role and influence of global trends and forces, such as postmodernism and globalization. Iversen argues fairly convincingly that local factors shape and domesticate macro movements. This is likely only part of the story. In relation to the gospel music movement, for example, I have argued that the Australian contextual analysis, which attempts to indicate a segue between African-American gospel music and Australian culture, does not relate to the widespread geo-cultural diffusion of gospel. The context does matter, but in many cases, social movements and religious thought patterns may best be understood as a synergy between micro and macro, local and global, national and international forces. Since the gospel music movement is, at least to some degree, calling into question the actual significance of contextualization in some cases, one wonders how it relates to Iversen's "park." One might be quick to assume that each individual is free to construct his/her own meaning in accordance with the parameters of the historical-cultural context. Perhaps this is true, yet gospel music, as a result of cross-cultural diffusion and reinforcement through a ritual process and mimesis, may also be infusing a type of spirituality based on kinesis, catharsis, and affectivity within the context of Christian expression which is not wholly recognized within extant Danish-religious categories. Given the aforementioned counter-cultural tendencies of the gospel constituency, one wonders if a religious analysis based solely on the micro-cultural perspective is myopic, or at least tells only part of the story. In this case, attention to larger trends is needed – to which this project now turns.

Notes

1. Denmark was the center of a huge controversy when one of the leading Danish newspapers, *Jyllands Posten*, published a series of cartoons depicting unfavorable caricatures of Muhammad. The hostile backlash among many Islamic nations, which featured media coverage of angry crowds burning Danish flags, assaults on Danish embassies, and Muslim boycotts of Danish exports was shocking to Danes.
2. I recall reading sources documenting linguistic analyses of the Danish language while in Denmark. Unfortunately, I can no longer locate these exact sources.
3. I have never actually been able to locate the source, though many Danes are able to recite Janteloven from rote.
4. Criticism of *Jantelovn*, among other things, is often expressed in Danish pop culture and among youth.
5. Stark's work is widely read in Danish religious studies and theological circles, and his books are commonly referenced in Danish religious studies publications.
6. Jenkins' book, *God's Continent*, argues that religious patterns in Europe may not be so unique after all.
7. Stories of Ansgar and King Harold "Bluetooth" are common folklore in grade school, which emphasize the importance of Christianization to the cultural identity of Denmark.
8. Jørgen I. Jensen's book, *Den fjerne kirke (The Distant Church)* provides an interesting perspective on the Danish Folk Church, positing that its primary purpose is the solidification of Danish cultural identity, rather than Christian indoctrination. This is particularly true of baptism, which he views as a cultural, not religious rite. In his view, the church is and should remain "distant" or non-imposing in regard to the conveyance of Christian meaning in relation to Christian rituals.
9. As a minister in a state-sanctioned Free church, it is likewise my pastoral duty to fulfill the state function of providing and storing official documents for my church members.
10. The image of "silhouette" originates with Jensen's book, *The Distant Church*.
11. By *pathos* I am referring generally to the state or condition of the collective "soul" of the audience (cf. Green 1997:555). *Logos* refers broadly to discourse, or the reasoning propelling one's argument (cf. Wells 2001:456), while *ethos*, in this context, refers to the nature and character of the church (cf. Baumlin 2001:263).
12. Højsgaard and Iversen's determination of what does and does not constitute a problem could and perhaps should be challenged, since their data indicates that twenty percent (one in five) of those polled are atheists (Højsgaard and Iversen 2005:13). This would place the percentage of Danes believing in God somewhere in the middle of all Western European countries, according to the European Values Study, which coincidentally records the Danish statistic somewhat lower (68.8 percent) (Davie 2002:7). Even if eighty percent of the population has faith in God, this number would be perceived as quite low in many contexts. Nevertheless, Højsgaard and Iversen's purpose is duly noted; the real issue is not "how many" people believe in God, but rather "what kind of belief" is found among those who do (2005:24-25).

as quite low in many contexts. Nevertheless, Højsgaard and Iversen's purpose is duly noted; the real issue is not "how many" people believe in God, but rather "what kind of belief" is found among those who do (2005:24-25).

Chapter 7

The Impact of Global Currents and Imported Spiritualities

The preceding chapter provides an analysis of Danish culture, including religious life, which serves as a background for understanding the people who are drawn to the gospel music movement in Denmark. In a way, the eccentricities of Danish culture serve as both a hindrance and a help to the adoption of gospel: a hindrance in that the gospel ethos runs counter to the valuation of understatedness, self-restraint, and subtlety, which are characteristics of Danish life, and a help in that the Christian logos itself is not a foreign concept due to the long history of Christianization. The irony of Christianization is that it serves to desensitize much of the populace to the actual content of Christianity, which in turn necessitates a re-imaging of the faith in order to create vibrancy and facilitate renewal. Gospel music seems to be doing this very thing for a number of the participants by using known (Christian) constructs and then prompting the construction of new meanings in association with known forms.[1] Although the presentation of Christianity through gospel music in Denmark is an obvious cultural import, the language and story-telling in many gospel songs have a general familiarity which is ingrained in the culture.

However, since the international transplantation of gospel music is made possible by global shifts in culture, the cultural-exegetical framework alone cannot tell the story of gospel music's impact, as well as the meaning constructions associated with the movement. This implies that another framework is needed, that is, a perspective that recognizes the impact of global currents in each social location. The primary global current that has been monitored especially in recent times, is related to the flow of information, ideas, beliefs, and goods that comprises the "umbrella" concept of *globalization*.

Globalization in Relation to Cultural Diffusion

The term globalization itself is diffuse. In covering topics ranging from economic development, to political shifts, to global ecology and the environment, to transitory and displaced populations, to religious trends, *ad infinitum*, it cannot be assumed that a "one-word-fits-all" label will even remotely correlate with the associated meanings on the part of the receptor. Add to it the gamut of emotional responses elicited by the concept – between highly favorable and highly "discontented" (as indicated by the title of Joseph Stiglitz's book, *Globalization and its Discontents*) – and one ends up in a quagmire of competing interpretations.

For the purposes of this discourse, globalization will be defined as "The rapidly developing and ever-densening network of interconnections and interdependence that characterizes modern social life" (Schweiker 2004:6). This interconnectedness affects all areas of life, and is not limited to certain regions of the world. As Ira Rifkin points out, this sort of interconnectivity is not a new phenomenon; what is unique is the pace at which the global interdependence is occurring (2003:4). As a result, a general perception of global "compression" is emerging as people from virtually every pocket of the world now possess instantaneous access to ideas and products from almost any other part of the world. This would, of course, include the cross-cultural diffusion of ethnic designators, such as customs, styles, language and artistic expressions.

The larger issues of economic and political impact as effectuated by the expansion of free markets and the emerging global economy are matters that demand ongoing monitoring. These issues are not necessarily central to gospel music diffusion and spirituality, but are not entirely peripheral. The primary impact of this interconnectedness on Danish culture in relation to the gospel ethos is understood on the level of cultural diffusion and innovation. The cultural impact of global trends has been pejoratively referred to as "McWorld," which implies the onslaught of Western cultural imperialism, such as McDonald's and Disney, at the expense of local and regional cultural expressions (I. Rifkin 2003:4).[2] One should note that such nomenclature is reductionistic, since all cultural diffusions cannot be lumped together in the same way. Likewise it is becoming clearer that the Western world is not in every diffusion "loop," which will likely become increasingly more so in the time to come. However, the impact of globalization in terms of the promulgation of consumerism, materialism, and the associated ontology, "I buy, therefore I am," does require a critical assessment of the impact of global economics on culture and the emerging trends which are changing the concept of human identity.

In contrast to the longstanding anthropological notion that cultures and religious beliefs are self-contained, somewhat static, and self-generating, the emerging global currents are presenting quite a different model by contending that culture is contingent, constructed, and contested (Rynkiewich 2002:301). Though, as Michael Rynkiewich asserts, the "breaching" of cultural boundaries is not something that suddenly emerged *ex nihilo* in the contemporary era, the phenomenon of globalization has clearly taken on an intensity, in light of the instantaneous dissemination of information, that is unparalleled in human history. The result is the construction of new identities that are based on the selective interpretations of the past, as well as the convergence of global trends in each regional and local context (Rynkiewich 2002:301).

Globalization theory in essence reverses the analytical perspective traditionally employed in cultural anthropology, shifting the view from the particularity of "national" culture to the universality of "international" trends. A contemporary analysis of culture cannot circumvent what Howard Snyder terms "Earth Currents," that is, the global trends which are impacting local contexts (Snyder 1995). These "currents," which include (among others) communication technology, global economic links, and ecological concern, are literally changing people's perspectives of everyday life and reconfiguring how people around the world perceive everything from technology, to politics, to popular culture, to relationships, to religion (Snyder 1995:25). A result is the growing recognition that culture is not as immutable as once was thought; rather, it is being constantly reconstructed by the people of that culture, in accordance with the perpetual global flow of objects, images, ideas, and populations (Rynkiewich 2002:315).[3] This means, even in societies once believed to contain stable cultural boundaries, that cultures, i.e., "systems of beliefs, feelings, values, and their correlated symbols, behavioral patterns, and products" (Hiebert 1999:374) are becoming more "fluid," while formerly believed-to-be solidified boundaries, even race and ethnicity, are being globally "appropriated" (Johnson 2003:2), "non-essentialized" (Hooks 1995:117), and "redefined" (Banks 1996:2).

There is little doubt that globalization has had a paradoxical effect in that earth currents have created a sort of retrenchment into traditional cultural identities (Lewellen 2002:91). This was clearly the case in Denmark, as mentioned, when the pressure to succumb to internationalism in relation to adoption of the new European currency caused a backlash of nationalism, where Danes voted (by a slight margin) unfavorably to the referendum on the Euro. This shows that one cannot underestimate particular and indigenous responses to hegemonic forces and global trends. Reactions throughout Europe to issues such as immigration policy, the spread of Islam, and maintaining indigenous languages rather than subsuming to the *lingua franca* of the globalized world (English) cannot entirely be separated from the desire to stem the impact of global currents on local cultures.

Globalization and Identity Formation

Of particular relevance to the discussion on the juxtaposition of global currents and the gospel music movement is the formation of identity. Ted C. Lewellen notes, "identity has been one of the most problematic and contentious fields within recent anthropology" (Lewellen 2002:90). The problem of identity is indeed exacerbated in the postmodern context, due to the "polymorphous versatility" and "identity diffusion" which Robert Jay Lifton refers to as "the protean style" (Lifton 1995:130-131).[4] The notion of "identity confusion," which was explored by noted psychologist Erik Erikson, is a form of psychological impairment that speaks to the tendency to identify too closely with a variety of perspectives without having any real sense of self (Lifton 1995:130). One might be described as wearing many "masks," which can be worn interchangeably and without any real sense of personal schism or "schizophrenia." The point that Lifton makes is that the capacity to "change shape" and adapt to differing contexts is actually an advantage in a world characterized by awareness of a multiplicity of contextual patterns and human experience (Lifton 1995:131). The tacit cultural sanctioning of multiple identities within a single entity, which are then subject to constant interchangeability and reconstruction, explains in part how gospel adherents, who otherwise may not confess allegiance to Christ, are not discouraged from singing and appropriating the "God-element" in gospel, since that particular identity can readily be segmented from more dominant identifications. What seems to occur is that individual identities become grafted together, as people become more adept at adopting and absorbing pieces of different cultures that can be educed at will, depending on the context (Lewellen 2002:99).

Other than the "protean style" characterization employed by Lifton, the concept of "hybrid" is often used to describe developments in identity formation in the emerging global context. Lewellen argues that "hybrid" is an unfortunate trope in globalization linguistics, given the associations with biological "tinkering," though Snyder wisely notes the growing preference for the model of "organism" rather than the "machine" model of Newtonian physics and the Industrial Revolution (Snyder 1995:36). The underlying reality is that human identity in the contemporary world is often fragmented, compartmentalized, and polymorphous, which explains in part why adaptability to a variety of contexts is becoming more preferable than monolithic stability in terms of personality formation. Becoming a hybrid could very well be regarded as a survival technique in a world where cultures, worldviews, and behavioral patterns are compressed into particular social locations as a direct result of shifting populations and other global currents. This means that wearing "masks" is no longer a sign of psychological maladjustment, but rather as an emerging phenomenon linked to the ongoing process of cultural diffusion.

As a thesis, the notion of hybridity is concomitant with Patrick Johnson's contention that "blackness" is being appropriated globally, primarily through the cooptation of music and performance styles (Johnson 2004). Johnson did not name it directly, but this pattern can be particularly observed in the area of hip-hop ("rap") music, especially among white urban teenage boys. The fact that so many youth adopt the music, language, symbols, and even behavioral patterns of a genre created and marketed within a particular ethnic and social class context that on the surface elicits no common ground with many of its consumers is a pertinent example of Johnson's thesis. One can readily observe that "blackness" is being appropriated by "white" culture internationally; yet it is globalization theory that provides the categories for understanding how the formation of identity, even if it is a "black" identity among "whites," is influenced by the phenomenon of cultural diffusion. In a similar manner, the transmission and marketing of religious and spiritual ideas in the global consumer context is facilitating openness toward new and "foreign" religious expressions, which suggests how gospel music diffusion has been able to promote a distinct identity, even among those who share no real commonality with African-American religion and ethnicity.

Denmark's Emerging Worldview: Postmodernism

The impact of globalization, particularly in the Western world, is likewise altering people's worldview. As Snyder points out, the impact of the so-called "Earth Currents" has been the emergence of a plurality of worldviews, which include a global economic perspective, a quantum scientific worldview, an ecological or "gaia" awareness, and a neo-determinism (Snyder 1995). The mere recognition of such plurality in worldview perspectives provides a segue to understanding perhaps the most compelling worldview (or "anti-worldview") in the current era: postmodernism. In an article about theology, culture, and hermeneutics, Kevin J. Vanhoozer quotes Carl F. H. Henry, who wrote: "No fact of contemporary Western life is more evident than its growing distrust of final truth and its implacable questioning of any sure word" (Vanhoozer 1993:1). This growing distrust, which has touched every field of knowledge, is having profound implications for theology and Christian praxis in Denmark and elsewhere. This relates particularly to the fact that it is becoming increasingly difficult for people to believe in the supremacy of a single revelation or metanarrative, which in turn would be regarded as the overarching paradigm by which life and truth would be gauged. Whereas Denmark has been regarded as a Christian country and therefore has at least nominally embraced Christian religious suppositions, the general spirit of the late-modern/postmodern mood seems more determined to question and even refute all authority, particularly if it even hints at any sort of exclusivist claim to ultimate truth.

A leading intellect, whose very name is coterminous with postmodernism in many academic circles, is Jean-Francois Lyotard. His book, *The Postmodern Condition: A Report on Knowledge*, catalyzed what is now a common assumption about the state of postmodernism as an "incredulity toward metanarratives" (Lyotard 1997:xxiv). As Europe is completing its transition into the postindustrial age, which commenced by the late 1950's, the entire realm of epistemology has been undergoing a general transformation (1997:3-4). The notion that there exists one overarching narrative, such as the Enlightenment/scientific worldview and the basic assumption that knowledge is an end in itself, has given way to the plurality of narratives, where each form of discourse has a certain legitimacy. In this scenario, knowledge is no longer an end, but rather a means to an end, since "truth" is something to be commodified and sold for the purposes of the catalyst circulating the knowledge (Lyotard 1997:5). The crisis of narratives which is indicative of the postmodern condition has forged a kind of de-centralization of knowledge and power, with the help of cybernetic instruments of information-proliferation (1997:xxiii, 3). Instead of centralizing sources of authority, such as the nation-state or some unifying philosophy (such as Marxism), the relativism of narrative and discourse has begun to shift the balance of power from hegemonic centralization to local groups and individuals, via the dissemination of universally accessible information.

The growing consensus among Danish scholars is that Danish culture is in a similar transition. When one considers Denmark's history as a mono-ethnic, mono-cultural, and mono-religious society, the movement toward multiculturalism, which is now evident in many aspects of Danish life, should be viewed as no less than a major paradigm shift. A recent research foray entitled "the pluralism project," was conducted under the leadership of Århus professor Viggo Mortensen. The significance of the project is that it demonstrates how religious life in particular is being impacted, since the once homogeneous culture forged by the Constantinian arrangement and guarded by the monopoly folk church is giving way to a different worldview – one that is pluralistic and multi-religious (Mortensen 2005:139). The effects of globalization are, in spite of the Danish Folk Church's continued position of dominance, perhaps moving Danes toward a free market approach to faith, in keeping with Rodney Stark's rational choice perspective (Mortensen 2005:144). This remains to be seen, since church life in general is not yet experiencing any significant renaissance, and the turn toward individualization and privatization in regard to faith is difficult to interpret. Nevertheless, in light of immigration and exposure to other forms of spirituality, Christian and otherwise, the foundational worldview of Danes and other Europeans is changing – from modernism to postmodernism.

One cannot overlook the irony of the term "postmodernism." In choosing this particular nomenclature, one is assuming a linear progression in order to categorize an epistemological shift that by nature defies such characterization. Paul Hiebert's *Missiological Implications of Epistemological Shifts* does much to perpetuate this irony, despite the helpful typologies he employs for the sake of approaching the foundations of knowledge missiologically. It is apparent that Hiebert uses modernist thinking, with its penchant for objective knowledge and categorizations, in describing the emergence of philosophical underpinnings that value subjectivity and the deconstruction of epistemological boundaries. Such attempts to objectify and systematize a particular type of thought that inherently engenders diametrically opposed assumptions is likely skewed in the sense that it endeavors to define that which is by definition incommensurable. Yet postmodernism itself in a way is reminding us that nothing can be known apart from the context in which it is embedded, thus supporting the notion that such an elusive and ambiguous term must be juxtaposed with the construct that it is reacting against – in this case, modernism. The irony of postmodernism (if it is indeed post- anything) is that it cannot be conceived in isolation from the cultural and epistemological hegemony that it advertently or inadvertently seeks to dismantle, and therefore must be inexorably linked with its own antithesis.

If one were to subsume to the type of linear categorizations so indicative of modernism, it is possible to trace the seismic epistemological changes that have shaped Western culture since before modernism. Although the term "premodern" may be overly problematic, given the reductionism involved in lumping together all of human thought prior to the fifteenth century, some defining features can be noted. The primary distinction revolves around the twin axioms of revelation and authority. Before the onslaught of the scientific age, the locus of truth and reality was mostly regarded as residing beyond the human mind. Although the Christian concept of theological anthropology has never been univocal, teetering constantly between the bipolar assertions of *imago Dei* and human depravity, the belief that humanity is part of some greater cosmic order that he/she was not responsible for designing was likely never seriously assailed. The worldview espoused in the Bible, including the supremacy of God, a multi-tiered universe, and the roles of the church and governing authorities as agents in the overall divine scheme were foregone conclusions for many centuries, at least in the Judeo-Christian "universe." Within this providentially sanctioned agenda the church was regarded as the ultimate arbiter in interpreting matters of truth and heralding revelatory knowledge. Although kings generally maintained an autocratic dominion over their subjects, the overall tenor of the Christianized premodern world was theocratic. The ultimate ruler was (allegedly) God, and the distinction between sacred and secular, which has been a normative bifurcation in more recent centuries, would have appeared nonsensical.

The genesis of the modern worldview coincides roughly with the onslaught of the Copernican revolution. The sixteenth century, which produced theological giants such as Luther, Calvin, Zwingli, and their ensuing Reformation movements, likewise witnessed an explosion of scientific insight, which eventually served to mitigate the role and influence of the church. Christians were forced on the defensive, often trying to defend arcane suppositions that no longer held credence in light of the burgeoning popularity of modern scientific thought. While the church was struggling to maintain her authority, the age of the Enlightenment was posing even greater challenges to Christian witness. Newtonian physics and the discovery of the natural laws of *cause and effect* began to displace purpose and teleology from common assumption (Newbigin 1995a:24). Kantian philosophy began to propound the supremacy of human reason and the *rational individual* as the exalted epistemological foundation. The birth of modern democratic thought and the accompanying philosophy of utilitarianism served to strengthen *individualism* by emphasizing rights, pursuit of happiness, and freedom, without clearly defining, in lieu of the new belief in human autonomy, what we are free from and what we are free to (Hauerwas 1993:33).

The rise of nationalism, the doctrine of *progress*, the dichotomy between fact/value, subject/object, and public/private spheres of existence, and the commitment to spread the Western cultural hegemony with missionary zeal all loom as trademarks of the modern project, which over time have displaced ecclesial authority and the previously unswerving conviction of the primacy of revelatory knowledge. In regard to the latter axiom, it was the unilateral impulse to remake the world in the image of the West that led to the systematic exploitation of the two-thirds world. The oppression of much of the world's population in the name of "progress" and "civilization" has been euphemistically referred to as *colonialism*. While an increasing stream of materials and narratives are now emerging from the continents of Africa, Asia, and South America, as well as the indigenous peoples of North America, all of which recount the particular effects of Western imperialism, the general colonial impulse can be related to the intrinsic belief of Westerners in their own cultural superiority. This in turn justified, in the minds of Westerners, the implementation of ideological suppositions, resulting in the institutionalization of cruelty. The slave trade, for example, as well as all of the other subtle and barbaric forms of cultural insensitivity is now casting retroactive aspersions on the modernist agenda, suggesting that the end product has greatly undermined the kind of world that Enlightenment harbingers likely assumed they would engender. The growing recognition of atrocities committed under the banner of scientific achievement and progress is in part responsible for the radical epistemological shift that is issuing in the postmodern era.

The Defining Features of Postmodernism

In reference to the aforementioned quote by Carl Henry, the emerging ideological climate presents the distrust, or negation of any sure word. This is interesting, not just for what it may be doing to the church in countries like Denmark, but for what it is doing to the longstanding hegemony of Western thought and culture. As the armor of Western dominance begins to crack, the era of globalization and pluralism is emerging as a rising star in the world. Yet what postmodernism actually means, and whether or not it applies outside of the Western context where postcolonialism seems to be a more appropriate paradigm and methodology, are debatable. It seems evident, in the very least, that postmodernism is affiliated with the rise of pluralism, not just as a *de facto* part of life, but as an overarching ideology. Philosophical pluralism fosters an extreme epistemology of subjectivity, which in part offers the corrective to the monolithic Western worldview that thinkers such as Lyotard, Michel Foucault, and Jacques Derrida have sought to deconstruct. In narrative terms, the transition to postmodernism constitutes the movement from a centralized story, controlled and disseminated by Western thinkers, to an emphasis on the uniqueness of each story, and the assumption that they all have intrinsic value. Thus the epistemological framework is shifting from "conceptual" to "contextual," as the universal hegemony of the West is being eclipsed by the particularity of social location.

Before his untimely death in 1992, David Bosch portrayed postmodernism in a favorable, almost utopian light, arguing that it constitutes a movement away from the shackles of Enlightenment or modernist ideology toward something much better. He offered it as a paradigm that would eventually supplant the axioms of modernity: expanded rationalism and narrative over rationalism; the "I/thou" scheme over the subject/object polarity; the rediscovery of teleology over natural cause and effect; the fiduciary framework of life over the fact/value dichotomy, and so on (Bosch 1991:349-362). Although Bosch's optimistic assessment has not (yet) come to fruition, there are elements in postmodernism that indeed are providing necessary correctives to the excesses of that which it defines itself against.

In an attempt to highlight the traits of postmodernism, Walter Truett Anderson's book, *The Truth About the Truth*, portrays the emerging worldview paradigm in all of its "multifaceted splendor." Instead of offering research-based arguments and definitive explanations about this emerging epistemological phenomenon which might serve to convince or appease linear thinking modernists, Anderson compiles essays and excerpts that, in the end, reveal the kaleidoscopic nature of postmodernism. In keeping with the postmodern mood, the contributions he collects from a variety of sources ultimately speak to the <u>experiential</u> rather than <u>conceptual</u> framework that characterizes the emerging epistemology. By presenting "splotches" from thinkers representing many disciplines, such as architecture, literature, the arts, sociology, philosophy, history, anthropology, and others, the reader is invited to experience postmodern thinking as a "collage," "pastiche," or tapestry, where almost any configuration or juxtaposition seems possible (Anderson 1995:23).

Of the many articles and essays included in Anderson's collection, an excerpt by Berger and Luckmann perhaps captures, as well as anything else, a good part of the essence of postmodernism. In theorizing that reality is a social construct that germinates within the human mind rather than externally in nature and then is "reified" in a way that paradoxically suggests that humans are shaped by dehumanizing forces, the sociologists lend additional credence to the instrumentalist nature of epistemology (Berger and Luckmann 1995:36-39). It is probably no exaggeration to assert that the notion of reality as "socially constructed" has become a sort of postmodern mantra. Although the emerging epistemology does not readily lend itself to the idea of unifying themes (except the unifying notion that there are no real unifying themes), there does seem to be a common thread that knowledge emanates subjectively and is consequently reified into objective systems, such as institutions, cultures, worldviews, symbolic universes, etc., which are then portrayed as being something other than socially constructed. Derrida picks up on this notion as well in his commentary on "substitution" (Derrida 1995:86-91). The underlying assertion that "there is nothing outside the text" in a way constitutes the canvas upon which postmodern thought is constructed – a theoretical framework in which there is no distinction between the signified and the signifier, and where ideas of transcendence are assumed to reveal more about the one who is expressing it than what is actually being expressed.

Of particular interest in postmodern thinking are writings which deal with the concept of selfhood. In the postmodern context, even the idea of gender is socially constructed and then reified in various cultural contexts through typification, which in turn leaves the impression that roles and gender-based behavior are determined by nature, rather than being byproducts of human construction. This would likewise imply that assuming the character traits of a particular ethnicity by a differing culture – *vis a vis* white culture assimilating the ethos of Black gospel – is not far-fetched in the postmodern world. As noted, Lifton's article on "the protean style" captures the redefining of personhood that is symptomatic of the postmodern age. By positing that human identity in reality is polymorphous and composite rather than singular and unified, Lifton seems to describe how people cope in light of the pluralism of contemporary life. Of course, the idea itself is hardly contemporary. Vanhoozer cites Shakespeare, who seemed to intuit the emergence of the protean being even at the outset of modernity:

> All the world's a stage,
> And all the men and women merely players.
> They have their own exits and entrances,
> And one man in his time plays many parts.
> (cf. Vanhoozer 1993:1)

This "new" concept of personhood can be perceived as negative (i.e., split identities indicate "rootlessness" and fragmentation) or positive (the protean self is more capable of dealing with the "otherness" and diversity that characterizes the postmodern world). Regardless, it seems to offer a poignant and accurate description of contemporary existence in the postmodern age, suggesting some keys to understanding the worldview that facilitates the phenomenon of Black gospel diffusion.

Is Denmark Really Postmodern?

The fact that the Danish Folk Church has not experienced any sort of mass exodus is cause to wonder whether Danes in general can be categorized as postmodern. Although allegiance to the church is not demonstrated in terms of active participation, the high degree of membership signifies that aside from the diversity of extant worldview perspectives, an overarching (albeit enervated) cultural hegemony may still remain intact. As has been stated, the role of the church in society, particularly the Folk Church, serves as a legitimating force designed to protect the boundaries of cultural identity within the nation-state. Since Denmark does not have any extensive history of multiculturalism, the cultural boundaries have been relatively tangible. This would include a worldview that even still has not been severed from its Christian heritage. The importation of other spiritualities has certainly created a more competitive religious market, as the spread of New Age spirituality and Islam, among others, might indicate. However, no other religious movement or philosophy, including secularism, has emerged to present the kind of alternative to the foundationalism of Cultural Christianity that one would rightfully expect in a truly postmodern context. Bishop Lindhardt's image of "scratch ticket" Christians is certainly rhetorical; nevertheless, there is likely a dimension of homogeneity in the Danish worldview and mentality that still resides, which may be underestimated according to analyses that use pluralism and global currents as methodological starting points. If one is to convincingly label Denmark and other similar countries as postmodern, one cannot assume that the vestiges of the past, be they modernism, Christendom, or the long-standing particularities of a shared culture, have been eradicated in the present and summarily replaced by an alternate worldview. Postmodernism in such a context should be viewed as a perspective that co-exists with other more stable and consequent social constructs within a given culture.

The kind of postmodernism found in countries like Denmark does not spring forth from contexts that were culturally, ethnically, and religiously heterogeneous to begin with. Rather, it is understood in the fact that plurality prevails in light of the existence, or at least semblance, of a unifying cultural coherence. This reality is evident in the churches, since a diversity of beliefs and even non-beliefs are encompassed by the membership of the Danish Folk Church (Mortensen 2005:95). Within the one, there are many, and the "right" to interpret or construct meanings in association with existent forms is largely unassailable. Whether one might more appropriately refer to this condition as "ultra"- or "late-modernism" rather than postmodernism is debatable. The underlying reality is that Danes in general have as much access to information as anyone else in the world, and the impact in terms of the relativism of narrative and worldview is likely as great as anywhere else. Although identification with a particular culture is still somewhat normative, the key shift in human identity in the postmodern world is toward consumerist ontology. It is the very commoditization of life, where desire is fulfilled instantaneously in the cybernetic marketplace and reality is a commodity to be shaped and constructed by individuals and groups that characterizes the postmodern world. This is, of course, a reality from which virtually no Dane is exempt.

Postmodern Implications for Black Gospel Diffusion

A primary nexus between postmodern theory and Black gospel diffusion involves the twin concepts of identity and meaning formation. In a context where life is characterized as "protean," the capacity not only to perform a foreign musical expression but to adopt its ethos through rhetorical exchanges, ritual process, and mimesis becomes distinctly possible. The history of Black gospel music has demonstrated its ability to speak to audiences across boundaries of culture and ethnicity, despite its rootedness in the particularities of the African-American experience. What distinguishes the current adoption of gospel music from earlier cases, such as minstrelsy, is the degree of flexibility inherited by those who are accustomed to a cultural climate characterized by the convergence of multiple identities. Minstrelsy often turned black culture into a type of parody by viewing it from a position of assumed cultural superiority – which by current standards is regarded as demeaning and ethnocentric (not to mention racist). The performance of Black gospel in postmodern contexts often reflects something quite different. In a context where an overarching metanarrative has given way to the legitimization of a plurality of narratives and discourses, one is free to appropriate the expression that is deemed most suitable or desirable. Many interviewees reflect an attitude that runs antithetical to former assumptions associated with Anglo-Saxon hubris. Gospel music and the culture from which it emerges are regarded with highest esteem, even to the point of romanticization. This can be just another form of ethnocentrism, but the postmodern condition has arguably created a context where respect for the uniqueness of each perspective is more possible than before. In a performance setting, the issue of authenticity will invariably rise to the surface, yet postmodernism has made it possible for participants to alternate identities with the ease of changing attire. This in turn has facilitated the diffusion of gospel music as a cultural commodity and has promoted the adaptation of it in a way that respects its legitimacy as a form of cultural and spiritual expression.

Postmodernism, in Denmark and elsewhere, is signaling the demise of an overarching metanarrative (except for the categorical assumption that there are no metanarratives). What seems to be emerging is a new form of knowledge – where epistemology is inseparable from hermeneutics – and an ontology that is decidedly pluralist. The shift toward radical subjectivity and acceptance of philosophical pluralism has likewise drawn the focus away from conceptual orientation to an experiential framework. This means that gospel music adherents in particular are less attentive to how the music makes them "think" than how it makes them "feel." It also helps one to interpret how people of varying faith and non-faith orientations can sing, clap, sway, and commune together in church and non-church settings, without any sense of theological disorientation. The emphasis is on the shared experience in addition to the ability of each individual to construct the meanings that he/she deem appropriate to the experience, in light of the formation that is implemented by gospel leaders.

The instrumental epistemology that is indicative of the postmodern condition can and should be critiqued. The religious content expressed in gospel music strongly suggests that participants should not passively acquiesce to the prevailing conditions of the dominant culture – conditions that often are characteristic of social pathology. In a climate where extreme subjectivity, for example, places the individual in the center of that person's universe, the endeavor to actually find meaning rather than perpetually search for and "construct" it becomes less satisfying. The goal of much of spirituality is to establish a connection with something greater than the self, which is also a major purpose in gospel music. Postmodernism may be paradoxically mainstreaming the gospel movement while concurrently undermining the connection to religious content in the minds of many of its participants. This is an issue that likely does not sit well with the leaders and change agents who seek to maintain the nexus between Christian forms and meanings inherent within the musical expression.

However, a cultural climate characterized by the nearly uncritical acceptance of pluralism does have distinct advantages. In a sense, the real benefit for gospel music diffusion is that the adaptation of an imported spirituality and ethnic cultural expression is no longer treated as an anomaly. It is, of course, commodified and appropriated in a fashion similar to other cultural imports. Like other forms of discourse and knowledge, it is a means to some other end. Yet for those searching for spirituality that re-images the Christian message in ways that circumvent the indigenous expressions which generally lack vitality, gospel music signifies something vibrant and appealing. It is not the only expression in the world of cross-cultural spirituality that is having this sort of impact in the postmodern context, but in light of the ontology of pluralism and the overriding respect for particularity rather than a hegemonic metanarrative, the gospel movement has been able to increasingly establish itself as part of the religio-cultural tapestry.

Notes

1. A discussion of meaning construction among gospel music adherents is the primary focus of Chapter Eight.
2. Rifkin credits Benjamin R. Barber for coining the term "McWorld."
3. Implied in the notion that cultures are being reconstructed is the seminal theory of Peter Berger and Thomas Luckmann, as postulated in their book, *The Social Construction of Reality*. The primary hypothesis is that human beings are themselves responsible for creating cultural constructs, including institutions, traditions, etc., that they in turn perpetuate, reify, and legitimate to the point that the social constructions become mechanistically assumed to have some transcendent origin.
4. Lifton coins the term "protean" in reference to Greek mythology. According to lore, "Proteus" was a sea-god capable of changing forms. The connotations for the adjective can either be positive – such as "flexible," "versatile," or "adaptable" – or negative – as in "elusive," "uncommitted," or "disingenuous." Lifton basically argues that a protean identity is indeed an asset in a postmodern world.

Chapter 8

Gospel Music's Power to Form Meaning through Emotional Experience and Sublimity

Thus far, the story of Black gospel music in countries like Denmark has been explained primarily as a trans-culturally diffused innovation. The diffusion itself has been auspiciously aided by macro-, or global trends, which also have facilitated access to (among other things) imported artistic expressions and spiritualities. As Chapter Four has indicated, gospel music has diffused and been adopted according to reasonably predictable patterns mapped out in accordance with diffusion theory. This sets Black gospel music development among Europeans, as well as others, in the context of other viable musical diffusions, such as jazz, rhythm and blues (R & B), ragtime, hip-hop, and others.

However, diffusion theory does not directly acknowledge the role and effect of constructs and phenomena that defy immediate categorization. In particular, the diffusion of innovation framework does not adequately answer the question of meaning formation. In fairness to Everett Rogers' work, issues revolving around the construction of meaning and solidification of identity in the process of adaptation are not really within the scope of his research on diffusion theory. Thus Rogers should not be held accountable for something he did not intend to address in the first place. Nevertheless, understanding meaning construction is a critical element in grasping the adaptation of gospel music in places like Denmark.

In light of the fact that gospel music is imbedded in a Christian worldview[1] that participants may or may not share, it is important to ascertain some familiarity with the conceptual frameworks that shape the perception and experience of singing/hearing the music. Interviews and observations reveal that the actual meaning of gospel music to participants and audiences is an intricate web, involving the convergence of divergent meanings and associations. One should note that this has been no less the case of Black gospel music in its original African-American context. Since the dawn of Negro spirituals, meaning constructions have never been singular and without ambiguity. The existence of coded messages in song texts written in the context of slavery, for example, has been well documented. What is surprising is the degree to which the hermeneutical openness engendered in Black gospel music likewise has applied to cross-culturally diffused contexts.

From a Christian theological standpoint, the existence of diverse associations with gospel semiology raises a fundamental question that has been at the heart of this dissertation: Is the experience and performance of gospel music in cultural contexts such as Denmark primarily an expression of Christian faith, or is it an aesthetic/artistic innovation with spiritual undertones that makes Christian faith one of several possibilities? The answer to this question is exceedingly complex, and thus necessitates an awareness of several theories regarding the formation of meaning itself.

The Framework of Ecology in Meaning Construction

Howard Snyder's *Earth Currents* provides some important groundwork in determining the nature and process of meaning formation. In an intriguing and relevant foray into "the meaning of meaning," Snyder espouses the term "ecology" in positioning his argument. By this, he asserts that meaning is not understood so much in the individual parts, but rather in the interaction of the parts themselves. In contrast to the "atomistic" ontology of modernity (that is, the assumption that individuals and things exist as self-contained entities, and thereby related only mechanistically), Snyder proposes that meaning itself is found in relationship (1995:242). The ontology presented here is decidedly "molecular" in that being itself is essentially corporate in nature, implying that individuals or "parts" are best understood as they relate and correlate to the whole, including the environment itself. Ecology, according to Snyder, implies two things: unity (wholeness) and diversity (distinction) (1995:244). The idea, which not coincidentally shares an affinity with Eastern Orthodox Trinitarian theology,[2] underscores that separate and distinct entities are to be acknowledged (and appreciated), but are understood ultimately as they contribute relationally to the larger ecosystem. By acknowledging the "parts," the concept of ecology differs from both monism and ideas often associated with Eastern religious philosophies, such as Hinduism, which subvert or annihilate the notion of selfhood.[3] On the other hand, the essence of an ecosystem contravenes the excessive emphasis on the individual, which is often characteristic of Western thought.

Ecology suggests furthermore that meaning involves both "correspondence and signification," which generally means that one thing is understood as it relates to other things (Snyder 1995:244). As a background to Snyder's thoughts on ecology, the notion of meaning arising from interconnectivity between two or more things has been widely investigated in accordance with the theory of structuralism. The name Ferdinand de Saussure in particular has become associated with the school of thought that studies the nature of structures and relationships in the context of linguistic analysis. According to Saussurian vocabulary, meanings are apprehended as a byproduct of the interaction of *sign, signifier* (the sound pattern of a word), and that which is *signified* (the concept of the word itself) within a particular structure (cf. Culler 1998:175, Schatzki 1997:185). Saussure's structural linguistics was subsequently transposed into the field of cultural anthropology by Claude Levi-Strauss, among others, and has since been applied to other social sciences and literature (cf. Schatzki 1997).

Although the philosophy of structuralism is convoluted, the primary gist of meaning formation involves the relationships and (perhaps more importantly) the contrasts that differentiate signs within a given system, and not the signs themselves (Culler 1998:174). References to "God" in gospel music, for example, can be understood in the Danish context in light of how the sign ("God") relates to the meaning projections in the music, the similar or contrasting attitudes and mental constructs of those who sing the discursive "signs," and the underlying religious structures inherited within Danish culture. Although divergent meanings and attitudes toward God and the religious vocabulary in gospel music are present, an overarching coherence exists within the system or structure that allows the usage of these particular signs and symbols.

It should be noted that structuralist thought, especially in postmodern contexts, has often yielded to the developments of poststructuralism. The ruminations of Jacques Derrida – in particular the neologism that he has termed *différance* – suggest that there is no necessary correlation between the signifier and what is signified. There is, in other words, "nothing outside the text" (Derrida 1995:89). In constructing the word, *différance*, Derrida proposes a cross between "temporization," or better yet, "deference," and "difference" as a way of arguing that meanings are constantly changing, and therefore ultimately unknowable (cf. Derrida 1982:6-8). What we may think of as a meaning construct is in actuality, according to poststructuralist thought, open-ended and elusive. This means that ideas such as "ecology" and "coherence" are related to something other than an imposed or closed system: they defer to the perpetual state of meaning formation and thought construction, which is otherwise characteristic of the culture of postmodern pluralism, not to mention the gospel music constituency.

It is difficult to position Snyder's notion of ecology in light of the structuralist-poststructuralist debate, and perhaps in the long run it is not altogether important to do so. What the ecology of meaning perspective does offer is a relational framework that points to the possibility that meaning construction – as diverse and chaotic as it may seem on the surface – also defers to some corporate or collective interpretation. In relation to Trinitarian thought and consequently the concept of *missio Dei*, the ecology paradigm relates to an ongoing synergy between the individual parts, which, in the process, engenders meanings that transcend the parts themselves.

On the most profound level, this synergy is found among the gospel constituency in connection to the gospel ethos itself. Whether participants are consciously aware of it or not, the attraction that facilitates the convergence of multiple identities has to do with the foundational values, character, dynamic, style, and persuasiveness which are intrinsic to the gospel culture. It is clear that people bring diverse belief patterns with them as they interact with both the music and other participants, which would perhaps be a source of tension and eventual dissonance if the participants did not have some greater collective allegiance. The allegiance in this case is to the fundamental gospel music values, such as the capacity for ("come-as-you-are") openness, possibility of catharsis, formation of interconnectivity among the participants, accentuation of affectivity's role in music, commitment to aesthetic excellence, appreciation of African-American cultural and religious heritage, adaptation of kinetics (swaying and clapping, for example) as an integral component in performance expression, prevalence of joy and praise, and so on.

Gospel music participants, for example, like the Danish populace in general, often complain that the church is dull, lifeless, and boring. It is therefore intriguing to hear, time and time again, members of gospel choirs state, *Gospel is my church*. Even one particular participant, Kirsten, whose spiritual leanings are more in favor of New Age expressions, finds her choir to be an embodiment of the church, because it regularly participates in benefit concerts and, during devotionals, there is prayer for the sick and needy. Many members of my current gospel choir, just like in the past one, will refer to the church in which the choir meets as "my church," even though the choir is their only point of reference. Although these and similar examples may seem trite to some, they do illustrate that there is an allegiance to an overarching gospel ethos, which then entails the construction of meanings in synergy with the dynamics of Christian faith and community.

The question from a missiological standpoint probes the extent to which this ethos is considered an authentic expression of the faith that gospel texts intentionally name. In other words, is the gospel ethos a Christian ethos? According to E. Patrick Johnson's analysis of the Australian gospel choir, the nexus between the shared values of the gospel constituency and the emphasis on community and social outreach imbedded in Christian praxis is often made, even among those who eschew religious dogma. Certain practices, such as gifts to charity, benefit concerts, and other expressions of social responsibility are often acknowledged for their rootedness in Christian ethical principles (Johnson 2003:176). This is an important observation since it explains how those who might be inclined to reject "Jesus" and the tenets of Christian faith as byproducts of conceptual packaging may be equally inclined to embrace them on some other level, such as charity and love for neighbor, as well as psychological benefits involving catharsis, gestalt, and affectivity. This means that while dogmatic use of particular religious language may continue to be unfashionable and even repugnant to some, the gospel ethos legitimates such language by couching it in terms, imagery, and experiences that are more widely accepted.

Conversations with non-Christian gospel participants in Denmark corroborate Johnson's findings in Australia, which suggest that interplay between the gospel ethos and Christian faith does exist. Interviews cited in Chapter Five, particularly with non-believers such as Henning, Niels, Trine, Helle, and others bear out that Christianity is influential to them on some level, despite their own meaning constructions that may, on another level, disassociate them from the faith. In reality, there is likely no ultimate or definitive answer to whether or not the gospel ethos constitutes Christianity, even in some "exotic" and non-traditional form. One could argue that certain aspects of this particular ethos represent nothing more than some nebulous sense of good will, although the desire for goodness could also be interpreted as a sign of prevenient grace. Either way, understanding the persuasiveness of the gospel movement in light of the general religiosity imbedded in Danish (and perhaps Australian) culture suggests that the gospel ethos offers an example of how Christianity might be better equipped to accommodate the conditions of the audience *(pathos)* by presenting faith in some revitalized form. Whereas certain elements of Christianity are involved in defining the essence of the gospel ethos, the dynamics, emotions, and influence engendered by gospel music participation serve as a positive hermeneutic of the Christian ethos, especially for those who, as a result of their cultural and religious scripting, have grown accustomed to a religious faith that lacks vitality and credibility. All in all, the synergy between faith and gospel music allegiance expresses how the ecology of meaning paradigm relates to the gospel music culture, since it is within this framework that the multiple identities and meaning formations which comprise the gospel music constituency appear to converge in a way that brings faith into the picture.

Constitutive Rhetoric and Collective Identity

The idea of a coherent (ecological) gospel ethos that inspires allegiance among the participants leads to consideration of the process of collectivization. As the individual constituents of the gospel music movement become involved in the presentation of a message through the medium of a Christian music genre, they share a common identity. This identity is rooted in a particular narrative and emanates from an African-American religious expression as filtered through a series of cultural variables. In the process, a common identity is formed, which is a byproduct of certain rhetorical exchanges.

A possible key to understanding the rhetorical process involved in identity formation is presented by the theory of constitutive rhetoric. The theory can be traced in Benedict Anderson's reflections on nationalism in *Imagined Communities* (1991), and it has gained particular notoriety via the writings of Maurice Charland. Typically, constitutive rhetoric has been employed in connection with the emergence of nations through the construction of a shared national identity; however, it applies equally to social movements of all types.[4] The gist of the theory purports that a fundamental collective identity is rhetorically enacted for a particular group through the use of narrative and other symbolic strategies – which not only define, but also demonstrate, that identity. The group is thereby called or "summoned" to act in a way that affirms that identity (Charland 1999:616). The process can be observed or experienced most blatantly in political campaigns, where audiences are touched by the discourse of the orator and the accompanying campaign slogans, and then moved to respond in a way that confirms allegiance to party-political or ideological affiliation. Identity is thus evoked or summoned forth by means of "interpellation" ("hailing"), which is a form of recruitment of subjects that transforms them by virtue of discourse and aesthetic feeling (Charland 1987:233-234, cf. B. Anderson 1991:141, and Radwan 2004:192).

Akin to the theories of structuralism and post-structuralism, the process of collectivization according to constitutive rhetoric is enhanced by outside forces which it seeks to define itself against. In this way, an identity is forged also by portraying the opposition as a threat and then by constructing a narrative that is more convincing than that of the opposition (Charland 1999:616). Hauerwas and Willimon, for example, capture the essence of the rhetorical process in the formation of a coherent Christian identity. In their book, *Resident Aliens*, the authors not only recognize the church as "an alternative community," but also as a "beachhead" that proclaims its story as an offensive against competing narratives, such as liberal accommodationism, consumerism, and the like (1993). The gospel music movement throughout Europe and Australia likewise may be benefiting from the scripting of Cultural Christianity because the proliferation of Christian knowledge not only has sown the knowledge that creates familiarity with gospel music meanings, but also provides the antithesis to the spiritual vitality demonstrated in the movement. Thus it also is important to name a common "enemy" in order to create an identity that can readily be embraced by an otherwise diverse audience.

Constitutive rhetoric accounts for the construction and formation of identity as something that is ascribed to an audience, which it in turn adopts and materializes through its actions (Charland 1999:616). The most common rhetorical explanation for such identity-adoption is offered by the *persuasion model*, which is rooted in rhetorical theory dating back to Aristotle. This particular approach, which consequently has been the model of preference among most Protestants throughout the periods of the Enlightenment and modernity, attempts to persuade an audience through the crafting of speech, which then calls upon respondents to render a judgment on the basis of carefully constructed argumentation. Listeners are thus ideally "persuaded" to form opinions and make decisions in accordance with the speaker's presentation, while the oration itself "exploits" the *pathos* of the audience – that is, its values, character, affective dispositions, and presumptions (1999:616).

However, the persuasion model does not really take into consideration the precursory steps that make persuasion possible. This means that it does not take factors such as language, culture, and history seriously enough. As Charland notes, the constitutive model recognizes discourse, not only for its ability to persuade, but for the capacity to actually produce identity, or, "The categories by which the world, and indeed the self, are understood" (1999:616). In relation to the idea of persuasion, serious studies on conversion often suggest that a series of other factors must also be present before an individual re-orients his/her thinking and personal identity as a response to some form of proclamation or oratory. Lewis R. Rambo, for example, notes that conversion takes place within a dynamic context, which in turn gives meaning to the "crisis, quest, encounter, commitment," and other elements that are integral to the process (Rambo 1993:20). Although Rambo's study may not relate directly to the formation of identity acknowledged by constitutive rhetoric, it does corroborate the notion that antecedent conditions are necessary to the actual act of persuasion.

The historical underpinnings of the constitutive approach can be traced back to the Sophists, particularly the oratory of Gorgias, who was a contemporary of Socrates. As Charland states, it was more than his ability to persuade an audience by addressing its reasoning faculty, but his capacity to <u>enthrall</u> by "poetically transforming its experience of being" that would become a primary distinction in the constitutive rhetorical approach (1999:616). Although it does not provide the antithesis to the persuasion model, it does recognize something that can be critically observed in the postmodern condition. Due to the general de-emphasis of rationality in favor of radical subjectivity in much of contemporary Western culture, audiences are recognized as not merely consisting of rational beings who can individually be persuaded to reach certain conclusions through reasoned arguments; rather, they are presumed to possess affective dispositions where collective identity must be posited and constituted before persuasion likely can occur.[5] Thus there is a paradox in that reality cannot be understood apart from the perception of reality. According to this approach, knowledge is contingent and therefore integrally related to the framing of a particular ethos or worldview, from which identification is produced (1999:616-617). It is the initial experience of being <u>enthralled</u> that produces the kind of shared identity that is precursory to intellectual consent and facilitates the process of collectivization.

In regard to meaning formation, the constitutive model would remind us that meaning is related to identity formation. Since meanings are not constructed in a proverbial "vacuum," it is important to analyze structures, categories, experiences, and motives in order to ascertain a complete picture of how belief patterns originate. This suggests that all discourse, including that which establishes meaning, is not just epistemological, but ontological in nature (Charland 1999:619). In other words, what a person believes is not just a matter of what they know or consent to, but an issue of who they are. Constitutive rhetoric is noteworthy at this point because of the attention it gives to identity as the framework from which meanings emerge and subjects are transformed.

A parallel foray dealing with the correlation of constitutive rhetoric and Contemporary Christian Music (CCM) is presented by Jon Radwan. In an article dealing with the rhetorical force of song texts in forging Christian identity, Radwan focuses explicitly on CCM artists the Newsboys' 1995 hit, "Shine." Radwan's treatment of the song contains some ideas that are helpful in understanding the process involved in identity formation by demonstrating how the song invites its audience to "develop shared definitions of Self and Other" (Radwan 2004:188). It also provides a potential "roadmap" into apprehending how the interpellation involved in the constitution of identity not only applies to the discursive narrative of song texts, but also to the dimension of aesthetic feeling inherent within various art forms, especially music (Radwan 2004:192). Since texts and music form a symbiosis, one can observe that songs work discursively through lyrics and more intuitively through music, which in turn "Evokes and makes present or available, an aesthetic style and a corresponding persona" (Radwan 2004:196). This separates music from propositional discourse, since symbols in music by design function to effect attitudes and emotions. Although the symbols in song lyrics are important, the ability of certain music to constitute identity involves the conjoining of both conceptual and affective dimensions, which then has the power to form a collective and stylized identity, in addition to a specifically denoted meaning (Radwan 2004:194). Based on the massive followings that certain music genres attract, including CCM and Black gospel, and the capacity for songs to actually alter behavior and re-orient allegiances, music itself can provide some potent examples of the principles enacted in the theory of constitutive rhetoric.

The Power of Gospel Music to Constitute Identity

The constitutive rhetorical model in communication theory is a helpful lens in interpreting the formation of identity, not only among CCM adherents, but also among the Black gospel music constituency. Even though gospel music participants come from diverse backgrounds in terms of lifestyle, faith, and ideology, a specific identity is indeed prescribed to all constituents, which, according to the idea of ecology, engenders coherence, synergy, and collectivity. This socially constructed and rhetorically constituted identity applies equally across the divides of gender, age, social position, sexual orientation, and religious affiliation. This is an integral part of the gospel music ethos: it establishes community based on the learning and performance of a Christian music style which is open and non-judgmental toward those who may not personally espouse the specific content of the songs. As a point of departure from the "us and them" Christian identity forged in the CCM song, "Shine,"[6] the gospel music discursive is usually much more bilateral in its portrayal of human beings in relation to the divine.[7] This implies that people are regarded as equals in both their struggles and joys, which is likewise a defining element in the gospel ethos (cf. Radwan 2004:214). The rhetoric in gospel music affiliation arguably creates a climate where acceptance (within the boundaries of a certain musical sensibility) is normative, and a persona of "joyful energy" constitutes the collective face of those who become part of the movement.

Perhaps the most conspicuous segue between gospel music and the constitutive model revolves around what Charland refers to as the capacity to enthrall. Although the degree of enthusiasm expressed for gospel music among the participants may vary, those who ascribe most ardently to the socially engineered gospel identity would testify to some emotional or aesthetic experience as the reason for adoption and continued activity. Whether it was through the feeling of awe inspired at a gospel festival, the cathartic release felt while attending a concert, the "pied piper affect" of a gospel leader, or some profound resonance with the message one heard in a gospel song, those who have become formed by this collective identity would cite an initial affective experience as critical to their engagement in the movement and acceptance of the ethos. The experience relates to categories known particularly in the realm of aesthetics, such as the numinous and the sublime. The relevance is that the drawing power of gospel music, choirs, and events pertains to rhetorical processes that begin with some sort of "encounter," which then facilitates persuasion and the acceptance of a prescribed identity that materializes in performance and rehearsal settings. It is the enactment of Christian symbols in the music and subsequently through acts of charity and "love for neighbor" that makes Christian faith a formative part of the constituted ethos as it is played out – from the point of enthrallment to the assuming of a collective identity.

In regard to meaning formation, constitutive rhetoric presupposes that meaning and identity are intertwined. This provides a plausible explanation regarding how gospel music constituents can oppose the Christian message on a personal-subjective level and embrace it on a collective-subjective level. Although non-Christian members may actively construct meanings that belie the prevailing semiology in gospel music, these participants are still incorporated by an ethos and a narrative, and are summoned to embrace an allegiance that transcends the presentation of the form of Christianity that they have consciously or unconsciously rejected. The motives among the constituents may be quite diverse, but the power of rhetoric to incorporate diverse individuals into a shared identity with common goals can readily be observed. Faith, in the context of gospel music, becomes part of the identity that is integral to the gospel narrative, albeit in a re-packaged and re-imaged form. In this case, it is a Christian identity that paradoxically may be casting a critical shadow on Cultural Christianity as well as some elements of traditional Danish culture, and which constitutes the matrix from which greater meanings are formed and established.

The Sublime

Interpretive theories, such as the ecology of meaning paradigm, structuralism/ poststructuralism, and constitutive rhetoric can and do shed light on gospel music from the vantage point of meaning construction and identity formation. In fact, these theories perhaps warrant more attention than they have been given in this study because of their value in helping to shed light on the complex yet critical issue of meaning. However, the experience of gospel music from the perspective of the participants suggests that other factors of an even more ethereal nature are involved. Since gospel music also educes strong emotional feelings that are related to religious experience and aesthetic beauty, one would be remiss not to incorporate categories of understanding that relate directly to affectivity. One such category for understanding might be the impulse of *praise*. In a book by Daniel Hardy and David Ford, *Praising and Knowing God*, for example, the authors cogently promote praise as that which "perfects perfection," that is, a mutual "delight" which in itself is something of worth (1985:6). In light of the "stoicizing" of faith, which is often indicative of Western European religiosity, and the inherent joy which emanates from gospel music participation, this particular category could yield valuable insights into the overall allure of gospel music among Christians and non-Christians alike. After all, praise relates not only to the emotions and spontaneity, but to something more primordial and transcendent in the human composition.

Another similar category is *desire*. As a framework that has received some attention in the writings of postmodernists, most notably Jean-Francois Lyotard, desire implies political assumptions ("libidinal politics," as Lyotard refers to it) by accounting for the plurality of desires that otherwise may be ignored or devalued in hegemonic systems (Gutting 1998:606).[8] This theory, which is a development of Derrida's notion of *différance*, might also provide a necessary corrective to the inordinate focus on collectivization inherent in the constitutive rhetorical approach.

However, the category that seems to elicit the most promise in interpreting the otherwise indefinable and ineffable feelings associated with the gospel experience is the *sublime*. The concept of the sublime has had an erratic history throughout the course of speculative thought, attracting interest at particular historical junctures, while remaining dormant during others. The idea can be traced back to ancient philosophy, especially in the thought of the first century AD Greek rhetorician, pseudonymously known as Longinus. His treatise, *On the Sublime*, points to a category for understanding "greatness" in literary language that transcends mere persuasion. In endeavoring to identify a language-based source of excellence that takes on a transcendent quality, Longinus writes:

> Sublimity is always an eminence and excellence in language; and that from this, and this alone, the greatest poets and writers of prose have attained the first place and have clothed their fame in immortality. For it is not to persuasion but to ecstasy that passages of extraordinary genius carry the hearer. (Longinus 1985:2)

In contrast to the reason-oriented approaches of Aristotle and Cicero, Longinus' visceral concept of sublimity ventures to address issues of style and emotion as integral to content (Oravec 2000:757). It would seem on the surface that he was preoccupied with literary greatness as the segue to the sublime, which ultimately would prove to be too narrow a reference, and which may in part explain why the idea was not subsequently developed until the neo-Classical period in the seventeenth century, and later in late eighteenth century Romanticism. However, there are indications that Longinus' scope was much larger than literary application in relation to the sublime. He wrote: "Our conceptions often pass beyond the bounds which limit it; and if a man were to look upon life all around, and see how in all things the extraordinary, the great, the beautiful stand supreme, he will at once know for what ends we have been born" (Longinus 1985:65). Though Longinus' writing contains seeds for expanding the concept deeper into the realms of aesthetics and religion, very few known sources endeavored to explore how sublimity is implicit to other areas of life until many centuries later.

The etymology of "sublime" is rooted in the Latin *sublimus*, a word that originally suggested "height." The connotation is linked to the cosmos – *sublimi feriam sidera vertice*, "with head uplifted I shall strike the stars" (Martland 1987:97). Although the idea is rarely related explicitly to religious understanding, it does imply acknowledgement of transcendence as an operative force in the human subconscious. Joseph Addison elevated the Longinian notion of transcendence in referring to the sublime, while Edmund Burke propounded the idea of "terror" and "self-preservation" as integral to the understanding of the concept (Crowther 1999:202). In his writing, *A Philosophical Enquiry into the Origin of Our Ideas on the Sublime and the Beautiful,* Burke recognizes the overemphasis of reason, noting that the source of greatness is something which "anticipates our reasonings and hurries us on by an irresistible force" (Burke 1968:57). The most profound source of sublimity comes from whatever excites the ideas of pain and danger, that is, whatever is "terrible" or is about terrible objects, thus operating analogously to terror (1968:39). In this sense, the sublime constitutes a crucible of sorts, producing out of the experience or apprehension of pain and death the strongest emotion that the mind is capable of feeling. Though other sources of sublimity do exist according to Burke – among them being confronted by immeasurable vastness, infinity, magnificence, and difficulty – the common characteristic is the awareness that the dimension of affectivity precedes and influences our reasoning capacity (Burke 1968:57).

The implications of Burke's concept of sublimity in relation to the sociohistorical circumstances from which gospel emerged are potent. The very defining theme of Black gospel – "Good news and bad times" – suggests how the sublime as arising from an encounter with "the terrible" can constitute a substantial category for interpreting its essential "greatness." However, subsequent ruminations have expanded this notion in ways that are perhaps more useful to the understanding of the cross-cultural diffusion of gospel. Immanuel Kant provides one such source. In the latter part of the *Critique of Judgment,* Kant posits different categorizations for apprehending the sublime. One such framework includes what Kant terms "the mathematically sublime." This is the name that he affixes to what is "absolutely great," that which is incomparable and ultimately beyond measure. According to Kant, we are able to ascertain only the semblance of how great anything is by reference to numbers, or approximate measurements; thus "the mathematically sublime" is essentially an aesthetic quantifier which points to that which is subjectively infinite (Kant 1955:498). This type of sublimity is not a pure concept of understanding or an intuition, or even a subcategory of reason (1955:497). Though devoid of form, it does convey a universally communicable "delight" which spawns the imagination. It is presented as a concept under the umbrella of aesthetics, but is done so only to explain the otherwise incommunicable concept in terms of ideas that are intelligible according to known structures of thought. This speaks to the notion of the sublime as representing a "subjective finality" that is not analogous to recognized objective categories (Kant 1955:497); in other words, the sublime can only be qualified as preeminent, and ultimately approached more in terms of via *negativa* (i.e., what it is not), rather than *via analogia.*[9]

Kant also made reference to the "dynamical (metaphysical) sublime," which he relates to forces of nature and the underlying sources of fear or reverence (1955:502-503). By alluding to the might of nature and the response it provokes, Kant demonstrates some affinity with Burke, while adding an ethical dimension in relating the sublime to "the law within" (Oravec 2000:759). Though Kant's writings at this point are exceedingly difficult to understand (cf. Kant 1955:502-504), one can sense the implications for studying the affect and evolution of meaning associated within the gospel movement, which in its very essence, is both spiritual/religious and musical. The fact that a large number of gospel music interviewees and conversation partners indicate that their actual experience is something that is not quantifiable or definable suggests they are attuned to something that defies immediate categorization. One might add that the root of the experience, and in turn the meaning behind it all, is not akin to the sense of beauty related predominantly to art, since beauty is connected with the actual form of some object. The sublime is not related to forms and boundaries; it involves something deeper, and is ultimately related to the sentiment of the mind rather than the virtue of the object to which one is relating (Kant 1955:504; cf. Radloff 2002:1).

In exploring other contours regarding how the sublime can suggest the nature of something that ultimately cannot be fully accessed via analogue or quantification, one can find clues in the writings of Søren Kierkegaard (S.K.). Although he did not employ the same taxonomy, one can find a nexus between the sublime and his musings on the notion of "indirect communication." In his writing, *Concluding Unscientific Postscripts to Philosophical Fragments*, Kierkegaard posits that language communication itself is dialectical, which points to the incongruence and disconnect that can occur between objective and subjective thinking (Kierkegaard 1991:75). In light of the ongoing intellectual conflict Kierkegaard had with some of the high ranking ecclesiastics of his day, including Grundtvig, as well as his general disdain for the dominant speculative philosophy of his day, Hegelianism, one could surmise that his theory was a polemic against the religious and philosophical ideas of his time. To him, they had more or less reductionistically prepackaged knowledge into directly attainable systems (cf. Thielst 1994:217-218).

For S.K., direct communication is a fraud toward God, towards oneself, toward others, and toward the entire gamut of thought (Kierkegaard 1991:75). Outward expressions do not capture the heart of true knowledge; truth is a matter for the subject, as reflected in inwardness and possession. Addressing the theory of direct and indirect communication in several of his writings, including *Opbyggelige Taler (Edifying Discourses)* and *Enten/Eller (Either/Or)*, S.K. demonstrated his brilliance by persuasively arguing against categorizations which insufficiently capture the essence of faith and knowledge (Perkins 1981:57). In a truly sublime work, *Frygt og Bæven (Fear and Trembling)*, for example, S. K. presents the reader with a glimpse into the ethical conundrum faced by Abraham on the verge of sacrificing his son, Isaac (Kierkegaard 1974). As the Biblical patriarch and archetype of faith is confronted with the God who would command him to destroy the very one whom God had given him as a sign of great blessing and affection, Kierkegaard explicates the essence of sublime terror in light of this astounding paradox, which then leads to an experience of God's "otherness" that contradicts all humanly constructed ethical systems. It is through such revelatory insights, such as the "suspension of the ethical," the use of irony, and indirect communication that one can discern in Kierkegaard recognition of some deeper religious experience – an experience that often remains latent and undetected by conventional wisdom and universal systems. These sorts of epiphanies render Kierkegaard's work relevant to ongoing discourse on the sublime.[10]

A work which more directly links the sublime with the notion of religious experience is *The Idea of the Holy*, by Rudolph Otto. Like Longinus, Burke, Kant, and others before him, Otto purports that there exists a category of incommensurability, which is apprehended affectively and supersedes rationalism. Though he carefully distinguishes his hypotheses from "irrationalism," which connotes something much different than what he intends to convey, Otto expounds on the problem of portraying God and religious experience primarily in rationalistic terms, while concurrently exposing the cultural bias toward rationalism (Otto 1971:1-4). Holiness, for example, is a category of interpretation in the sphere of religious thought which cannot be explained solely in the preexisting frameworks dictated by the Enlightenment penchant for reason. Though it is often taken to mean "completely good" with moral significance, Otto understands that there is an "unnamed something" at work in the Holy – a living force that is beyond human taxonomy and classification (1971:6). This leads to Otto's now well-known reference, which he calls the *numinous*. As an interpretive framework, Otto reminds us that the essence of holiness, or the Holy, cannot be measured against known systems; it is absolutely primary, completely "other," *sui generis*. It is something which cannot be taught – only evoked, stirred, or awakened in the mind (1971:7).

The expression for the sense of the Holy is what Otto refers to as the *mysterium tremendum* (Otto 1971:12). Recalling somewhat the writings of Burke on the sublime, the *mysterium tremendum* conveys both the hidden, esoteric nature of the Other, and the terror, dread, and awe which accompanies religious experience. The response is emotional, and can be manifest in a tranquil mood of deepest worship or a frenzy characterized by a sudden eruption (1971:12-13). It evokes an element of urgency, vitality, energy, passion, emotional temper, force, movement, excitement, and activity; it is, simply stated, the impetus for religious response that emerges from a state of worship and communion with God (1971:23). The primary emphasis once again is on feelings rather than reason, which Otto also links to supreme fascination, as well as boundless awe and wonder (1971:41).

Otto does not commingle the numinous and the sublime, though the two concepts are analogous. The fundamental difference for Otto is that the sublime is a frame of reference taken from aesthetics rather than religion, which one senses, according to Otto, renders the concept more diminutive by comparison. Nevertheless, there is correlation between the two constructs in that they cannot be unfolded or systematically explained. Both the numinous and the sublime exhibit a dialectical character by invoking diametric responses: intimidation and attraction; humility and exaltation; fear and rejoicing; and circumscription and transcendence (1971:41-42). The primary implication to be found in Otto for the gospel music movement is that the sublime becomes the most effective means of expressing the numinous in art, which includes music. Though his writings on the subject have many implications, the gist of his idea in this context is that sound and the accompanying feelings that are associated with music have the potential to unleash a subjectivity that overrides rational categorization while pointing to the Holy (Otto 1971:65-70). The sublime and the numinous are not coterminous, yet the aesthetic dimension known as sublimity does allude to that which is transcendent in Otto's thought, and is therefore useful in ascertaining the depth of religious meaning that may be associated with the gospel experience.

Beyond Rudolph Otto and his interplay between aesthetics and religion, the concept of the sublime has experienced a renaissance of sorts in the writings of postmodernists/poststructuralists – most notably Lyotard. In *The Postmodern Condition: A Report on Knowledge*, Lyotard posits that narratives in general are in crisis, which he expresses in what now has become a postmodern axiom: "an incredulity toward all metanarratives" (Lyotard 1997:xxiv). Even the "narrative" of scientific discourse, which has enjoyed hegemonic status in Western culture since the emergence of Enlightenment epistemology, can no longer be legitimated and regarded as immune to critique. In the absence of a unifying and hegemonic discourse, another universalizing narrative has paradoxically become elevated in society, albeit a de-centered and de-constructed narrative – namely, pluralism. It is the demand for diversity and difference that now provides the axiomatic supposition of plurality's "transcendence" in lieu of the negation of other absolutes. As Lyotard states: "Postmodern knowledge refines our sensitivity to differences and reinforces our ability to tolerate the incommensurable" (1997:xxv).

It is within a context lacking in metanarratives that Lyotard draws upon the concept of the sublime. In light of the de-legitimating of metanarratives, as society is characterized by "instability and accelerating complexity" (Crowther 1999:204), it is the sublime that provides the aura of transcendence, where complexity, rapid change, the breakdown of categories, and the general deconstruction of truth claims can actually be embraced – even enjoyed (Crowther 1999:202).

For Lyotard, the sublime is concomitant with poststructuralism. In contrast to Saussure's construct of sign, signified, and signifier, where an idea contains a direct correlative in terms of some physical manifestation, especially in language, Lyotard, like Derrida and others, contends that such correlations do not always exist. The sublime presents just such a case. It occurs when the imagination fails to project an object that adequately depicts or conveys the concept, thus relating to the recognition of incommensurability (Lyotard 1997:78). The idea is that the sublime refers to a reality that cannot be concretized; if it could, then it could not appropriately make reference to that which lies beyond. Citing Kant, who himself quoted the biblical injunction, "Thou shalt not make graven images" as the most sublime verse in Scripture, there is the recognition that the Bible itself forbids iconic presentations of the Absolute, thereby enshrining that which is beyond measure (Lyotard 1997:78).

Lyotard connects the sublime with aesthetics as applied predominantly to art, particularly avant-garde expressions. One could easily contend, however, that the concept has the potential for speaking to the world of music as well as art. In relation to what many people have experienced in connection with gospel music, for example, it has been argued that the enthralling-persuasiveness of the movement goes much deeper than the song texts, which some might glibly characterize as simplistic verses that are repeated in mantra-like fashion when performed. The power, the sense of awe, and the ability to draw followers while evoking a variety of emotions, even religious ones, among a spiritually eclectic gathering, perhaps relates to an unseen and unmeasured category that has no real equivalent in structuralist, modernist, and systems thought. In truly postmodern fashion, Lyotard explains how the aesthetic category of the sublime "rejects the terror of totality while celebrating the play of diversity" (Oravec 2000:760), which suggests how the gospel movement can be an appealing Christian expression in a postmodern context by virtue of its non-threatening, non-judgmental, and indirect nature.

Some Implications of Sublimity to Meaning Formation in the Gospel Movement

The relationship between Negro spirituals and the sublime is patently clear. As an expression of incommensurable religious experience in light of the "terror" of slavery, racism, oppression, and hardship in general, the musical expressions of African Americans in earlier centuries is much more visceral than mere rhythm, song meter, and text; they allude to something far greater. Colonel Thomas W. Higginson, a nineteenth century abolitionist, minister, and Harvard graduate who was in part responsible for the preservation of the spirituals, articulated the profundity of the music: "There is no parallel instance of an oppressed race thus sustained by the religious sentiment alone. These songs are but the vocal expression of the simplicity of their faith and the sublimity of their long resignation" (Darden 2004:99). Similar statements by more contemporary vanguards of Black gospel music contend that the impact and meaning of the expressions cannot be properly understood without making reference to categories such as the numinous and the sublime (cf. A. Jones 1993:16, 64 and Darden 2004:44).[11]

Although Danish gospel choir participants and audiences do not even remotely share the socio-political conditions that gave rise to such sublime expressions, there is nevertheless evidence that something deeply profound and immeasurable is at work in the gospel movement. One particular sign is the extent to which gospel music effectuates an emotional catharsis among participants and listeners. It is relatively normal, for example, to witness tears streaming down the faces of people in attendance at a gospel concert. When asked to describe the experience, respondents often indicate that they do not possess the vocabulary to do so. Interviewees and conversation partners have responded similarly to questions regarding meaning and appeal, and even when they did respond, it was common to hear them say that "the answer does not do justice to the actual experience." This does not necessarily prove that an ethereal category, such as sublimity, is crucial to the interpretation of meaning in gospel music, but it does underscore the presence of something deeply affective and subjective in the overall experience.

Another phenomenon in gospel music participation that opens the dialogue up to the sublime is the ability of the music and events centering on the music to awaken religious sentiments. The fact that Danish people, who are otherwise reputed for being reserved and dispassionate about religious matters, find legitimation for these sentiments in this particular musical expression presents some evidence that the essence of gospel relates to formless categories that are noumenal and primordial in nature. This is, of course, not the case for every gospel music participant and audience member; in fact, it may not be the case for the majority. Nevertheless, since a highly noticeable percent are aroused, incited, and enthralled by the experience, the sublime – which would also include the potential relation of sublimation and the subliminal – is a plausible category in the context of gospel music expression.[12]

Musicology and Affectivity

Thus far in this chapter, the power of gospel music to shape meaning has been explored in accordance with theories involving ecology of meaning, constitutive rhetoric, and the sublime. Together, they offer an interpretative framework regarding how an otherwise diverse constituency can find some semblance of coherence in the overall gospel ethos while experiencing, at least in many cases, something of great profundity on an affective level. Such a presentation harkens what William James once referred to as "The One and the Many:" in the midst of seemingly irreconcilable difference, there is an overriding harmony – and vice versa. In gospel music contexts, there is immeasurable latitude to appropriate meanings in whatever way the subject seems inclined, and yet there exists within the mix of meaning constructions incommensurable forces – rhetorical, aesthetic, and spiritual – which provide common ground on some deeper level for many of the participants.

Without intending to deviate from this interpretive framework, an obvious fact has of yet remained unstated: music in itself is unassailably recognized for its impact on the emotions. Writings on the sublime and the numinous in particular open up a dialogue on meaning construction as related to issues of incommensurability and transcendence. It should not be overlooked, however, that musicological forays also ruminate on the nexus between music and the non-rational dimension of human existence. In fact, the discipline of musicology generally includes affectivity as a valid area of consideration, in addition to rhetorical dimensions of and uses for music (Radwan 2004:191).

Some studies of note have worked explicitly with the subject of music, affectivity, and transcendence, and thereby can at least incidentally illuminate the subject of meaning formation in gospel music. In a still widely recognized work dealing with the meaning behind music in general, entitled *Philosophy in a New Key*, Suzanne Langer takes a deeper look at the factors involved in the transmission of feeling from presenter to audience in music, while raising the question of where the true aesthetic essence really lies (1951:204, 214). In an especially articulate statement, Langer demonstrates why musical/aesthetic symbols cannot be confused with discursive forms of communication:

> Music is revealing, where words are obscuring, because it can have not only a content, but a transient play of contents. . . The assignment of meanings is a shifting, kaleidoscopic play, probably below the threshold of consciousness, certainly outside the pail of discursive thinking. . . Not communication but insight is the gift of music; in very naïve phrase, a knowledge of 'how feelings go'. (Langer 1951:243-4)

What musical expressions may in actuality affect in listeners is exceedingly difficult to pinpoint; whether the source of feeling lies predominantly with the composer, the listener, the relationship of the two, some outside factor(s), or a combination of these elements remains a matter of conjecture. The main point is that even provisional answers to such questions begin by acknowledging the depth, transience, and effusiveness of emotions as a guiding force in human activity.

Langer's work was subsequently enhanced by Malcolm Budd, who in his book, *Music and the Emotions*, also considers the impact of music from many different angles. Included in his analysis is the experience of emotion as a "simple expression" with no other components, as a compound or composite experience, and beyond (Budd 1985:1). Although Budd's perspective at times appears "odd" by virtue of its modernist systematization of that which intrinsically is aloof to such categorization – namely, the emotions – it does raise issues dealing with the rhetorical categories of *ethos*, *logos*, and *pathos*. These are important considerations in apprehending the nature and impact of music upon affectivity, as well as the understanding of music as "unconsummated symbol," relating clearly to states of mind, character, attitudes of life, and other cognitive conditions (Budd 1985:104). Although Budd does not refer to the sublime directly, his analysis couches music theory in a way that envisages such a development by recognizing that emotions in music are radically subjective and indefinable in nature (1985:16-17).

As a related field, ethnomusicology furthermore explores cultural expressions of music, which among other things leads to the subject of *world music* and raises questions regarding the "transcendent" appeal of particular music genres on human intuition, imagination, and affectivity. Although ethnomusicology does, in the words of Leonard Meyer, demonstrate that meaning in music is "referential" and therefore not universally innate, there do seem to be some general consequences of music's impact on the emotions that apply cross-culturally (Meyer 1968:2). Of course, Meyer's analysis came too early to assess the impact of globalization in terms of the streamlining of musical genres cross-culturally within local contexts. The point is that musicology, as studied across boundaries of culture and ethnicity reveals that music is intrinsically able to charge the emotions in ways that little else can, and thereby influence how meaning is constructed and construed.

In general, the combination of musicology and the transformative missiological impulses inherent within the gospel music movement suggests an interpretation that emphasizes the nexus between affectivity and the divine. Renowned writer and philosopher, Mircea Eliade, was particularly preoccupied with this sort of interpretation of reality in recognizing the ability of art to suspend the traditional sense of time and space. For Eliade, art expresses the fundamental human instinct for transcendence (Eliade 1986:xi-xii). Of course, the power to enthrall and incite, which is indicative of Eliade's understanding of art, applies more than equally to the realm of music. Another music researcher, Lawrence E. Sullivan, examines in his book, *Enchanting Powers: Music in the World's Religions,* the universal impact of music on the cultures and religions of the world. Citing the insights of Renaissance humanist, Marcilio Ficino, who attributed "magical" qualities to music, Sullivan focuses on the unleashing of imagination, which he regards as a faculty of the divine spirit (Sullivan 1997:1). Music, according to Sullivan, is the most "malleable and profound expression of the power of imagination" (1997:1), which, from a Christian perspective, springs from Creation.

In reflecting upon the integration of music into the very fabric of the created universe, Jeremy Begbie articulates the matter of emotions in music theologically: "Human creativity is supremely about sharing through the Spirit in the creative purpose of the Father as he draws all things to himself through his Son" (Begbie 1991:179). In a way that perhaps ties in with Snyder's notion of the ecology of meaning due to its relational and Trinitarian foundation, Begbie implies that music and other art forms can provide inherent opportunities for animating praise, worship, spiritual freedom, and redemption, which are believed to be at the core of humanity's relationship to God. In proposing how Creation itself unleashes the imagination as typified in music, one finds in Eliade, Begbie, and Sullivan reflections relating theologically to the likes of Martin Luther and other Reformers (cf. Växby 2003:42), as well as a recognition of the "sacred" impulses in the symbols of music. Particularly in Begbie's interpretation, the impulses are related to the "Triune God," whose very being is relational and involves the outpouring of ecstatic love from one to the other (Begbie 1991:181).

In light of assertions regarding music's universality as expressed in the particularities of culture and personal preference, it is important to place the gospel movement within the grander scale of music's general impact on affectivity. As an expression of what I have earlier termed *missiomusicology*, gospel music is illustrating the power to impact emotions, forge meaning constructs, and shape identity in ways that for many, leads to a Christian encounter – in some cases, conversion. This does not always happen; what is perceived as sublime by some may be regarded as profane by others. Nevertheless, for those who are most impacted by the music, the experience is deeply emotional, and at times ecstatic.

The insight regarding the connection between affectivity in music and religious faith is peripherally supported by Paul Hiebert, who speaks of the neglected "middle zone" of human ontology (Hiebert, et al. 1999:49). The implication, based on studies of primal and folk religions, is that actions and thoughts are generally catalyzed by emotions which reside in the level of being that is especially neglected in a context where Western Enlightenment suppositions are predominant. These studies are corroborated by the work of neurologist Antonio Damasio, who in *Descartes Error* (2000) argues from the vantage point of neurobiology that human emotion and passion are at least as essential to brain function as reason. Although Hiebert and Damasio did not explicitly mention music, their conclusions corroborate musicological findings, which recognize music as a direct channel to feelings and intuition. This is indeed part of its "enchanting power" and consequent relation to the sublime. It is through emotion that one begins to relate to grandiose ideas, such as the numinous and the sublime, of which music constitutes the instinctual longing for transcendence, as well as what some might regard as a conduit to the "divine" (Hone, et al. 1996:54). Music can also be credited as being "The part of living that has the power to awaken in us sensations and emotions of a spiritual kind," touching on a dimension in the psyche that little else can reach (Onwachei 2001:134). One wonders why certain types of music are more inherently capable of arousing these sensibilities than others, as well as why certain genres exhibit the power to impact people cross-culturally. This enhances the fascination with Black gospel music, which is displaying this very ability to animate spiritual feelings and evoke religious experiences among culturally and spiritually diverse audiences.

Emotions in Gospel Music and the Issue of Control versus Spontaneity

In relation to the essence and impact of gospel music, a certain question arises as a result of general studies relating to music, emotion, and meaning in a religious context. This matter of aesthetic and religious concern is whether or not a vital musical/artistic expression should be manipulated as a means to an end, such as the employment of gospel music in service to Christian evangelism. Or, should the music and the ensuing movement simply be acknowledged and appreciated for what it is on its own merit? In an article, "New Sounds of Faith," John Hurst addresses the issue by using the example of the musical "Jesus Christ, Superstar," which was (and still is) a commercially successful venture that happened to call attention to Christ through the medium of unadulterated art (1998:339). Hurst points out that the motives of the composer/artist in this case did not necessarily determine the perception and the emotional impact of the music. Generally speaking, the composer will always lose control of the text and composition, which is keenly indicative of the postmodern condition where meaning in general is acknowledged as socially constructed.

In understanding the partnership of music and theology (as Hurst presents it), it could be argued, especially in light of the experience of gospel music in cross-cultural contexts, that evangelization is likely to occur intrinsically. If the movement is indeed emanating something of great relevance in terms of sublimity and emotional transcendence, then reconfiguring or harnessing the essence of the gospel movement to comply with an overt evangelistic thrust may ironically mitigate the movement's capacity to allure and transform people in accordance with Christian suppositions. This hypothesis would find a "soul mate" in Kierkegaard's preference for the subtlety of indirect communication rather than (what some might consider) the bombastic direct approach of overt evangelism.

The management or control of emotions in gospel music and other artistic expressions in order to serve an explicit missional end contravenes the "indirect evangelization" approach engendered by the gospel music movement. In fact, part of the appeal of the gospel music experience among its spiritually eclectic constituency is its spontaneity, which might become seriously compromised if it becomes detectably managed. Attempts to harness gospel music emotions by promoting certain meaning-associations are likely inevitable, but it would be wise to proceed in ways that are contextually relevant, such as through the configuration of a ritual process.

Borrowing from James Smith's ruminations on aesthetics in his book, *Introducing Radical Orthodoxy*, gospel music seems to imply a participatory (or, "creational") ontology, which implies the liturgical sacramentality of the created order (Smith 2004:222-223). Viewed from this perspective, music takes on a doxological dimension that leads to the affirmation not just of sacred arts, but the arts in general (2004:223). By presupposing goodness in creation, or in Wesleyan terminology, <u>prevenient</u> grace, as well as the dynamic interplay of the incarnation and resurrection, it becomes theologically preferable to allow the music and its impact to stand on its own merits. It is likely the perpetual capacity to defer meaning (in the poststructuralist sense) that paradoxically leads to the sublime encounter in gospel music, especially since the meaning constructs in association with gospel music semiology ("Jesus," "God," "salvation," "freedom," etc.) have been culturally coopted. At some point, it may become warranted to act as a hermeneutic of Christian identity in the context of gospel music expression in a way that does not compromise the gospel ethos, which includes the gospel music axiom that participation precedes confession ("belonging before believing"). One particular approach to the application of gospel music to Christian identity formation that does not jeopardize this essence can be understood via the paradigm of ritual process theory, which comprises the final section of this project.

Notes

1. It is debatable, at least from a cultural anthropological point of view, whether Christianity can be considered as an autonomous worldview, or should be more appropriately regarded as an agent that either seasons or challenges other worldviews. Although Christian faith is generally inseparable from the influences and affects of culture, I am assuming in this particular context that there exists a biblical-theological framework from which gospel music expression germinates.

2. Eastern Orthodoxy in general emphasizes the inter-relatedness of the Father, Son, and Holy Spirit, rather than stressing the individual parts themselves.

3. The annihilation of selfhood is fully expressed, for example, in the Hindu and Buddhist concept of Nirvana. The image of a drop of water returning to the ocean is often used to convey the ultimate course of existence, according to these religious philosophies.

4. Charland's writing on "The Case of the Peuple Québécois" provides an excellent example of constitutive rhetoric's application to the formation of national identity by analyzing the 1980 rhetoric of the Quebec sovereignty movement. Benedict Anderson's book, *Imagined Communities*, addresses the issues of nationalization in a more general sense. In Anderson's thesis, the principles of constitutive rhetoric are more implied.

5. The idea that human beings are not first and foremost rational but emotional is posited from a neurological standpoint by Antonio R. Damasio in his book, *Descartes Error: Emotion, Reason, and the Human Brain* (2000).

6. The chorus of the Newsboys' hit song, *Shine*, proclaims: "Shine, make ém wonder what you've got, Make 'em wish that they were not, On the outside looking bored. Shine, Let it shine before all men, Let 'em see good works and then, Let 'em glorify the Lord" (Newsboys).

7. Radwan refers to the Henry W. Johnstone's work on bilateral ethics, which means, in a rhetorical context, that all parties in the exchange must deal with each other as equals. Radwan offers this as a potential criticism of the lyrics in "Shine," since they portray a one-sided relationship between Christians (i.e., those who "shine"), and "others" (Radwan 2004:214).

8. Lyotard expounds on this category in his book, *Le Differend*. The concept has particular relevance when attempting to exegete and develop conclusions on the postmodern cultural context in which gospel is imbedded.

9. The concept of "via negativa," or the idea of apprehending something by understanding what it is not, calls to mind certain medieval Jewish scholars, such as Moses Maimonides. The implications for Maimonides' writings to the sublime have not, to my knowledge, been adequately explored.

10. Samuel McCormick has written an unpublished paper entitled, "On Awakening the Numinous in Others," in which he positions the "indirect communication" of Søren Kierkegaard as an alternative to Rudolph Otto's devaluation of discourse in connection with religious experience. McCormick's insight into Kierkegaard's use of paradox and reflection on the ineffable and unknowable reality that lies behind "ordinary communication" suggests (for me) that Kierkegaard is expressing some aspect of the sublime.

11. Arthur C. Jones makes reference to W. E. B. DuBois and Vincent Harding, and Robert Darden quotes William Turner, among others – all of whom eloquently contend that spirituals and gospels reflect some sense of the numinous and/or the sublime.

12. Graham Ward asserted in his book, *Cultural Transformation and Religious Practice* that "there is no Christian love which cannot be justly labeled as sublimated, highly refined eroticism" (2005:56). This particular quote raises the thought that some juxtaposition may exist between the sublime, the subliminal, and the sublimated. Although I have not dealt with it directly, the idea that sensual and erotic impulses are present in the overall gospel experience is not implausible.

4. Charland's writing on "The Case of the Peuple Québécois" provides an excellent example of constitutive rhetoric's application to the formation of national identity by analyzing the 1980 rhetoric of the Quebec sovereignty movement. Benedict Anderson's book, *Imagined Communities*, addresses the issues of nationalization in a more general sense. In Anderson's thesis, the principles of constitutive rhetoric are more implied.

5. The idea that human beings are not first and foremost rational but emotional is posited from a neurological standpoint by Antonio R. Damasio in his book, *Descartes Error: Emotion, Reason, and the Human Brain* (2000).

6. The chorus of the Newsboys' hit song, *Shine*, proclaims: "Shine, make ém wonder what you've got, Make 'em wish that they were not, On the outside looking bored. Shine, Let it shine before all men, Let 'em see good works and then, Let 'em glorify the Lord" (Newsboys).

7. Radwan refers to the Henry W. Johnstone's work on bilateral ethics, which means, in a rhetorical context, that all parties in the exchange must deal with each other as equals. Radwan offers this as a potential criticism of the lyrics in "Shine," since they portray a one-sided relationship between Christians (i.e., those who "shine"), and "others" (Radwan 2004:214).

8. Lyotard expounds on this category in his book, *Le Differend*. The concept has particular relevance when attempting to exegete and develop conclusions on the postmodern cultural context in which gospel is imbedded.

9. The concept of "via negativa," or the idea of apprehending something by understanding what it is not, calls to mind certain medieval Jewish scholars, such as Moses Maimonides. The implications for Maimonides' writings to the sublime have not, to my knowledge, been adequately explored.

10. Samuel McCormick has written an unpublished paper entitled, "On Awakening the Numinous in Others," in which he positions the "indirect communication" of Søren Kierkegaard as an alternative to Rudolph Otto's devaluation of discourse in connection with religious experience. McCormick's insight into Kierkegaard's use of paradox and reflection on the ineffable and unknowable reality that lies behind "ordinary communication" suggests (for me) that Kierkegaard is expressing some aspect of the sublime.

11. Arthur C. Jones makes reference to W. E. B. DuBois and Vincent Harding, and Robert Darden quotes William Turner, among others – all of whom eloquently contend that spirituals and gospels reflect some sense of the numinous and/or the sublime.

12. Graham Ward asserted in his book, *Cultural Transformation and Religious Practice* that "there is no Christian love which cannot be justly labeled as sublimated, highly refined eroticism" (2005:56). This particular quote raises the thought that some juxtaposition may exist between the sublime, the subliminal, and the sublimated. Although I have not dealt with it directly, the idea that sensual and erotic impulses are present in the overall gospel experience is not implausible.

Chapter 9

The Application of Ritual Process in the Formation of Gospel Identity

The issues of meaning construction and identity formation in relation to the gospel music ethos may invoke ongoing discussions on the broader areas of ecology of meaning, rhetorical exchange, the sublime, and affectivity. These areas of study, in a way, provide groundwork for unique phenomenological interpretation of the experiences observed among the gospel music constituency. Together, these approaches are helpful because of their capacity to explain the intangible forces at work in constituting meaning and identity, as well as the spontaneity and play on emotions involved in their constitution.

As we now move from interpretive theory to praxis, we observe that gospel music identity, as influenced by abstract and ethereal concepts such as constitutive rhetoric and the sublime, is concretized by the tangible actions and use of symbols that are repeated mimetically over the course of time. This points in general to the function of ritual in the overall process of identity formation. Although gospel music is particularly noted for its emotional impact, the experience can also be mundane and ordinary. Not everyone who hears and sings gospel music perceives it as euphoric and sublime. This means that those participants, as they continue their association with the movement, generally find some form of connectedness, even when they do not "feel it." Analogous to weekly celebration of the Eucharist, the rituals enacted during gospel rehearsals and performances function to create points of reference for all participants, regardless of their emotional disposition. It is the relevance of the ritual process in gospel gatherings to the continuation of the gospel movement that comprises the focus of this chapter.

Studies in the practice of ritual are, to put it euphemistically, quite varied. The diversity by which rituals have been explained and applied, as well as the attitudes toward rituals by the scholars who have studied them – ranging from, phenomenological acceptance to critical condescendence[1] – render the discipline sometimes confusing (Zeusse 1987:405). It is certainly not within the scope of this discussion to explain in detail the different approaches, although as one might at this point suspect, my "bias" will favor interpretations that couch religious symbols, rituals, and ceremonies in a favorable or phenomenological light. This could include, among others, Mircea Eliade, who in the development of the concept of *hierophany*, proposes that ritual acts are a response to the manifestation of sacred realities in the context of the natural or "profane" world (Eliade 1987:11). Eliade's work draws heavily from Rudolph Otto, whose speculative analysis in *The Idea of the Holy*, including ruminations dealing with the numinous and the sublime is based on the presupposition that holiness is a category of intrinsic value (Otto 1971). This is an important assumption, since rituals involved in gospel music gatherings, like more traditional religious meetings, actively seek to "transform the banality of ordinary life" through the use of symbols and patterned behaviors (Zeusse 1987:405).

Rite of Passage as an Operative Framework in Understanding Gospel Gatherings

Although targeting only one specific ritual studies theory may be reductionistic, Victor Turner's ritual process model may provide the best explanation as to how identity formation is strengthened through continual participation in gospel gatherings. The rite of passage theory, originally published by Arnold Van Gennep and later developed by Turner, certainly constitutes an interpretive lens by which gospel choir association can be understood. However, for the purposes of this discourse, it will be examined as a proposal for how gospel identity can be intentionally solidified by leaders in a way that facilitates meaning constructions and experiences of enthrallment, and does not contradict the gospel ethos.

As Turner notes, rites of passage embody a kind of paradox that all of us experience as we live out the tension between nature and culture (Turner 1987a:381). Certain passages are determined by biology, such as birth, reproduction, and death; yet prescribing how people define and embrace these events within their particular context is an issue of culture, or subculture. Rites of passage rituals are recognized for providing meanings that both satisfy individual aspirations and sustaining identity as part of a social group (Turner 1987a:381). Thus these culturally determined rituals are performed during life's transitional stages and in communal gatherings in order to facilitate an initiation process and solidify individual and collective membership.

The ritual process as interpreted according to the rite of passage framework generally features three distinct phases, which often accompany transformative times in life in connection with change of place, state in life, social position, and age (Turner 1997:94). Turner refers to these transition phases as 1) separation, 2) margin (liminality), and 3) aggregation (incorporation or reintegration). Based largely on the research of Van Gennep (1958), the tripartite process explains how initiates pass through a series of stages that lead to an alteration in identity, status, and affiliation, as well as outlining how people associate prescribed meanings with certain symbols through the use of ritual.

Although the process traditionally has been connected with studies in tribal ceremonies (apropos Turner's focus on the rituals of the *Ndembe* people of northwestern Zambia), it applies cross-culturally to events that involve solidification of identity and meaning, such as what occurs during retreats, religious gatherings, and other similar events.[2] The first phase, separation, involves the process where initiates are removed from ordinary circumstances or their "old status" in order to establish time and space for the introduction of new symbols and a new mental framework (Zahniser 1997:92). The subsequent stages of liminality and reincorporation further separate the initiates from their old state by promoting transition and eventual reintegration into society as changed beings through the intentional use of distinct symbols and rituals. A. H. Mathias Zahniser explains the three-stage process by employing the image of a lock complex, comparing the process to a ship that makes a passage along a river from one level to another through a system of locks (1997:93). The image is a good one since it also implies that the passage involves a combination of natural occurrences and human engineering.

Turner's distinct contribution to rite of passage theory, which is likewise relevant to the process involved in gospel choir involvement, revolves around his elaboration of the concept of liminality and the accompanying "unstructured state" that he refers to as *communitas*. As a phase that is described as "betwixt and between" (cf. Turner 1987), liminality deals with the disengagement from what once was, while not yet experiencing attachment to what is to come. It is likened to death or being in the womb, or perhaps more metaphorically to a trapeze artist who, while hurdling in the air, has released one bar, while not yet taking hold of the next one. In certain rites, liminality is represented as dispossessed and possessing nothing (Turner 1997:95). It may furthermore be characterized by weakness and passivity, submissiveness and silence, and can be referred to as the *tabula rasa* stage. The latter referral connotes a blank slate upon which the collective wisdom and knowledge of the group is inscribed upon the "neophyte" in order to lead eventually to reintegration and attainment of new status. While removed from the old status, initiates generally bond with others who share the same state of "lowliness and sacredness, homogeneity and comradeship" – which is, according to Turner, the unstructured social state of communitas (Turner 1997:95-96).

As differentiated from the concept of community, which implies indiscriminately all who we live with or among, communitas is comprised of those who bond by sharing no status in relation to the larger social structure. They are thus yoked by a common state of disconnectedness or displacement. Although communitas is not always predicated on the state of liminality, the members share a common characteristic in terms of marginalization and occupation of what Turner calls the "lowest rung" (1997:125). It is the lack of social structures in liminality that creates the conditions for communitas, which then becomes a sort of social structure for those without social structure (1997:126-127).[3] This offers some explanation as to how the status of gospel choir members, who otherwise represent virtually every social class and professional station in the larger society, has no real relevance when it comes to their gospel music affiliation. Members of my current choir bear witness to this reality as they comprise teachers, administrators, a bank clerk, a real estate broker, students, custodians, a politician, nurses, a social worker, teenagers, unemployed, mentally ill, a recovering addict, and two pastors, to name a few. When the choir meets, everyone is on a first name basis and recognition of status in the ordinary world is a non-factor.

Historical Precedents for Rite of Passage Ritual in Relation to Identity Formation

Before jumping ahead to the application of ritual process in the fortification of gospel music identity, one would be remiss not to reference how this process has been employed, consciously or inadvertently, to facilitate meaning constructions and identity formation. As noted, rites associated with birth, passage to adulthood, marriage, and death highlight formative stages of passage. In each case, societies employ rituals and accompanying symbols that give these passages culturally appropriated meaning in accordance with the tripartite phases explicated by Van Gennep and Turner. Yet the rite of passage framework has also been utilized to constitute meanings and identities that are particular, sustained, and counter-cultural in nature. The priestly traditions in the Old Testament may offer such an example. One can observe in the Priestly accounts in the Torah as well as the Chronicles, Ezra, and Nehemiah, a program of strict rituals involving eating customs, sexual habits and taboos, worship patterns, doctrinal affirmations, holiday celebrations, sacrifice rituals, and the like. They were most likely established by the Israelites to strengthen minority group identity during times of Exile and Diaspora. In this case, the ritual process was present, not only to establish meaning and identity during major life changes, but also to renew identity in a manner that was ongoing and repetitive.

A recent study has demonstrated the validity of the rite of passage framework to the constitution of counter-cultural identity and renewal among Christians in Taiwan. In an article dealing with the application of the rite of passage structure to the solidification of Christian identity in that country, missionary Jim Courson explains how the phases of separation, liminality, and incorporation can be used to facilitate bonding to Christian meaning in a part of the world where Christian converts often wind up leaving "through the back door" (Courson 1998:301). Although the structure is generally observed in rites that build upon culturally sanctioned norms, such as ancestral veneration or Buddhist temple worship, Courson suggests how a program that incorporates indigenous symbols while promoting Christian meanings into the rite of passage framework can actually stem the tide of defections among those who initially make a Christian confession. One of his primary findings is that those who perceive evangelism not as a one-time event but as a prolonged process that includes compensating for the loss of status through sustained bonding to a dynamic Christian fellowship (communitas), are much more apt to persevere in their decision. For them, faith becomes "a way of life" more so than "a way of belief" (Courson 1998:306).

In a similar article, Thomas M. Finn illuminates the effectiveness of the rite of passage structure, describing how the three-stage process was intuitively designed by the third century church. In order to solidify Christian identity against the backdrop of Roman hostility, early Christianity actually flourished in spite of systematic persecution as a result of the ritual process prescribed in the catechumenate. Referring to the document of *The Apostolic Tradition of Hippolytus*, Finn surmises that the liminal status of Christians in the Roman Empire together with the elaborate and long-term catechism facilitated the enculturation of catechumenates into the enduring bonds of Christian fellowship (Finn 1989:79). The rites, which included a time of inquiry, oral instruction, exorcism, and baptism, took place over a three year period. During this time, converts were able to separate from society by forming kinship networks and new status within the liminal Christian community (1989:72-77). Once again, it was the process of separation, liminality, incorporation into a social network driven by a common ethos, and reintegration into the larger society with changed status that deepened the sense of transformation, thus effectuating a proficient discipleship program.

Jumping ahead to a more contemporary example, Ronald Schouten argues that the rite of passage model can be observed in the renewal process that has taken place in a phenomenon that hardly would be linked to any kind of ritual structure – namely, the *Toronto Blessing*. As an evangelical movement emphasizing a direct encounter with the Holy Spirit, the *Toronto Blessing* started in January 1994 during a Vineyard Church conference in which the congregation began to display all manner of bodily manifestations, including trance-like walking, laughing uncontrollably, and even imitation of animal noises. Leaders and participants of the movement perceived these actions and the frequency of their occurrence as signs of the Holy Spirit's immanence and power. Although the kinds of occurrences associated with the *Toronto Blessing* have been documented in earlier Pentecostal movements and even the Wesleyan Revival, the intensity of the movement has been somewhat distinct, not least because it has been propitiously aided and sustained by the use of modern technology, such as video, satellite-television, and internet (Schouten 2003:25). During the next few years after its inception, renewal meetings were held on a regular basis at the Toronto Airport Church, attracting pilgrims from around the world (including delegates from many of the Danish Free churches). Sojourners to Toronto from my own Methodist conference, for example, have given accounts of extraordinary experiences, which were credited for their own renewed Christian commitment and vitality.

Schouten claims in his article that it has been the combination of ritualization (the repetition of certain actions until they become ritual), liturgy, and celebration that is at the heart of a collective process which has shaped identity and formed meaning among the participants. Even though the experiences are highly personal, the process of collectivization could be observed through the ongoing ritual actions and the services that have been offered on a monthly or weekly basis. For Schouten, the special emphasis on the phase of liminality and the expression of the anti-structural communitas germane to Turner's analysis shed interpretive light on the *Toronto Blessing* by explaining the forces at work during services and small group meetings. Schouten's article does not provide much detail regarding the actual rituals that have emerged in this context, although he credits them for giving the participants a collective sense of divine intervention in addition to facilitating bodily manifestations. As Schouten stated, "In communitas, all seekers are together worshipping God, and at the same time they are individuals waiting for the Holy Spirit to come" (2003:30).

As suggested, the presence of ritualized actions is somewhat ironic at a Charismatic or Pentecostal service, given the proclivity of adherents to define their worship as anti-ritualistic. In fact, Mary Douglas in her classic work, *Purity and Danger*, notes the strong presence of anti-ritual bias inherent in Protestantism on the whole as a backlash against the tendency to codify and institutionalize religious conduct, and to displace religious feelings (Douglas 1996:62; cf. Grimes 2000:62). This is likewise the sentiment that Schouten rightfully attributes to charismatic expressions of Christianity (2003:29). Yet the presence of a ritual process that incorporates the tripartite phases of separation, liminality, and reintegration into the overall *Toronto Blessing* worship experience reveals that rituals themselves can and are being renewed.

The common ground between the articles by Courson, Finn, and Schouten is the deliberate or intuitive employment of a ritual process aligned to the rite of passage framework, which then facilitates the reorientation and fortification of identity. In each case, initiates (congregants) are addressed both affectively and cognitively, while led on a "journey" of sorts that takes them through a process of detachment-liminality-reorientation. Although the process in each of these examples is not related to rite of passage in the primary sense (birth, adulthood, marriage, etc.), it does reveal a secondary application of the process to events and situations where repeated exposure to it can effectuate change of heart and mind. This offers some perspective in terms of the social construction that is (or can be) characteristic of the gospel ethos and identity.

The Application of the Ritual Process to the Gospel Movement

Returning to Patrick Johnson's analysis of the Australian gospel choir, *The Café of the Gate of Salvation*, one can detect a strong awareness of Turner's ritual process theory and its relevance to the formation of gospel identity. Particularly in relation to the state of liminality, Johnson suggests that the "psychological and spiritual dissonance" experienced when singing gospel is reflective of a liminal stage, as members reside "between the sacred and the secular, the divine and the profane" (Johnson 2003:178). This is a cogent insight since it explains, at least in part, the ability of choir members to live comfortably with the apparent contradictions involved in the adaptation of Black gospel music among white constituents, as well as the appropriation of a Christian ethos by those who otherwise disavow Christianity. Viewed from the state of anti-structure, which is descriptive of the phase of liminality and the associated formation of communitas, the conflicts that have been categorized by societal structures have no bearing on those residing in the betwixt-and-between spaces recognized by the ritual process. Since societal expectations, mores, and categorizations are not determinative, the liminal stage characteristic of gospel choir involvement enhances the opportunity for reconstruction of cultural and social values.

Johnson goes further in pinpointing the act of performance as providing the space for social and cultural reflection and critique, since the enactment of a foreign ethnic/religious expression transgresses "the strictures of white hegemonic systems that sanction behaviors, beliefs, and attitudes" (Johnson 2003:207). It is primarily in the "transformative act of performance" (2003:212) that members, through mimesis and ritualization are able to appropriate meanings and a sense of identity that the general society would not likely be inclined to acknowledge or appreciate. Even though Johnson's agenda deals primarily with the "appropriation of blackness" by a non-African-American culture, his recognition of the inner workings of ritual stages in a gospel choir reveals the possibilities involved in applying ritual process theory to the gospel movement in general.

In the Danish context, it is likewise apparent that symbols, ceremonies, and the rite of passage framework are pivotal tools in embracing the disparity between form and meaning, as well as the related issue of syncretism. In the case of Danish gospel choirs, the strengthening of Christian identity within the gospel context might be enhanced by recognizing the unwitting impact that rituals, symbols, and ceremonies already are affecting. In light of Turner's research, it is clear that gospel choirs have developed an elaborate array of rituals, which have served not only to solidify the gospel music identity, but in many cases have paved the way for meaning constructions that correlate with Christian meaning.

Looking at gospel choir rehearsals alone through the epistemological lens of Van Gennep and Turner, one can observe and/or propose a microcosm of the rite of passage experience each time the participants gather. The phases of separation, liminality, and reintegration can be played out with regularity, leading people through a transition from world, to the time of undifferentiated communitas (Turner 1997:96), to reentry into the world with an altered status. Once again, the application does not refer to the large-scale rite of passage framework, but rather to a secondary usage of the process.

As people gather during evenings of rehearsal, for example, the process of separation can be perceived as they come out of their work-a-day worlds, catch trains, buses, or bike to the church or rehearsal venue. Since urban dwellers in Europe are not overly reliant on personal vehicles, they are likely to depend on public transportation, which requires deliberate planning. Choir members will sometimes travel substantial distances, taking up to an hour or more in cities like Copenhagen to reach their destination. If this sort of planning is interpreted as a phase of separation, then it becomes a testimony to the level of commitment and desire to experience the routinized transition from "chaos to cosmos," and from world to sacred space on a weekly basis (cf. Eliade 1987:29).

As people enter, the process can then lead to a gradual transition into the phase of liminality. At this point, all measures of worldly status, importance, work, career, etc. are reduced to lesser significance. As noted from the example of my current choir, the members can be wealthy or poor, young or old, career-minded or unemployed, Christian or non-Christian; once rehearsals commence, they are formed into an egalitarian and cohesive unit that is subject to the same rituals, the same instruction, and the same demands. In Turner's words, this liminal state offers a blend of "lowliness and sacredness, of homogeneity and comradeship," which is the essence of communitas (1997:96). If choir leaders and organizers are inclined to interpret the process in this way, then the entire gathering can be viewed as a state of anti-structure. The fact that choir participants bond, for example, not on the foundation of status in the outside world, but on the basis of a common experience in a musical context, often creates a cohesiveness that even the most unified congregations would hope to emulate. In keeping with the analysis of Van Gennep and Turner, a different sort of hierarchy emerges out of the liminal state, which in the case of gospel gatherings, is rooted primarily in musical ability. Certain vocalists, for example, are better suited to be soloists than others, a status which is completely unrelated to mental aptitude, training, and other worldly talents. Choir leaders also experience status elevation since they are, in the context of sacred time and liminality, endowed with authority, which has nothing to do with their income, beauty, or other common measurements of worldly significance.

Liminality can also be expressed in the array of rituals that characterize rehearsals. Warm-ups, from a rite of passage perspective, can and do constitute a segment where inhibitions are cast out amid a humorous string of tongue exercises, facial contortions, and bizarre tonal inflections, which produce the same hilarious responses each time they are practiced. It is doubtful that these warm-up exercises can actually produce better singers, but leaders perhaps may recognize intuitively the value of "humiliation" in the rite of passage process in order to promote better group cohesiveness and sense of common purpose. Warm-ups are in some choirs followed by a devotional and time of prayer. Whether devotionals are held at the beginning or end of the rehearsal, they can be viewed as the primary segment in which Christian formation in connection with gospel music is emphasized unambiguously. It is the time when the spiritual foundation of gospel music can be interpreted, though preferably in a way that is not importunate, rigid, or dogmatic.

Learning and rehearsing gospel songs is sometimes an arduous and tedious process; in other words, it can be hard work. In that sense, it is reflective of liminality in general, which can at times be emotionally and psychologically taxing. The temptation to lose focus, especially as each voice section (soprano, alto, tenor, and bass) learns their part separately, can sometimes be overwhelming. Yet the eventual arrival at a finished product is contingent upon each person maintaining the necessary discipline to listen, learn, and support the other groups as they go through the tedious process of turning an inchoate string of tones and phrases into an expression of musical artistry. If the process was viewed in light of the rite of passage framework, it conceivably might impart meanings and positive associations, especially for those who do not intuitively grasp the importance of the process.

As choir practice winds down, the members may prepare themselves for reintegration into profane space and time. The cycle can be completed as people begin to think about bus and train schedules, and calculate when they must leave the church in order to reach the nearest station on time. As they go, however, one might observe that, in light of the impact of the process, they are transformed by the experience. The songs may linger in their minds, and they might even hum the melodies while at work or school the next day. Recollections of conversations may remain vivid. On the whole, the impact of the evening upon one's affective sensibilities can be interpreted as transformative. This is evidenced by the fact that so many maintain a high level of enthusiasm, even after years of participation. As implied in interviews, conversations, and observations in Chapters Four and Five, the impact of the rite of passage process during special events, such as concerts and festivals, can be so intense that it can elicit a truly transformative moment in a person's life.

Gospel Symbols in Christian Identity Formation

As one might expect, the world of gospel choirs is laden with symbols which might be employed to strengthen the nexus between the gospel ethos and Christianity. In connection with the prior discussion on "Musicology and Affectivity" (p. 146ff), it should not be taken for granted that music itself constitutes one of the most forceful symbols known within human experience. Zahniser notes: "Music is one of Christianity's most consistent symbolic connections between the sensory world of human life and the meaning of Christian faith" (1997:84). When employed in the proper context, it effects profound and positive transformation in attitudes and relationships, which is most certainly true in the case of gospel music (cf. Zahniser 1997:189).

Music, from a theomusicological or missiomusicological perspective, is a gift from the God of the universe, and though it often creates division in light of the fact that people have their own musical preferences, it also unites people, even inter-culturally and inter-racially (Scott 2000:9). It offers an appeal that goes to the heart of Creation (Johansson 1998:8). It is, again, naïve to suggest that music is a universal language, especially since there is no universal music any more than there is a universal language (Scott 2000:8). Yet certain genres, such as gospel music, are able to resonate deeply within the affective dimension of many, creating a sort of primordial connection to a spiritual reality that lies within and beyond the individual. I have, in this discourse, ventured to call it the sublime. It seems that many choir participants experience the music in such a way, which explains why gospel is more than a peripheral part of life and worship for many – it is integral. As a symbol, music has the capacity to penetrate the depths of one's being in ways that are largely unparalleled. Therefore, gospel music, together with the integral and primordial symbol of rhythm, has the intrinsic capability of being one of the more powerful instruments of the Christian Gospel currently employed in the European context.

Music is always accompanied by an array of auxiliary signs and symbols, although they may not necessarily convey the sense of transcendence as overtly as the discursive and non-discursive symbols in the music itself. Choir directors, for example, employ a host of signs, such as a balled fist (last refrain), a raised index finger (first refrain), a pat on the head (from the top), a circling motion (repeat the refrain), and countless other hand gestures, which are intended to provide direction to the choir. It would be interesting to think through how these gestures might be contextualized in terms of a strategy to shape Christian identity. When the choir raises their hands, claps, and sways to the music and rhythm during a performance, for example, the opportunity exists to make a connection between these kinetic expressions and the true focus of worship and praise. Although choirs sometimes use these symbols to mimetically reproduce the gospel style, they have the potential to point to something beyond the gestures themselves. When the director points to his/her eyes as a sign to watch and stay focused, it might be effective to draw a correlation with "staying focused on God and God's love." Opportunities abound for promoting Christian meaning by instilling a connection between seemingly mundane signs and the message to which they may point.

Other instrumental symbols could possibly be viewed as keys to deepening Christian identity. Coffee and tea thermoses, for example, are common symbols in Denmark. Times of fellowship and meaningful conversation often take place during informal breaks and after worship services, where refreshments, including coffee, tea, and pastries, are always present. The mere sight of these symbols sets off a warm feeling of companionship and, as explained in Chapter Six, *hygge* (coziness). They are almost always expected during gospel choir gatherings in Denmark. This is indeed an experience that has profound cultural significance, and constitutes an area of reflection when considering how to reach out to the Danes in ways that are culturally indigenous.

In general, the symbols associated with gospel music may offer an as of yet untapped goldmine of opportunity for Christian leaders and practitioners to relate the Christian Gospel to gestures, signs, objects, sounds, and motions which already are indelibly ingrained in the gospel music experience. Since most gospel choirs in Denmark, at least for the time being, are still connected with the church, it is possible to utilize specific Christian symbols and rituals, such as Communion, worship services, the Cross, and others, in an effort to maintain the affinity between gospel music symbols and Christian faith. A potential problem, as explicated in the section dealing with Danish religiosity (Chapter Six), is that Christian symbols have to a greater or lesser extent been coopted in favor of national cultural identity. However, it is quite possible that gospel symbols, when working synergistically with innately Christian symbols, might facilitate a deeper experience of the sublime and transcendence in ways that circumvent the religiously and culturally domesticated meaning associations, from which the majority of the gospel constituency seems to distance themselves.

Implications for Future Use of Ritual in Gospel and Christian Identity Formation

As the rite of passage framework is used to provide the structures and mechanics from which meaning construction and identity formation can emerge, its usage in general may have great promise in places like Denmark. Since the Danish Folk Church is largely perceived as a rite of passage church, the concept is not really alien to their cultural identity. The primary difference is that, rather than promoting a passive Christian identity that subjugates Christianity to a national agenda, the gospel music rite of passage process inducts its participants into a world of excitement and energy that has the potential for expressing Christian faith in ways that ameliorate rather than suppress the affective domain. Music reaches the heart, and gospel music arguably is intended to take this particular expression of Christian faith as far as the music and the power to which it defers can reach.

The fact that the gospel movement contains counter-cultural elements can be viewed as both an advantage and a challenge. Since Christian expressions in the mother tongue are often attached with feelings and associations that are less than inspiring, the "foreignness" of gospel provides a vehicle for communicating Christianity in ways that circumvent the standard categories and mental constructs indigenous to the Danish worldview. In this sense, the gospel movement constitutes a new paradigm in Christian life, worship, and expression, and is therefore to be studied and appreciated as a phenomenon that possibly could come to facilitate missionary and evangelistic efforts in ways that yet are unimagined. The fact that English ultimately is not the heart language may imply that gospel music may eventually need to wrestle with how to find other indigenous expressions, lest the semiology in gospel music result in an "exotic" but not "intimate" encounter with Christian spirituality. The reality of syncretism must be addressed at some level, not so much because constituents are free to construct their own meanings, which is at the core of the gospel ethos, but due to the proclivity in Danish and European societies on the whole to subvert Christian faith to a cultural and national agenda. As long as the music and the experience continue to enthrall its constituency and symbols of Christian faith remain part of the mix, then it will likely continue to re-image (and re-imagine) the faith, even in parts of the world where Christian influence is largely considered a spent force.

The primary key in Christian identity formation among the gospel constituency in places like Denmark is leadership. The capacity to maintain and promulgate a connection between the forms of gospel music and the meanings associated with Christian faith will unfortunately not occur without vision and implementation on the part of those entrusted with leadership authority. It is, after all, the change agents in the movement that have the opportunity to establish the habits, practices, and ritual behaviors that create the sort of platform that is conducive to spiritual development. Since most gospel musicians and leaders still acknowledge their indebtedness to the African-American and British gospel movements, which remain indisputably rooted in Christian worship, the tendency to truncate Christian faith and worship altogether is not yet critical. However, leadership training in the future may become a pivotal factor in assuring that Christian ritualization in accordance with the gospel music ethos is in some way practiced, while continuing to create space for ongoing construction of meaning.

The challenges to identity formation in the Danish context, as well as other areas, necessitate deeper reflection on how best to engineer the inherent symbols, rituals, and practices in ways that both advance faith and embrace diversity. Yet the challenge is actually an opportunity. Since the gospel music phenomenon is becoming recognized as one of the more effective secondary Christian movements to take place in Northern and Western Europe in recent decades, it comes down to a matter of recognizing, in terms of its energy and vibrancy, what is providentially and spontaneously already taking place.

Notes

1. Zeusse notes that psychoanalytic theory often equates religious rituals in particular with "neurotic compulsions" (Zeusse 1987:405). Victor Turner recounts a similar bias engendered by one of the leading scholars in the field of ritual studies during his student days, Lewis Henry Morgan, who regarded primitive religions as "grotesque and intelligible" (Turner 1997:1).

2. Turner has written an article entitled, "Ritual, Tribal, and Catholic," which suggests that the Eucharist, for example, can also be understood in accordance with ritual process theory (1976). Mathias Zahniser names the "Walk to Emmaus" retreat and Marriage Enrichment seminars as potential field studies for the enactment of the rite of passage stages in contemporary Western society (1997:91).

3. The liminality phase and accompanying state of communitas share some affinity with the ordering of society in accordance with rites of sacrifice. Other ritual theorists, such as Rene Girard have appropriately argued that the idea of sacrifice is germane to virtually all cultures, which in ritual reenactment symbolizes mediation between the sacrificed and the designated deity (Girard 1979:6). Although this does not really provide the most appropriate framework for understanding how gospel choir members form identity, the idea of the sacrificial process relates to liminality in that there occurs a separation of the "victim" from those for whom the victim becomes a substitute, while concurrently creating associations with other "victims," thus promoting a sense of similarity (i.e., communitas) (cf. Girard 1979:39). This suggests that the solidification of identity in accordance with ritual theory also relates to primordial impulses that among other things, involves placating violent urges as well as providing the contours within which a group can connect with that which is considered sacred and holy.

Chapter 10

The Future of the Gospel Music Movement in Denmark and Beyond

In the time frame that has elapsed since the beginning of this project, a number of noteworthy developments have taken shape in the world of diffused gospel music. First, gospel music seems to be, slowly but surely, attracting the interest of researchers. As mentioned, Trine Berg Nielsen has completed a master's project dealing with the relationship between church-based choirs and mission (2006). Carsten Morsbøl's book *Gospel for Gospelfolk* (2003) is still circulating, and is challenging gospel choirs to consider the maintenance of a Christian identity appropriate to the gospel music culture. The Gospel Factory homepage has been monitoring the development of choirs by providing quantitative data, as well as disseminating articles and information on the gospel movement in Denmark. Each year, papers and bachelor level theses are written, and others are on the way, dealing typically with some aspect of the gospel music movement in the Danish context. Similar research forays are likewise emerging from the neighboring countries of Sweden, Norway, and Germany. As gospel music continues to expand, it seems like only a matter of time before additional scholars from inside and outside Northern Europe will begin to apply their analytical and interpretive insights to the movement. It would be especially enriching to hear accounts and reflections from countries in the parts of Asia where gospel choirs are showing some stability and where the cultural scripting of Christendom is either minimal or nonexistent. Hopefully, this study will serve to spawn dialogue and further interest among researchers from various fields of study and divergent cultural contexts.

Second, the spontaneity, vibrancy, and freshness which characterized the movement in the earlier years is issuing in a spirit of reflection and speculation about its future direction. A question that seems to be on the tip of the tongue among Danish church leaders and change agents is, "Where do we go from here?" Especially since pastors and laypersons are slowly becoming resigned to the fact that choir members may not become active church members after all, earlier visions and strategies are of necessity giving way to new ones. This may ultimately mean that leaders and strategists should take to heart the simple yet profound statement that I have heard repeatedly in my association with the movement: "Gospel is my church."

Of course, the capacity to accept such a proposition may depend on one's definition of "church." If preaching, administration of the sacraments, and reciting of creeds are non-negotiable components, then most gospel choir gatherings do not appear very church-like. However, other components of a missional nature are often present. Whether it is *kerygmatic* communication through gospel songs, devotionals, gospel worship services, or conversations; *koinonia*, as experienced in the gatherings and times of fellowship; *diakonia*, as practiced in acts of good will toward fellow constituents or the larger community in terms of benefit concerts and charitable contributions; or *martyria* ("witness") as observed among those who have taken the gospel music message to wider arenas, even when the reception has bordered on hostile; gospel choirs often function as churches or para-churches, despite not wearing the label. Friend and colleague, Carsten Morsbøl, warned a 2007 audience that the idea of "gospel church" is inherently limited and therefore flawed, because the movement has difficulty attracting men (about eighty percent of most choirs are women) and because centering exclusively on one music genre is too narrow a focus. It may furthermore be unwise, given the general aversion to the concept of church in Denmark as a result of cultural factors, to officially sanction a nomenclature that many adherents would find ambiguous, even disdainful. Nevertheless, this particular topic is exemplary of the sort of dialogue and introspection that we now are witnessing.

It can be added, at this particular juncture in gospel music's young history in Denmark, that three dominant strategies can be delineated. A first strategy entails precisely the idea of gospel church. Though it is not yet established and the concept is still amorphous, it is gaining momentum. As reported in Chapter Four, the Copenhagen Free Church is the location of just such a congregation. In addition to the aforementioned caveats, the gospel ethos, among other things, is by nature very casual and based more on desire than commitment; therefore it is presently difficult to imagine how such an ecclesial structure could emerge, particularly in a country where church involvement is excessively passive. However, the idea may ultimately prove to be as simple as calling at least some gospel choirs what they pragmatically and functionally already are: congregations. As gospel worship services and events continue to draw their own crowd and appeal to a specific subculture, it might be suggested that, if the idea is sown over a period of time, it eventually will come to fruition.

As a second strategy, gospel-involved pastors and laypeople still utilize gospel choirs in the hope that they will continue to revitalize existing congregations. According to this perspective, choirs are recognized for instilling an energy and vitality in Folk and Free churches by their mere use of the facilities and occasional involvement in worship services and other activities. Although choir members are not joining the host churches in significant numbers, congregations are purportedly impacted positively by the life that gospel music and its constituency bring. As noted again in Chapter Four, the situation in Odense Methodist

Church, which houses the choirs *Nardus, Emmaus,* and *Joy Sticks,* provides a cogent and dynamic example of this model.

As a third strategy, there remains the pragmatic (and perhaps more secular) assumption that gospel music singing is no more and no less than a recreational activity. According to the structuring of Danish society, gospel choirs are often advertised as a "spare time" activity in local and community catalogues, on a par with swimming lessons, dance classes, and sports clubs. School-based choirs are particularly representative of this model. Many participants are introduced to the world of gospel music, not because of any spiritual inclinations, but simply because they like to sing. Thus the image of "parks and recreation" is the most appropriate metaphor according to this model, since it is a given that people of all persuasions will converge, and that the Christian advantage will be neutralized. Each strategy, of course, presents its own set of missiological challenges and opportunities, especially for those who are concerned about the overall constitution of meaning and formation of identity.

In addition to research and introspection, a third area of recent development has been the establishment of children's and youth gospel choirs. Only within the past few years has gospel music breeched generational boundaries in a very noticeable way. The fact that pre-adults also are drawn to the vibrancy of the music and choose to join choirs, not to mention participate in newly established gospel festivals and workshops which target this age group, is a telling sign of gospels music's diffusion in general. Although it is still too soon to empirically demonstrate whether the gospel movement has staying power or will eventually fade like Big Band music or the electric typewriter, the interest being shown by the "next generation" certainly encourages one to be optimistic in the assessment of gospel's immediate future, at least in Denmark.

Some (Still Unconcluded) Conclusions about the Gospel Movement

In the course of researching and writing on gospel music in Denmark, there is, here at the end, still much to ponder. As I reread several of the hypotheses stated at the beginning of this project, one thing has become conclusive: the conclusions will likely lead to more questions. In terms of one primary area of consideration, namely, the Christian themes and symbols in the music and performance, it can be stated that they are present, but just how consequential they are in shaping religious belief patterns remains "in the eye of the beholder." What is at stake in interpreting the impact and overall experience of gospel music is no less than a comprehensive analysis of the constitution of meaning itself. The interfacing of Christian symbols and Danish cultural factors, which includes religious-cultural scripting and reactions to global imports, reveal that meaning constructions are ongoing and unending. In the end, we can say that Christian influence is part of the creative mix in gospel music, and is at times a powerful and life-altering element for some of the participants. For many others, however, it is not determinative. In this case, the religious element in the music is syncretistic – that is, it is being coopted by some other agenda. But this is not necessarily a bad thing. It merely suggests that the Christian witness in the music is, in the context of the supermarket culture of postmodern pluralism, ever part of the equation. For those who are interested in contextual and "ethos appropriate" evangelization, the opportunities are challenging, but also exciting.

When it comes to adoption of and adaptation to a cultural import, especially one with spiritual overtones, it will generally involve meaning construction. As useful as diffusion of innovation theory is in explaining the mechanics of the diffusion process, it is not particularly illuminating in relation to the area of meaning. Useful developments in this theoretical framework might emphasize greater awareness of cultural determinants and the construction of meaning to the process of diffusion/adoption. Since such constructions come out of a culture characterized by shared values and relationships (apropos "ecology"), and where the culture itself is increasingly contingent, the attachment of meaning to signs and symbols will be ongoing. This is paradoxically a factor that creates a high degree of diffusion favorability, and it likewise constitutes the matrix out of which additional categories, such as the *mysterium tremendum* and the sublime, can emerge. Diffusion theory, especially in poststructuralist/ postmodern contexts might consider this.

The meaning constructions among gospel music participants likewise highlight how, in a particular culture, they are reconfiguring a global diffusion into something more contextual. The term "glocal" is now being used as a revision in globalization theory, suggesting how global imports are shaped by the particularities, complexities, and histories of the local situation.[1] As a case study, the gospel music movement might suggest how the concept of "glocalization" could be nuanced in relation to the constitution of meaning. Part of the nuancing, of course, would involve the dimension of affectivity, which is related to a complex array of factors, ranging from cultural conditioning to personality idiosyncrasies. Like diffusion of innovation theory, glocalization theorists would do well to consider how emotions, and their role in terms of larger constructs such as sublimity, collectivization, and identity formation, impact the interplay between global and local impulses.

Rite of passage theory likewise reveals important aspects of identity formation. Although I have not interpreted it in the traditional sense as it relates to significant passages in the life cycle, Turner's theory has value when applied in a more cursory and ordinary manner. Among other things, it sheds light on how otherwise mundane experiences, such as choir rehearsals and other less than climactic events are and can be transformed in accordance with the values and dynamics that the leaders and change agents desire to implement. As a supplement to the other meaning construction and identity formation theories dealt with in these pages, the rite of passage framework constitutes the structure within which exciting things are taking place. It therefore merits further attention.

Final Thoughts

There are some general truths that the gospel movement is manifesting, which will be of particular interest for those who consider practicing Christian mission in a part of the world where Christian witness has largely been enervated. One such truth, as trite as it may sound, is that the communication of the Christian Gospel is more effective in contexts where belonging precedes believing. George G. Hunter has insightfully captured the essence of this precept in *The Celtic Way of Evangelism* (2000). Just as Patrick and the ensuing Celtic movement established a paradigm for involving the fifth to tenth century people of Ireland in monastic life where they in turn discovered faith, gospel choirs are providing similar opportunities for adherents to participate without first insisting on a faith-based litmus test. Since the encounter with Christianity and Christian people in accordance with the gospel ethos of "come-as-you-are" openness is resulting in positive transformation, including first time confessions of faith, there is evidence that the approach may be paradigmatic in a context where Christianity is widely perceived as little more than a cultural inheritance.

The relationship of constitutive rhetoric and the sublime to the gospel movement presents another profound truth: people in general must be enthralled as well as persuaded. In a part of the world where Christian information is not sparse, it becomes excessively crucial that faith is conveyed experientially and affectively, and not only conceptually. Donald Soper's old adage, "faith is better caught than taught," has application here. Music is certainly a primary springboard for promoting this approach, and gospel music in particular is noted for enthralling people not just as individuals, but as a group. This is part of the genius of the movement, and is one of the reasons why it is, in many cases, effectuating Christian renewal. The experience of joy, energy, vitality, life, and a connection with "something greater" is not a small thing, even when the source of the experience is unnamed or unknown. There comes a time when the facilitators of gospel music will be charged to act as a hermeneutic of the faith from which the music blooms; the leaders of the movement must be careful not to neglect this important responsibility, lest the musical expression becomes severed from the very spiritual foundation that accounts for its power and dynamic. However, the message is best communicated when people, perhaps more so than just hearing it on a propositional level, encounter it on an affective level.

Since some sort of encounter with the Triune God is (arguably) an inherent spect of the gospel music experience, it is incumbent for Christian leaders to facilitate rather than manipulate the spontaneity of the movement. Throughout much of Western Europe, Christian faith has been pacified and privatized as a result of its (sometimes sordid) religious past and the ongoing program of Cultural Christian indoctrination. For authentic renewal to take place, people in this context need some deeper sense of emotional and spiritual liberation and catharsis, which not inconsequently are prevailing themes in gospel music. It is no secret that evangelistic efforts in the West often have been dominated by a management-oriented approach, which thinks in terms of strategies and programs to attain a desired result. Although the gospel movement has benefited exponentially from the organizational masterminds behind festivals, workshops, camps, and the like, these innovations have not functioned to strangle the movement, but rather to nurture its life and spontaneity.

Speaking in terms of Christian thought constructs, it may be wiser for leaders to embrace a theology that is more creational/natural than revelational. This means that one is attuned to what God is doing through this musical expression, and then allowing it to unfold, instead of judging it on the basis of exclusive theological suppositions, and then trying to change it. A related idea is understood in terms of the Wesleyan concept of prevenient grace, implying that all are created in the image of God, and therefore endowed with some limited measure of goodness and grace. Again, the diffusion of gospel music and proliferation of gospel choirs in countries like Denmark constitutes "new wine." Evangelists and missionaries to the movement should be cautious about imposing a "pre-packaged" Christian agenda that would end up associating gospel music expressions and symbols with religious constructs that many have already distanced themselves from. This would only amount to restricting the new wine to "old wineskins."

Missiologists should take note that the gospel movement may be demonstrating the limitations of the traditional contextualization paradigm, particularly in parts of the world where the Christian *logos* has already been thoroughly contextualized. At various points throughout this study I have suggested that contextualization theory, especially in areas where Christian proclamation has taken root over a long period of time, needs to be nuanced. An "un-nuanced" approach might purport that the proper cross-cultural communication of religious narrative is inordinately contingent upon learning the worldview, language, and cultural idioms of a people, and then appropriating the Gospel in ways that respect and utilize these particularities. The inherent flaw, especially in cultures where the seeds of Christendom have been sown over a long period of time, is that the religion of cultural inherence, i.e., "the contextual version," paradoxically acts as an impediment to a more engaging form of faith.

I have argued that gospel music's ability to re-image and re-imagine Christian faith is related to elements in the movement which are counter-cultural in nature. It may be overstated, given the insights provided by cultural diffusion and "glocalization" theory, to say that gospel music is completely "a-contextual." What is taking place likely speaks to the capacity of cultures and subcultures to adopt foreign innovations, and then, through a complex series of events, make them uniquely their own. Since gospel music and other related music forms were already present to some extent, it would be inaccurate to propose that some prescriptive type of contextualization was not already in process. However, the appeal of gospel music and its relevance to spiritual reflection in essence "rewires" missiological thinking. It does this by contending that contextualization in the Western context is not the key; the real story involves the ability of the movement to tap into something more central to the human condition, even if it means circumventing certain aspects of the existing culture and worldview.

Again, this does not at all mean that cultural exegesis, including an understanding of the history and patterns which shape people's thoughts, feelings, and actions is not important. It is, in fact, critically important. What the gospel constituency instead seems to be revealing is that the general "version" of Christian expression that has developed as a result of centuries of contextualization is not wholly sufficient. This may be at the very root of why the thousands of participants who are enthralled by the music and the identity that Black gospel music affiliation constitutively forms, so readily adopt a foreign religious mythology, even if they themselves are professing non-Christians. Could it be that this mythology contains important elements that are neglected by their own? In this case, the primary concern is revitalization, or the recontextualization of Christian faith in ways that circumvent some of the cultural patterns and historical idiosyncrasies that have domesticated it over a long period of time. At any rate, contextualization theory is not wholly applicable in areas where Christendom is the established paradigm; a more appropriate theory might instead be christened "postcontextualization."[2]

The question regarding whether or not the gospel ethos constitutes a Christian ethos or whether the diffusion of gospel music represents a definitive Christian movement, again, does not elicit a conclusive answer. The evidence can only suggest that it is a distinct possibility. Since Christian themes and symbols are obviously present, and since faith-oriented transformation does occur, it is hard to deny that missiological impulses are a decisive part of the mix. However, the attachment of non-Christian meanings to these themes and symbols makes it equally difficult to deny that syncretism will always be a formidable element in the equation. How this will play out in the time to come is hard to determine, and will likely be contingent on the attitudes and spiritual dispositions of the leaders, both present and future.

In the northernmost part of Denmark on the Jutland peninsula, there exists an architectural and geological phenomenon, which metaphorically epitomizes the current situation. In the nineteenth century, a Danish folk church was built on a sandbar, and subsequently, due to constant high winds and shifting terrain, it was eventually engulfed by sand. Only the upper half of the church is visible today. Appropriately, this tourist attraction is simply called, "The Sandy Church." In reference to the ongoing development of the gospel music movement, one must hope that it does not eventually become so engulfed by the sands of secularism and marginalized by competing spiritualities that it loses its vitality as a recontextualized expression of Christian renewal.

In the meantime, those who have become enriched and even transformed by the gospel music phenomenon should unhesitatingly acknowledge their gratitude to the leaders, change agents, and aficionados who have been engaged in promoting what has transpired in the name of the Triune and missionary God. Standing at the heart of the movement are talented and visionary people – some of whom have been interviewed or referred to in connection with this project, and many others who have not. The impact and success of what has taken place in recent decades has been contingent upon the contributions of all of them. Perhaps what we also are discovering is that, among the pantheon of missionary archetypes that have been forged throughout Christian history, a new one is being added. In this case, it is the image of the gospel music psalmist, armed with song sheets, extraordinary musical ability, a joyful and energetic persona, a passion for the music, and an engaging faith, who is helping to "compose" a model of Christian renewal in a challenging religious and cultural context.

Notes

1. I became acquainted with the term "glocal" in an article by J. Nelson Jennings entitled, "Christian Mission and Glocal Violence in 2007 A.D. / 1428 H."
2. Thanks to Dr. Terry Muck for suggesting the term "postcontextualization."

Bibliography

Abbott, Lynn
    1992   "'Play That Barber Shop Chord': A Case for the African American Origin of Barbershop Harmony." *American Music 10,* Fall, 1992. Pp. 289-319.

Anderson, Barbara G.
    1990   *First Fieldwork: The Misadventures of an Anthropologist.* Prospect Heights, IL.: Waveland Press.

Anderson, Benedict
    1991   *Imagined Communities: Reflections on the Origin and Spread of Nationalism.* New York: Verso.

Anderson, Walter Truett
    1995   *The Truth About the Truth: De-confusing and Re-constructing the Postmodern World.* New York: Tarcher/Putnam Books.

Bachika, Reimon, ed.
    2002   *Traditional Religion and Culture in a New Era.* New Brunswick, NJ: Transaction Publishers.

Banks, Marcus
    1996   *Ethnicity: Anthropological Constructions.* London: Routledge.

Barker, Joel Arthur
    1992   Paradigms: The Business of Discovering the Future. New York: Harper Collins Publishers.

Baumlin, James
    2001   "Ethos." *Encyclopedia of Rhetoric.* Thomas O. Sloane, ed. London: Oxford University Press. Pp. 263-277.

Begbie, Jeremy S.
    1991   *Voicing Creation's Praise: Towards a Theology of the Arts.* Edinburgh, UK: T & T Press.
    2000   *Theology, Music and Time.* Cambridge, UK: Cambridge University Press.

Bell, Gerome
    2005   Interview with U.S. American gospel leader, Gerome Bell, October 2005.

Bennett, Lerone Jr.
    1983 *Before the Mayflower: A History of the Negro in America 1619-1964*. Revised edition. Middlesex, England: Penguin Books Ltd.

Berger, Peter L.
    1969   *A Rumor of Angels: Modern Society and the Rediscovery of the Supernatural*. Garden City, NY: Doubleday and Company, Inc.
    1990   *The Sacred Canopy: Elements of a Sociological Theory of Religion*. Orig. Pub. in 1967. New York: Anchor Books.

Berger, Peter L., and Thomas Luckmann
    1967   The *Social Construction of Reality: A Treatise in the Sociology of Knowledge*. New York: Anchor Books.
    1995   "The Dehumanized World." *The Truth About the Truth: De-confusing and Re-constructing the Postmodern World*. Walter Truett Anderson, ed. New York: Tarcher/Putnam Books. Pp. 36-45.

Bevans, Stephen B.
    2002   *Models of Contextual Theology*. Revised and Expanded Edition. Maryknoll, NY: Orbis Books.

Bevans, Stephen B. and Roger P. Schroeder
    2004   *Constants in Context: A Theology of Mission for Today*. Maryknoll, NY: Orbis Books.

Biesecker-Mast, Susan and Gerald Biesecker-Mast
    2000   *Anabaptists and Postmodernity*. Telford, PA: Pandora Press.

Bjerager, Erik
    2006   *Gud bevarer Danmark: Et opgør med sekularismen*. (trans. *God Preserve Denmark: A Showdown with Secularism*). Gylling, Denmark: Gyldendal Publishers.

Black Gospel Website
    2005   "Artist Spotlight: Interviews with a Variety of Black Gospel Artists." Accessed March 23, 2005. Available from: http://www.blackgospel.com/interviews/index.htm

Blumer, Herbert
    1969   *Symbolic Interactionism*. Englewood Cliffs, NJ: Prentice Hall.

Bosch, David
    1991   *Transforming Mission: Paradigm Shifts in Theology of Mission*. Maryknoll, NY: Orbis Books.

Boyer, Horace Clarence
    1995   *How Sweet the Sound: The Golden Age of Gospel*. Washington, D.C.: Elliott & Clark Publishing.

Brittan, Arthur
    1998   "Symbolic Interaction." *Routledge Encyclopedia of Philosophy*, vol. 9. Edward Craig, general editor. London: Routledge. Pp. 243-245.

Brubaker, Pamela K.
    1999   *Globalization at What Price? Economic Change and Daily Life*. Cleveland, OH: The Pilgrim Press.

Budd, Malcolm

1985 *Music and the Emotions: The Philosophical Theories.* London: Routledge and Kegan Paul.

Burdett, Silver
2006 "African American Music: Spirituals and Gospel Music." Accessed August 3, 2006. Available from: http://www.sbgmusic.com/html/teacher/reference/styles/spirituals.html

Burke, Denis John
2005 "Ireland Finds New Soul in Gospel Music." Interview with several gospel groups in Dublin. Accessed November 16, 2005. Available from: http://english.ohmynews.com/articleview/article_print.asp?menu=c10400&no=253453&rel_no=1&isPrint=print

Burke, Edmund
1968 *A Philosophical Enquiry into the Origin of Our Ideas of the Sublime and Beautiful.* Orig. Pub. in 1757. J.T. Boulton, ed. Notre Dame, IN: University of Notre Dame Press.

Burnim, Mellonee V.
1980 "The Black Gospel Music Tradition: Symbol of Ethnicity." Ph.D. Dissertation, Indiana University.

Burnett, David
2000 *World of the Spirits: A Christian Perspective on Traditional and Folk Religions.* London: Concorde House.

Cahoone, Lawrence, ed.
2003 *From Modernism to Postmodernism: An Anthology.* Malden, MA: Blackwell Publishing.

Cameron, Etta
2006 Interview with Etta Cameron, November 2006.

Campos, Albert
2005 "Positive Soul Gospel Choir." Accessed January 23, 2005. Available from: http://www.positivesoul.com/gospelkor.htm

Celebration of Gospel
2005 Program aired on Black Entertainment Television (BET), February 24, 2005.

Chadwick, Owen
1975 *The Secularization of the European Mind in the Nineteenth Century.* London: Cambridge University Press.

Charland, Maurice
1987 "Constitutive Rhetoric: The Case of the Peuple Québécois." *Quarterly Journal of Speech,* 73:133-150.
1999 "Politics: Constitutive Rhetoric." *Encyclopedia of Rhetoric.* Thomas O. Sloane, ed. London: Oxford University Press. Pp. 616-619.

Clapp, Rodney
1996 *A Peculiar People: The Church as Culture in a Post-Christian Society.* Downers Grove, IL: InterVarsity Press.

Cone, James H.
1972 *The Spirituals and the Blues: An Interpretation.* New York: Seabury Press.

Copenhagen Gospel Festival

2005 "Copenhagen Gospel Festival." Accessed January 21, 2005. Available from: http://www.cgf.dk/

Copher, Charles B.
1986 "Biblical Characters, Events, Places, and Images Remembered and Celebrated in Black Worship." *Journal of the Interdenominational Theological Center* 14. Fall '86/Spring '87. Pp. 75-85.

Courlander, Harold
1964 *Negro Folk Music, U.S.A.* New York: Columbia University Press.

Courson, Jim
1998 "Deepening the Bonds of Christian Community: Applying Rite of Passage Structure to the Discipling Process in Taiwan." *Missiology*. 26(3):301-313.

Craddock, Fred B.
1978 *Overhearing the Gospel.* Nashville, TN: Abingdon Press.

Cragg, Kenneth
1998 *The Secular Experience of God.* Harrisburg, PA: Trinity Press International.

Crowther, Paul
1998 "The Sublime." *Routledge Encyclopedia of Philosophy*, vol. 9. Edward Craig, general editor. London: Routledge. Pp. 201-205.

Culler, Jonathan
1998 "Structuralism." *Routledge Encyclopedia of Philosophy*, vol. 9. Edward Craig,
general editor. London: Routledge. Pp. 174-177.

Cusic, Don
1990 *The Sound of Light: A History of Gospel Music.* Bowling Green, OH: Bowling Green University Popular Press.

Damasio, Antonio R.
2000 Descartes Error: Emotion, Reason, and the Human Brain. New York: Quill.

Darden, Robert
2004 *People Get Ready: A New History of Black Gospel Music.* New York: The Continuum International Publishing Group.
2004a "All Things Considered: A History of Gospel Music." Michelle Norris. Interview on National Public Radio (NPR), December 17. http://www.npr.org/templates/story/story.php?storyId= 4233793

Dargan, William Thomas
1983 "Congregational Gospel Songs in a Black Holiness Church: A Musical and Textual Analysis." Ph.D. Dissertation, Wesleyan University.

Davie, Grace
1994 *Religion in Britain Since 1945: Believing Without Belonging.* Oxford, UK: Blackwell.
2000 *Religion in Modern Europe: A Memory Mutates.* London: Oxford University Press.
2002 *Europe: The Exceptional Case: Parameters of Faith in the Modern World.* London: Darton, Longman, and Todd Ltd.

Derrida, Jacques
1982 *Margins of Philosophy.* Translated by Alan Bass. Chicago, IL: University of Chicago Press.

1995 "The Play of Substitution." *The Truth About the Truth: De-confusing and Re-constructing the Postmodern World.* Walter Truett Anderson, ed. New York: Tarcher/Putnam Books. Pp. 86-91.

Dixon, Christa K.
1976 *Negro Spirituals: From Bible to Folk Songs.* Philadelphia, PA: Fortress Press.

Douglas, Mary
1996 *Purity and Danger: An Analysis of the Concepts of Pollution and Taboo.* First published in 1966. London: Routledge.

Du Bois, W. E. B.
1989 *The Souls of Black Folks.* Originally published in 1903. New York: Bantam Books.

Dupree, Sherry Sherrod and Herbert C.
1993 *African American Good News (Gospel) Music.* Washington, D.C.: Middle Atlantic Regional Press.

Dyer, Ervin
2002 "Some Soul to Keep." *The New Crisis*, Jan/Feb. 2002. Accessed May 5, 2005. Available from: http://www.findarticles.com/p/articles/mi_qa3812/is_200201/ai_n9079623

Eliade, Mircea
1986 *Symbolism, the Sacred, and the Arts.* New York: Crossroad Publishing Company.
1987 *The Sacred and the Profane: The Nature of Religion.* San Diego, CA: Harvest Book. Originally published in 1957.

Eskew, Harry, James C. Downey and H. C. Boyer
2001 "Black Gospel Music." *The New Grove Dictionary of Music and Musicians.* Stanley Sadie, ed., John Tyrell, exec. ed. Vol. 10. Pp. 177-185. London: Macmillan Pub. Ltd.

Facey, Solomon and David Elevique
2005 Interview with British gospel leaders Solomon Facey and David Elevique, October 2005.

Ferraro, Gary
2001 *Cultural Anthropology: An Applied Perspective.* 4th edition. Belmont, CA: Wadsworth / Thomson Learning, Inc.

Finke, Roger and Rodney Stark
1992 *The Churching of America: Winners and Losers in our Religious Economy.* New Brunswick, NJ: Rutgers University Press.

Finn, Thomas M.
1989 "Ritual Process and the Survival of Early Christianity: A Study of the Apostolic Tradition of Hippolytus." *Journal of Ritual Studies.* 3(1):69-89.

Fisher, Miles Mark
1967 *Negro Slave Songs in the United States.* New York: Russell and Russell.

Flanagan, Kieran
2003 "Ritual." *Encyclopedia of Religion and Society.* William H. Swatos, Jr., Editor. Accessed April 22, 2005. Available from: http://hirr.hartsem.edu/ency/Ritual.htm

Fletcher, Richard

1999 *The Barbarian Conversion: From Paganism to Christianity.* Berkeley, CA: University of California Press.

Foucault, Michael
1967 *The Order of Things.* Trans. A. Sheridan. London: Tavistock.

Franklin, E. Frazier
1975 *The Negro Church in America.* Orig. published in 1964. New York: Schocken.

Frostin, Per
1985 "The Hermeneutics of the Poor – The Epistemological 'Break' in Third World Theologies." *Studia Theologica.* 39(1985):127-150.

Gill, Sean, Gavin D'Costa and Ursula King, eds.
1994 *Religion in Europe: Contemporary Perspectives.* Kampen, The Netherlands: Pharos Publishing House.

Girard, René
1979 *Violence and the Sacred.* Translated by Patrick Gregory. Baltimore, MD: The Johns Hopkins University Press.

Goines, Leonard
2005 "Gospel Music and the Black Consciousness." Accessed November 16, 2005. Available from: http://artemis.austincollege.edu/acad/hwc22/Greek/Gospel/gospelmusic.html

González, Justo L.
1999 *Christian Thought Revisited: Three Types of Theology*, 2nd ed. Maryknoll, NY: Orbis Books.

Gospel Factory
2005 "Syng i Gospelkor!" (trans. "Sing in a Gospel Choir!") A list of all registered gospel choirs in Denmark. Accessed January 21, 2005. Available from: http://gospelnet.sequelsite.dk/default.asp?id=427

2005a "Gospelkirke." (trans. "Gospel Church.") Accessed March 3, 2005. Available from: http://gospelnet.sequelsite.dk/default.asp?id=1117

2007 "Syng i Gospelkor!" (trans. "Sing in a Gospel Choir!") A list of all registered gospel choirs in Denmark. Accessed January 24, 2007. Available from: http://gospelnet.sequelsite.dk/default.asp?id=427

2007a "Gospelkirke." (trans. "Gospel Church.") Accessed January 24, 2007. Available from: http://gospelnet.sequelsite.dk/default.asp?id=1117

Gospel Flava
2005 "Gospel Around the World: Germany (Part 1: History)." Accessed January 20, 2005. Available from: http://www.gospelflava.com/articles/gospelaroundtheworld-germany1.html

2005a "Gospel Around the World: Germany (Part 2: Influences)." Accessed March 23, 2005. Available from: http://www.gospelflava.com/articles/gospelaroundtheworld-germany2.html

2005b "Gospel Around the World: Norway." Accessed March 3, 2005.

Available from:
http://www.gospelflava.com/articles/gospelaroundtheworld-norway.html

2005c   "Gospel Around the World: Sweden." Accessed March 23, 2005. Available from:
http://www.gospelflava.com/articles/gospelaroundtheworld-sweden.html

Gospel Music in Denmark
    2005   "Gospelmusikken – Historien om Gospel." (trans. "Gospel Music: The History of Gospel"). Accessed February 20, 2005. Available from: http://www.gospel.dk/gospelmusikken/

Green, Lawrence
    1997   "Pathos." *Encyclopedia of Rhetoric*. Thomas O. Sloane, ed.. London: Oxford University Press. Pp. 554-569.

Greinacher, Norbert and Norbert Mette, eds.
    1991   The New Europe: A Challenge for Christians. London: SCM Press.

Grell, Ole Peter
    1995   *The Scandinavian Reformation: From Evangelical Movement to Institutionalisation of Reform*. Cambridge, UK: Cambridge University Press.

Grimes, Ronald L.
    1995   *Beginnings in Ritual Studies*, revised edition. Columbia, SC: University of South Carolina Press.
    2000   *Deeply into the Bone: Reinventing Rites of Passage*. Berkeley, CA: University of California Press.

Grimmel, Bernd and Sebastian Hentsch
    2005   Interview posted on website. Accessed January 21, 2005. Available from: www.gospelflava.com.

Gutting, Gary
    1998   "Post-Structuralism." *Routledge Encyclopedia of Philosophy, vol. 7*. Edward Craig, general editor. London: Routledge. Pp. 596-604.

Hackett, Rosalind I. J.
    1996   *Art and Religion in Africa*. London: Cassell.

Hall, Edward T. and Mildred Reed Hall
    1990   "Key Concepts Underlying Structures of Culture." *Understanding Cultural Differences*. Yarmouth, ME: Intercultural Press, Inc.

Hansen, Judith Friedman
    1976   "The Anthropologist in the Field: Science, Friend, and Voyeur." In *Ethics and Anthropology: Dilemmas in Fieldwork*. Michael A. Rynkiewich and James P. Spradley, ed. New York: John Wiley and Sons. Pp. 123-134.

Harbsmeier, Eberhard and Hans Raun Iversen
    1995   *Praktisk teologi (trans. Practical Theology)*. Frederiksberg, Denmark: Forlaget ANIS.

Harding, Vincent
    1990   *Hope and History: Why We Must Share the Story of the Movement*. Maryknoll, NY: Orbis Books.

Hardy, Daniel W. and David F. Ford
    1985   *Praising and Knowing God*. Philadelphia, PA: Westminster Press.

Harris, Michael W.

- 1992 *The Rise of Gospel Blues: The Music of Thomas Andrew Dorsey in the Urban Church.* New York: Oxford University Press.
- 1992a "Conflict and Resolution in the Life of Thomas Andrew Dorsey." *We'll Understand it Better By and By.* Bernice Johnson Reagon, ed. Washington, D.C.: Smithsonian Institute Press.

Harvey, Louis-Charles
- 1987 "Black Gospel Music and Black Theology." *Journal of Religious Thought.* 43(Fall-Winter):19-37.

Hauerwas, Stanley
- 1981 *A Community of Character: Toward a Constructive Christian Social Ethic.* Notre Dame, IN: University of Notre Dame Press.
- 1983 *The Peaceable Kingdom: A Primer in Christian Ethics.* Notre Dame, IN: University of Notre Dame Press.
- 1991 *After Christendom?* Nashville, TN: Abingdon Press.
- 1993 *Dispatches from the Front: Theological Engagements with the Secular.* Durham, NC: Duke University Press.

Hauerwas, Stanley, and William H. Willimon
- 1993 *Resident Aliens: Life in the Christian Colony.* Originally published in 1989. Nashville, TN: Abingdon Press.

Hawn, C. Michael
- 2003 *Gather into One: Praying and Singing Globally.* Grand Rapids, MI: Eerdman's Publishing Company.

Heilbut, Tony
- 1969 *The Gospel Sound: Good News and Bad Times.* New York: Simon and Schuster.

Heitzenrater, Richard P.
- 1995 *Wesley and the People Called Methodists.* Nashville, TN: Abingdon Press.

Hiebert, Paul G.
- 1976 *Cultural Anthropology.* Philadelphia, PA: J. B. Lippencott Company.
- 1994 *Anthropological Reflections on Missiological Issues.* Grand Rapids, MI: Baker Book House.
- 1999 "Cultural Differences and the Communication of the Gospel." *Perspectives on the World Christian Movement: A Reader,* 3rd edition. Ralph D. Winter and Stephen C. Hawthorne, eds. Pasadena, CA: William Carey Library.
- 1999a *Missiological Implications of Epistemological Shifts: Affirming Truth in a Modern/Postmodern World.* Harrisburg, PA: Trinity Press International.

Hiebert, Paul G., R. Daniel Shaw and Tite Tiénou
- 1999 *Understanding Folk Religions: A Christian Response to Popular Beliefs and Practices.* Grand Rapids, MI: Baker Books.

Hillsman, Joan R.
- 1990 *Gospel Music: An African American Art Form.* Washington, D.C.: Middle Atlantic Regional Press.

Højlund, Henrik

1999 "Resten skal han bare gi faen i." (Trans. "Leave the Rest the Hell Alone"). In *Ny Mission nr. 1: Kulturkristendommen og kirken*. Jørn Henrik Olsen, ed.. Valby, Denmark: Unitas Publishers. Pp. 52-62.

Højsgaard, Morten Thomsen and Hans Raun Iversen, eds.
2005 *Gudstro i Danmark* (trans. *Danish Faith in God*). Copenhagen, Denmark: Forlaget ANIS.

Hone, Timothy, Jeff Astley and Mark Savage
1996 "Variations on a Theme: Towards a Theology of Music?" *Modern Believing*. 37(4):54-62.

Hooks, Bell
1995 "Postmodern Blackness." *The Truth About the Truth: De-confusing and Re-constructing the Postmodern World*. Walter Truett Anderson, ed. New York: Tarcher/Putnam Books.

Hopkins, Dwight N., Lois Ann Lorentzen, Eduardo Mendieta, and David Batstone
2001 *Religions / Globalizations: Theories and Cases*. Durham, NC: Duke University Press.

Horstman, Dorothy
1975 *Sing Your Heart Out, Country Boy*. New York: E.P. Dutton.

Hunsberger, George
2002 "The Church in the Postmodern Transition." In *A Scandalous Prophet: The Way of Mission After Newbigin*, Thomas F. Foust, et al., editors. Grand Rapids, MI: Eerdmans Publishing Company. Pp. 95-106.

Hunt, T. W.
1987 *Music in Missions: Discipling Through Music*. Nashville, TN: Broadman Press.

Hunter, George G., III
1996 *Church for the Unchurched*. Nashville, TN: Abingdon Press.
2000 *The Celtic Way of Evangelism: How Christianity Can Reach the West . . . Again*. Nashville, TN: Abingdon Press.
2003 *Radical Outreach: The Recovery of Apostolic Ministry and Evangelism*. Nashville,TN: Abingdon Press.
2004 "The Church Grows in Six Ways." Unpublished draft of July 8.

Hunter, Leslie Stannard, ed.
1965 *Scandinavian Churches: A Picture of the Development of the Churches of Denmark, Finland, Iceland, Norway, and Sweden*. London: Faber and Faber.

Hurst, John
1998 "New Sounds for Faith." *Theology*. 101(Sept.-Oct.):338-345.

Iversen, Hans Raun
1982 *Tro, håb og kærlighed: sekularisering og socialisation grundtvigsk forstået*. (trans. *Faith, Hope, and Love According to a Grundtvigan Understanding*). Århus, Denmark: FK- tryk.
1997 "Five Recent Papers on Church and Culture in Denmark." *Religion and the SocialOrder*, vol. 7. David G. Bromley, series editor. Greenwich, CT: Jai Press.
1998 "Leaving the Distant Church: The Danish Experience." *Religion and the Social Order*, 7:139-158.
1999 "Kulturkristendom, kirkekristendom og karismatiskkristendom:

Kristendomsformernes baggrund og samspil i folkekirken." (trans. "Cultural Christianity, Church Christianity, and Charismatic Christianity: The Background of Christian Formation and Interplay in the Folk Church"). In *Ny Mission nr. 1: Kulturkristendommen og kirken*. Jørn Henrik Olsen, ed.. Valby, Denmark: Unitas Publishers. Pp. 6-43.

2005 "Gudstro i den danske religionspark." (trans. "Faith in God within the Danish Religious Park.") *Gudstro i Danmark*. Højsgaard, Morten Thomsen and Hans Raun Iversen, eds. Copenhagen, Denmark: Forlaget ANIS. Pp. 103-123.

2006 "How can a Folk Church be a Missional Church?" Lecture arranged by International Research Consortium Congregational Mission and the Social Sciences, Friday, March 3, 2006 at the Norwegian School of Theology.

Jackson, Joyce Marie
    1995 "The Changing Nature of Gospel Music: A Southern Case Study." *African American Review*. 29(2):185-201. Accessed April 28, 2006. Available from: http://www.questia.com/PM.qst

James, William
    1997 *The Varieties of Religious Experience: A Study in Human Nature*. New York: Simon and Schuster Inc.

Jenkins, Philip
    2002 *The Next Christendom: The Coming of Global Christianity*. Oxford, U.K.: Oxford University Press.
    2007 *God's Continent: Christianity, Islam, and Europe's Religious Crisis*. Oxford, U.K.: Oxford University Press.

Jennings, J. Nelson
    2007 "Christian Mission and Glocal Violence in 2007 A.D. / 1428 H." *Missiology*, 35(4):397-415.

Jensen, Jørgen I.
    1996 *Den fjerne kirke*. (trans. *The Distant Church*). Viborg, Denmark: Samleren.

Job, Reuben P., chair
    1989 *The United Methodist Hymnal*. Nashville, TN: The United Methodist Publishing House.

Jochimsen, Hans Christian
    2006 Interview with Hans Christian Jochimsen, July 2006.

Johansson, Calvin M.
    1998 *Music and Ministry: A Biblical Counterpoint*. 2nd edition. Peabody, MA: Hendrickson Publishers, Inc.

Johnson, E. Patrick
    2003 *Appropriating Blackness: Performance and the Politics of Authenticity*. Durham, NC: Duke University Press.

Jones, Arthur C.
    1993 *Wade in the Water: The Wisdom of the Spirituals*. Maryknoll, NY: Orbis Books.

Jones, Lisa C.
    1995 "Are Whites Taking Gospel Music?" *Ebony*. 50(9):30.

Jüngel, Eberhard

1993   "The Gospel and the Protestant Churches of Europe: Christian Responsibilities for Europe from a Protestant Perspective." *Religion, State and Society*, 21(2):137-149.

Kaney, Pamela and Carol J. Smith
    1998   "The Power of Music to Help and Heal." *Christian Counseling Today*, 6(4):14-17.

Kant, Immanuel
    1955   *The Critique of Judgement*. Great Books of the Western World, volume 42. Orig. Pub. in 1790. Robert Maynard Hutchins, editor in chief. Chicago: William Benton, Publishers. Pp. 459-612.

Katz, Bernard, ed.
    1969   *The Social Implications of Early Negro Music in the United States*. New York: Arno Press and New York Times.

Kefas
    2007   Homepage for gospel choir Kefas. Accessed January 24, 2007. Available from: www.kefas.dk

Kierkegaard, Søren
    1974   *Fear and Trembling and Sickness Unto Death*. 5th Printing. Translated by Walter Lowrie. Princeton, NJ: Princeton University Press. Orig. published in 1843 under the title, *Frygt og Bæven*.
    1992   *Concluding Unscientific Postscripts to Philosophical Fragments*. Volumes. 1 and 2. Edited and translated by Howard V. Hong and Edna H. Hong. Princeton, NJ: Princeton University Press. Orig. published in 1846 under the title, *Afsluttende uvidenskabelig Efterskrift*.

Kirk-Duggan, Cheryl A.
    1997   *Exorcizing Evil: A Womanist Perspective on the Spirituals*. The Bishop Henry McNeal Turner/Sojourner Truth Series in Black Religion, volume 14. Maryknoll, NY: Orbis Books.

Kline, Brett
    2003   "Putting the Accent on Gospel." Accessed March 29, 2006. Available from: http://www.expatica.com/source/site_article.asp?channel_id=4&story_id=1544

Knower, Rosemary
    2004   "World-Class Choir Takes Russia by Storm." <u>Baltimore Sun</u>, Special section – Education. Feb. 22. Pp. 1 and 11.

Kuhn, Thomas S.
    1970   *The Structure of Scientific Revolutions*. Chicago, IL: University of Chicago Press.

Küng, Hans
    1981   *Art and the Question of Meaning*. New York: Crossroad.

La Cour, Peter
    2004   "Danskernes Gud i krise." (trans. "The God of the Danes in Crisis.") *Gudstro i Danmark*. Højsgaard, Morten Thomsen and Hans Raun Iversen, eds. Copenhagen, Denmark: Forlaget ANIS. Pp. 59-81.

Lawrence-McIntyre, Charshee Charlotte

1987   "The Double Meaning of the Spirituals." *Journal of Black Studies.* 12(4):379-401.

Lee, Jung Young
1995   *Marginality: The Key to Multicultural Theology.* Minneapolis, MN: Fortress Press.

Leffel, Gregory Paul
2004   "Faith Seeking Action: Missio-Ecclesiology, Social Movements, and the Church as a Movement of the People of God." Ph.D. Dissertation. E. Stanley Jones School of World Mission and Evangelism, Asbury Theological Seminary.
2007   *Faith Seeking Action: Mission, Social Movements, and the Church in Motion.* Lanham, MD: The Scarecrow Press, Inc.

Lévi-Strauss, Claude
1963   *Structural Anthropology.* Trans. C. Jacobson and B.G. Schoepf. New York: Basic Books.

Levine, Lawrence
1977   *Black Culture and Black Consciousness.* New York: Oxford UP.

Levinson, David, editor in chief
1992   *Encyclopedia of World Cultures*, volume IV: Europe (Central, Western, and Southeastern Europe). Boston, MA.: G.K. Hall & Co. Pp. 88-91.

Lewellen, Ted C.
2002   *The Anthropology of Globalization: Cultural Anthropology Enters the 21st Century.* Westport, CT: Bergin and Garvey.

Lewis, Christopher
2005   Polish Soul: Church-planting gets turned upside down in Poland." Avant Ministries. Posted October 2005. Accessed November 16, 2005. Available from: http://www.avantministries.org/content/page_print.asp?id=412&article

Lewis, Mark W.
2004   "Gospel Choirs: A Meeting Ground Between Christians and New Age Adherents." A working paper submitted to the Issue Group on "Religious and non-Religious Spiritualities in the Western World," for the Lausanne Conference on World Evangelization held Sept/Oct 2004, in Pattaya, Thailand. Accessed September 3, 2006. Available from: http://www.areopagos.org/lausanne/Gospel%20Choirs%20%20A%Meeting%20Ground%20Between%20Christians%20and%20Nw%20Age%20Adherents.doc.

Lifton, Robert Jay
1995   "The Protean Style." *The Truth About the Truth: De-confusing and Reconstructing the Postmodern World.* Walter Truett Anderson, ed. New York: Tarcher/Putnam Books. Pp. 130-135.

Lindhardt, Jan
2005   *Folkekirke?Kirken I det danske samfund.* (trans. *Folk Church? The Church in Danish Society*). Copenhagen, Denmark: Hovedland.

Linton, Michael
1998   "The Music of 'Having Church'." *First Things.* 81 (March 1998):17-18.

Løbner, Svend

2006 *Frikirke for alle.* (Trans. *Free Church for Everyone*). Copenhagen, Denmark: FrikirkeNets Forlag.

Longinus
 1985 *On the Sublime.* Translated by James A. Arieti and John M. Crosset. New York: The Edwin Mellen Press.

Lubbock on Line
 2005 "Europeans Develop Fondness for American Gospel Music." Accessed March 23, 2005. Available from: http://www.lubbockonline.com/news/021697/european.htm

Lüchau, Peter
 2005 Danskernes gudstro siden 1940'erne: Sekularisering eller individualisering?" (Trans. "The Faith of the Danes since the 1940's: Secularization or Individualization?") *Gudstro i Danmark.* Højsgaard, Morten Thomsen and Hans Raun Iversen, eds. Copenhagen, Denmark: Forlaget ANIS. Pp. 31-58.

Lusangi Gospel Choir
 2007 Lusangi Gospel Choir Homepage. Accessed January 24, 2007. Available from: http://www.lusangi.dk

Lyhne, Jette
 2006 "Fem store point til Etta." (Trans. "Five Stars for Etta.") An interview with Danish-American Gospel singer Etta Cameron in *Ældre Sagen.* (trans. The Matter of Aging). June 3, 2006. Pp. 18-21.

Lyotard, Jean-Francois
 1991 *Phenomenology.* Brian Beakley, trans. Albany, NY: State University of New York Press.
 1997 *The Postmodern Condition: A Report on Knowledge.* Translation from the French by Geoff Bennington and Brian Massumi. Minneapolis, MN: University of Minnesota Press.

Lyotard, Jean Francois, and Eberhard Gruber
 1999 *The Hyphen: Between Judaism and Christianity.* Amherst, NY: Humanity Books.

Marquand, Robert
 2002 "Asia Adopts Christmas." The Christian Science Monitor. From the December 23, 2002 edition. Accessed April 3, 2006. Available from: http://www.csmonitor.com/2002/1223/p01s04-wogn.html

Martland, T. R.
 1987 "The Sublime." *The Encyclopedia of Religion,* volume 14. Mircea Eliade, editor in chief. New York: Macmillan Publishing Company. Pp. 97-99.

Mbiti, John S.
 1968 *African Religions and Philosophy.* New York: Anchor Books.

McCormick, Samuel
 2004 "On Awakening the Numinous in Others." A Working Paper.

McGavran, Donald
 1990 *Understanding Church Growth*, 3rd edition. Revised and edited by C. Peter Wagner. Grand Rapids, MI: Eerdmans Publishing Company.

McLeod, Hugh
 1981 Religion and the People of Western Europe, 1789-1970. Oxford, UK: Oxford University Press.

McLeod, Hugh, and Werner Ustorf, ed.
    2003   The Decline of Christendom in Western Europe, 1750-2000. Cambridge, UK: Cambridge University Press.

McClain, William B.
    1981   "Preface." *Songs of Zion: Supplemental Worship Resources 12.* J. Jefferson Cleveland and Verolga Nix, eds. Nashville, TN: Abingdon Press.

McGee, Gary B.
    2000   "Pentecostal Missions." *Evangelical Dictionary of World Missions.* A. Scott Moreau, general editor. Grand Rapids, MI: Baker Book House.

Meyer, Leonard B.
    1968   *Emotion and Meaning in Music.* 8th impression. Chicago, IL: University of Chicago Press.

Moreau, A. Scott, Harold Netland, and Charles Van Engen
    2000   *Evangelical Dictionary of World Missions.* Grand Rapids, MI: Baker Book House.

Morsbøl, Carsten
    2004   *Gospel for Gospelfolk.* (trans. *Gospel Music for Gospel* People). Thisted, Denmark: Kurér Forlaget.
    2006   Interview with Carsten Morsbøl, October 2006.

Mortensen, Jørgen
    2007   Interview with Pastor Jørgen Mortensen, August 2007.

Mortensen, Viggo
    2005   *Kristendommen under forvandling: Pluralismen som udfordring til teologi og kirke I Danmark* (trans. *Christianity in Transition: Pluralism as Challenge to Theology and Church in Denmark*). Århus, Denmark: Univers.

Most, Glen
    1998   "Mimesis." *Routledge Encyclopedia of Philosophy,* vol. 9. Edward Craig, general editor. London: Routledge. Pp. 381-382.

Mudge, Lewis S. and Thomas Wieser, eds.
    1998   *Democratic Contracts for Sustainable and Caring Societies: What Can Churches and Christian Communities Do?* Geneva, Switzerland: WCC Publications.

Myerhoff, Barbara G., Linda A Camino, and Edith Turner
    1987   "Rites of Passage." *The Encyclopedia of Religion,* vol. 12. Mircea Eliade, editor in chief. New York: Macmillan Publishing Company

National Institute for the Renewal of the Priesthood
    2005   "Part B: What Do We Mean By 'Renewal'?" Accessed April 22, 2005. Available from: http://www.jknirp.com/renewal.htm.

Nelson, David
    1999   "Crossing the Musical Threshold." *Evangelical Mission Quarterly,* 35(2):152-155.

Newbigin, Lesslie
    1986   *Foolishness to the Greeks: The Gospel and Western Culture.* London: SPCK.
    1989   *The Gospel in a Pluralist Society.* London: SPCK.
    1994   *A Word in Season: Perspectives on Christian World Mission.* Grand Rapids, MI: William B. Eerdmans Publishing Co.

1995 *The Open Secret: An Introduction to the Theology of Mission.* Revised edition. Grand Rapids, MI: William B. Eerdmans Publishing Co.
1995a *Foolishness to the Greeks.* 5th edition. London: SPCK press.

Ngugi Wa Thiong'o
2002 *Decolonising the Mind: The Politics of Language in African Literature.* First published 1986. Oxford, UK: James Curry, Ltd.

Nida, Eugene A.
1990 *Message and Mission: Communication of the Christian Faith.* Revised Edition. Pasadena, CA: William Carey Library.
1997 *Customs and Cultures: Anthropology for Christian Mission.* Eugene, OR: Wipf and Stock Publishers.

Niebuhr, H. Richard
2001 *Christ and Culture.* Orig. published in 1951. San Francisco, CA: Harper San Francisco.

Nielsen, Trine Berg
2006 "What can church based gospel activity do in terms of in-reach mission to its Danish participants – and what can it not do?" M.A. Dissertation (unpublished), University of Sheffield at Cliff College.

Nørlykke, Lene Matthiesen
2006 Interview with Lene Matthiesen Nørlykke, July 2006.

Oh Happy Day
2004 A Danish film directed by Helle Joof.

Ong, Walter J.
1989 *Orality and Literacy: The Technologizing of the Word.* London: Routledge.

Onwochei, Pic
2001 "Music: Its Religio-Social and Medical Uses." *Svensk Missions Tidskrift*, 89(1):133-141.

Oravec, Christine L.
1998 "The Sublime." *Encyclopedia of Rhetoric.* Thomas O. Sloane, ed. Oxford, UK:Oxford University Press. Pp. 757-761.

Otto, Rudolf
1971 *The Idea of the Holy.* Originally published in 1923. Trans. by John W. Harvey. London: Oxford University Press.

Patterson, Lindsay, ed.
1968 *The International Library of Negro Life and History: The Negro in Music and Art.* New York: Publishers Company, Inc.

Perkins, Robert L.
1981 Kierkegaard's *Fear and Trembling: Critical Appraisals.* Birmingham, AL: University of Alabama Press.

Petersfield, W. R.
1995 "Established Churches, Free Churches, Religious Communities: Their Contemporary Social Setting." *Expository Times.* 106:110-113.

Pratt, Ray
1991 *Rhythm and Resistance: Explorations in the Political Uses of Popular Music.* New York: Praeger Publisher.

Raboteau, Albert J.
1978 Slave Religion: The Invisible Institution in the Antebellum South. Oxford, UK: Oxford University Press.

Radloff, Bernhard
    2002   Sublime Repetitions." *University of Toronto Quarterly.* 71(2), Spring 2002. Accessed April 23, 2006. Available from: http://www.utpjournals.com/product/utq/712/712_radloff.html

Radwan, Jon
    2004   "Religious Identity via Pop Music: 'Shine'." *The Journal of Communication and Religion.* 27(2):187-216.

Rambo, Lewis R.
    1992   *Understanding Religious Conversion.* New Haven, CT: Yale University Press.

Ramsey, Guthrie P., Jr.
    2003   *Race Music: Black Cultures from Bebop to Hip-Hop.* Berkley, CA: University of California Press.

Reid, Jennifer I.M., ed.
    2003   *Religion and Global Culture: New Terrain in the Study of Religion and the Work of Charles H. Long.* Lanham, MD: Lexington Books.

Riedel, Johannes
    1975   *Soul Music Black and White: The Influence of Black Music on the Churches.* Minneapolis, MN: Augsburg Publishing House.

Rifkin, Ira
    2003   *Spiritual Perspectives on Globalization: Making Sense of Economic and Cultural Upheaval.* Woodstock, VT: Skylight Paths Publishing.

Rifkin, Jeremy
    2000   The Age of Access: The New Culture of Hypercapitalism, Where all of Life is a Paid-for Experience. New York: Jeremy P. Tarcher/Putnam.
    2004   *The European Dream: How Europe's Vision of the Future is Quietly Eclipsing the American Dream.* New York: Jeremy P. Tarcher/Penguin.

Risher, Dee Dee
    1997   "Singing for My Life: An interview with Yoaye M. Barnwell." *The Other Side,* 33(July-Aug):44-47, 50-51.

Robinson-English, Tracey
    2005   "The Healing Power of Gospel Music." *Ebony.* 61:1, December 2005.

Rogers, Everett M.
    2003   *Diffusion of Innovations,* 5th edition. New York: Free Press.

Rublowsky, John
    1971   *Black Music in America.* New York: Basic Books, Inc.

Russello, Gerald J., ed.
    1998   *Christianity and European Culture: Selections from the Work of Christopher Dawson.* Washington, D.C.: The Catholic University of America.

Rynkiewich, Michael A.
    2002   "The World in My Parish: Rethinking the Standard Missiological Model." *Missiology,* 30(3):301-321.

Schaller, Lyle E.
    1993   *Strategies for Change.* Nashville, TN: Abingdon Press.

Schatzki, Theodore R.

1997   "Structuralism in Social Science." *Routledge Encyclopedia of Philosophy*, vol. 9. Edward Craig, general editor. London: Routledge. Pp. 184-189.

Schreiter, Robert J.
1984   "Culture, Society, and Contextual Theologies." *Missiology* 12(3):261-273.
2002   *Constructing Local Theologies*. Maryknoll, NY: Orbis Books.

Schwarz Lausten, Martin
2002   *A Church History of Denmark*. Translated by Frederick H. Cryer. Burlington, VT: Ashgate Publishing Company.

Schweiker, William
2004   *Theological Ethics and Global Dynamics: In the Time of Many Worlds*. Malden, MA.: Blackwell Publishers.

Scott, Joyce
2000   *Tuning in to a Different Song: Using Music as a Bridge to Cross Cultural Differences*. Pretoria, South Africa: The Institute for Missiological and Ecumenical Research.

Smith, James K.A.
2004   *Introducing Radical Orthodoxy: Mapping a Post-secular Theology*. Grand Rapids, MI: Baker Academic.

Snyder, Howard
1995   *Earth Currents: The Struggle for the World's Soul*. Nashville, TN: Abingdon Press.
1996   *The Radical Wesley and Patterns for Church Renewal*. Orig. Pub. 1980. Eugene, OR: Wipf and Stock Publishers.
1997   *Signs of the Spirit: How God Reshapes the Church*. Eugene, OR: Wipf and Stock Publishers.

Sölle, Dorothee
1990   *Thinking About God: An Introduction to Theology*. Philadelphia, PA: Trinity Press International.

Spencer, Jon Michael
1990   *Protest and Praise: Sacred Music of Black Religion*. Minneapolis, MN: Fortress Press.
1993   *Theological Music: Introduction to Theomusicology*. New York: Greenwood Press.

Spradley, James P.
1979   *Participant Observation*. New York: Holt, Rinehart, and Winston.

Stark, Rodney
1997   *The Rise of Christianity: A Sociologist Reconsiders History*. Princeton, NJ: Princeton University Press.
2001   Efforts to Christianize Europe, 400-2000." *Journal of Contemporary Religion*. 16:1, January 2001. Pp. 105-123.

Stark, Rodney and William Sims Bainbridge
1984   *The Future of Religion: Secularization, Revival, and Cult Formation*. Berkley, CA: University of California Press.
1997   *Religion, Deviance, and Social Control*. New York: Routledge.

Steinvig, Peter
2004   Interview with Peter Steinvig, July 2004.

Stiglitz, Joseph E.

Bibliography

    1999   *Globalization and its Discontents.* New York: W. W. Norton and Company.

Storti, Craig
    1999   *Figuring Foreigners Out: A Practical Guide.* Yarmouth, ME: Intercultural Press, Inc.
    2001   *The Art of Crossing Cultures, 2nd edition.* Yarmouth, ME: Intercultural Press, Inc.

Sullivan, Lawrence E.
    1997   *Enchanting Powers: Music in the World's Religions.* Cambridge, MA.: Harvard University Press.

Thielst, Peter
    1994   *Livet forstås baglæns – men må leves forlæns: Historien om Søren Kirkegaard.* (trans. *Life is Understood Backwards – But is Lived Forwards: The Søren Kierkegaard Story*). Haslev, Denmark: Gyldendal.

Thurman, Howard
    1975   *Deep River and the Negro Spiritual Speaks of Life and Death.* Richmond, IN: Friends United Press.

Tokyo Journal
    2000   "Today on Tokyo Journal – Gospel." Accessed January 21, 2005. Available from: http://www.tokyo.to/gospel/

Towler, Robert ed.
    1995   *New Religions and the New Europe.* Aarhus, Denmark: Aarhus University Press.

Turner, Victor
    1976   "Ritual, Tribal and Catholic." *Worship* 50(1976):504-526.
    1987   "Betwixt and Between: The Liminal Period in Rites of Passage." In *Betwixt and Between: Patterns of Masculine and Feminine Initiation.* Louise Carus Madhi, Steven Foster, and Meredith Little, eds. Lasalle, IL.: Open Court.
    1987a   "Rites of Passage." *The Encyclopedia of Religion,* vol. 12. Mircea Eliade, editor in chief. New York: Macmillan Publishing Company.
    1997   *The Ritual Process: Structure and Anti-Structure.* Orig. Pub. 1969. New York: Aldine De Gruyter.

Van Engen, Charles
    1996   *Mission on the Way: Issues in Mission Theology.* Grand Rapids, MI: Baker Books.

Van Gennep, Arnold
    1958   *The Rites of Passage.* Monika B. Vizedom and Gabrielle L. Caffee, trans. French edition, 1909. Chicago, IL.: The University of Chicago Press.

Vanhoozer, Kevin J.
    1993   "The World Well Staged? Theology, Culture, and Hermeneutics." *God and Culture:* Essays in Honor of Carl F. H. Henry. Grand Rapids: Eerdmans Publishing Co.

Växby, Hans
    2003   "Gudstjänstens språk och musik." (trans. "The Language and Music of Worship.") M. Div. Dissertation (unpublished), Överås Theological Seminary, Gothenburg, Sweden.

Vidler, Alec R.

Walker, Wyatt Tee
    1990   *The Church in an Age of Revolution: 1789 to the Present Day.* London: Penguin Books Ltd.

Walker, Wyatt Tee
    1979   *"Somebody's Calling My Name:" Black Sacred Music and Social Change.* Valley Forge, PA: Judson Press.

Wallace, Anthony F.C.
    1956   "Revitalization Movements." *American Anthropologist.* 58:264-281.

Ward, Andrew
    2000   *Dark Midnight When I Rise: The Story of the Jubilee Singers Who Introduced the World to the Music of Black America.* New York: Farrar, Straus, and Giroux.

Ward, Graham
    2000   *Cities of God.* London: Routledge.
    2005   *Cultural Transformation and Religious Practice.* Cambridge: Cambridge University Press.

Wells, Susan
    2001   "Logos." *Encyclopedia of Rhetoric.* Thomas O. Sloane, ed. Oxford, UK: Oxford University Press. Pp. 456-468.

Wessels, Anton
    1994   *Europe: Was it Ever Really Christian?* London: SCM Press.

Whiteman, Darrell L.
    2003   "Anthropology and Mission: The Incarnational Connection." The Third Annual Louis J. Luzbetak, SVD Lecture on Mission and Culture. Chicago, IL: CCGM Publications.

Wilson-Dickson, Andrew
    1996   *The Story of Christian Music: From Gregorian Chant to Black Gospel.* Minneapolis, MN: Fortress Press.

Wolffe, John, ed.
    2003   *Global Religious Movements in Regional Context.* Milton Keynes, UK: The Open University.

Zahniser, A. H. Mathias
    1997   *Symbols and Ceremonies: Making Disciples Across Cultures.* Monrovia, CA: MARC Publishers.

Zuesse, Evan
    1987   "Ritual." *The Encyclopedia of Religion,* vol. 12. Mircea Eliade, editor in chief. New York: Macmillan Publishing Company. Pp. 405-422.

Index

Abbott, Lynn, 39
Aborigines, 51
Addison, Joseph, 141
Apostolic Church, 109
Adopter categories, 41-42, 46, 53, 71-73, 101-102
Affectivity, 41, 74, 80, 81, 146-150
African origins, 31-34, 46
African worldview, 33-34
African-American church, (see Black church)
African-American history/ethnicity/culture, 7, 9, 29, 43, 51, 61, 72, 134
Alcohol addiction/Alcoholics Anonymous, 82
Alsted, Christian, 64
Analytical myopia, 103
Andersen, Hans Christian, 96, 98
Anderson, Benedict, 135-136, 151
Anderson, Walter Truett, 124-125
Ansgar, 105
Anthropological method, 12
Anti-structure (see communitas)
Aristotle, 136, 140
Atheists, 4, 81
Australia, 48-52
Azusa Street Revival, 40

Bailey, Bob, 64
Banks, Marcus, 119
Baptist, 109
Barber, Benjamin R., 129
Barbershop Quartet, 39
Baumlin, James, 115

Beecher, Henry Ward, 37
Begbie, Jeremy, 27, 148
Belgium, 1
Believing and belonging, 107
Bell, Jerome, 46, 63-64
Bellah, Robert, 114
Berger, Peter and Thomas Luckmann, 125, 129
Bevans, Stephen B., 24-26, 44, 46
Bjerager, Erik, 104, 108-109
Black church, 23, 42, 45
Black Entertainment Television, 30, 45
Black exodus, 38, 40
Black gospel beginnings, 38-42
Blixon, Karen, 98
Bohr, Niels, 98
Bornholm, 4
Bosch, David, 124
Brahe, Tycho, 98
Budd, Malcolm, 147
Burke, Edmund, 141
Burnim, Melonee, 29-30

Café of the Gate of Salvation, 48-52,
Cameron, Etta, 62-63, 67
Campbell, Lucie, 13, 39
Campos, Albert, 64
Catharsis, 41, 50, 81, 102, 145, 169
CAYA (Gospel choir), 49
Celtic influences, 106, 169
Change agent, 54, 61, 63
Charland, Maurice, 135-137, 151

China, 1, 17
Christian ethos, 48
Christian foundationalism, 111
Christian heritage, 106
Christian symbols, 9
Christianization, 117
Church, 166 (see also Danish Folk Church and Free Church)
Church/State relations, 104, 108
Cicero, 140
Cleveland, James, 42
Coded messages, 36-37
Collectivization, 135-137, 140, 157, 168
Come-as-you-are (see gospel ethos)
Communication channels, 60-61
Communitas, 155-156, 159-160 (see also rite of passage)
Cone, James, 29-30
Confirmation rituals, 106-107
Confirmation step (see innovation-decision process)
Consequences (of gospel), 73-74
Constitutive rhetoric, 18, 135-139, 169
Constantinian Christianity, 104-105, 108
Contemporary Christian Music, 16, 137
Contextual theology (gospel music as), 43-45
Contextualization, 2, 26-27, 105, 170-171
Conversion theory, 136-137
Copenhagen Free Church, 166
Copenhagen Gospel Festival (CGF), 3, 60-61, 63, 65, 69-70, 79
Copenhagen Gospel Voices, 64, 65
Copher, Charles B., 44
Counter-cultural (gospel as), 44-45, 163
Courson, Jim, 156
Creation theology, 170
Critical contextualization, 112

Crouch, Andrae, 3, 42
Cultural anthropology, 119
Cultural Christians/Christianity, 3, 5, 9, 17, 49, 126, 136, 139, 169
Cultural diffusion (see diffusion)
Cultural identity, 107
Cultural imperialism, 118
Cusic, Don, 31-32

Damasio, Antonio, 149, 151
Danish Folk Church (National Church), 3, 5, 8, 57, 63, 74, 104, 106-110, 126-127, 163
Danish culture, 8, 57-60, 62, 93-116, 117, 122, 133, 167
Danish language, 97
Danish religiosity, 102-105, 110-115, 162
Danish worldview, 95, 126
Darden, Robert, 31-32, 33, 34, 37, 46
Dargan, William T., 44
Davie, Grace, 2, 104, 107-108, 110, 112
Dawson, Christopher, 111
Decision step (see innovation-decision process)
Denmark 1, 119
Derrida, Jacques, 124, 125, 133
Desire, 140
Différance, 133, 140
Diffusion (of innovations), 2, 29, 37, 52-75, 64, 118-119, 131, 168
Discursive narrative, 137-138, 147
Distant church, 107, 115
Dixie Hummingbirds, 42
Dorsey, Thomas A., 13, 40-42, 46
Douglas, Mary, 158
Dual kingdoms, 109
Duke University, 63

Early adopters (see adopter categories)
Earth currents, 119, 121, 132-135

Eastern Orthodox theology, 131, 151
Ecology (of meaning), 132-135, 168
Election, 23-24
Eliade, Mircea, 148, 154
Emotions (in music) (see affectivity)
Energy (see also gospel ethos)
Enthrall, 137, 169
Epistemology, 122, 128
Ethnic designators, 118
Ethnohistorical, 9, 12, 15-16, 29-46
Ethnomusicology, 147-148
Ethos-logos-pathos, 147, 170 (see also gospel ethos or Christian ethos)
European Values Study, 5, 108, 116
Evangelists, 170
Evangelization/evangelism, 17, 150, 168, 169

Faith, 81-82
Feelings (see affectivity)
Ferraro, Gary, 52
Ficino, Marcilio, 148
Finn, Thomas M., 157
Fisk Jubilee Singers, 37, 38
Fletcher, Richard, 104
Folk Church (see Danish Folk Church)
Form and meaning, 26, 43
Foucault, Michel, 124
France, 1
Franklin, Aretha, 79
Franklin, Kirk, 42, 67, 79
Free church(es), 95, 101, 108, 109, 115

Germany, 1
Girard, Rene, 164
Glocal(ization), 168, 170
Globalization, 16, 34, 114, 117, 118-121
God (belief in), 113-114

Going Up (Gospel Choir), 64
Gonzalez, Justo, 24
Gorgias, 137
Gospel choir rehearsals, 14, 75
Gospel church, 26, 82, 166
Gospel ethos, 14, 49, 80, 82, 83, 101-102, 117, 134-135, 138, 150, 158, 166, 169, 171
Gospel Factory, 4, 55-56, 64, 75
Gospel festivals/workshops, 14, 57, 64, 170
Gospel in Denmark, 62-70
Gospel music (definition), 13
Gospel worship services, 14
Grace (Gospel choir), 63
Great Depression, 38
Green, Lawrence, 115
Grundtvig, N.F.S., 98
Grundy, Ricky, 42, 79

Hackett, Rosalind, 31
Hammond, Fred, 42
Hairston, Jester, 62
Hall, Edward T. and Mildred, 94, 98
Hansen, Judith, 78, 97
Harbsmeier, Eberhard, 109
Hardy, Daniel and David Ford, 139-140
Harris, Michael, 31, 41
Harvey, Louis Charles, 44
Hauerwas, Stanley, 27, 108, 136
Hawkins, Edwin, 3, 13, 42
Heilbut, Tony, 43
Henry, Carl F. H., 121
Hiebert, Paul, 50, 112, 119, 122, 149
Hierophany, 154
Higginson, Thomas W., 145
High context/low context culture (see primary message systems)
Hip Hop, 67
Højsgaard, Morten Thomsen, 110-111, 116
Holiness churches, 40

Index

Holy (Idea of), 143-144
Homophilous/heterophileous contacts, 60
Hooks, Bell, 119
Hunter, George G. III, 169
Hurst, John, 149-150
Hybrid (see identity formation)
Hygge, 101

Identity formation, 119-120, 125, 127, 131, 136, 137, 153-164, 168
Immigration, 114
Individualism, 58-59, 107
Individualistic/communal, 95-99Individualization, 111
Innovation-decision process, 54, 61-70, 73
Inoculation program, 109
Internet, 61
Interview (analysis), 79-92
Invisible churches, 34-35
Ireland, 1
Iversen, Hans Raun, 97, 100, 101, 107, 109-111, 113-114

Jack-leg preacher, 39
Jackson, Irene, 44
Jackson, Joyce, 32
Jackson, Mahalia, 42, 46, 62, 79
Japan, 1, 17, 50
Janteloven, 58, 99-101, 115
Jenkins, Philip, 2
Jensen, Jørgen I., 107, 115
Jesus Christ, Superstar, 149
Johnson, E. Patrick, 47-52, 74, 119, 134, 158-159
Johnstone, Henry W., 151
Jones, Arthur C., 151
Joseph narrative, 22-24
Jim Crow, 29, 35, 38
Jochimsen, Hans Christian, 8, 18, 64-66, 75, 81
Jochimsen, Lars, 64
Jones, Arthur, 33

Jones, Lisa C., 29-30
Joy, 80, 81

Kant, Immanuel, 141-142, 144
Kefas gospel choir, 5, 56-57, 60, 63, 64-65, 66, 68, 80
Key, John P., 42
Kierkegaard, Søren, 14, 98, 142-143, 150
King Christian III, 106
King Harald Bluetooth, 105

La Cour, Peter, 112-113
Laggards (see adopter categories)
Langer, Suzanne, 147
Late adopters (see adopter categories)
Leadership, 65-68, 163-164, 169
Lee, Jung Young, 28
Leffel, Gregory, 18
Levi-Straus, Claude, 133
Lewellen, Ted C., 119-120
Lifton, Robert Jay, 120, 125, 129
Liminality, 74, 156, 158-160 (see also rite of passage)
Lindell, Julie, 65
Lindhardt, Jan, 108, 126
Linguistic analysis, 133
Literary method, 13
Løbner, Svend, 109
Logos (see ethos-logos-pathos)
Longinus, 140-141
Lüchau, Peter, 107, 110-114
Lusangi gospel choir, 56
Lutheran Church (see also Danish Folk Church), 1, 106, 114
Lyotard, Jean-Francois, 121, 124, 140, 144-145, 151

Marriage/cohabitation, 95-96
MBUF, 66
McClain, William, 43
McCormick, Samuel, 151
McLeod, Hugh, 111-112

Meaning (of gospel music), 77-92
Meaning construction (formation), 9, 26, 127, 131-150, 156, 168
Meaning differential, 52
Metanarrative, 127-129, 144
Methodist, 4, 39, 109
"Middle zone" (of human ontology), 149
Mimesis, 11, 14, 18, 115, 159
Minstrelsy, 38, 127
Missio Dei, 22, 133
Missiologists, 170
Missiology, 15, 21-28
Missiomusicology, 15, 27, 148, 161
Missionary (archetypes), 170, 171-172
Modernism (see also worldview)
Monism, 131
Morsbøl, Carsten, 64, 165,166
Morality/moral standards, 96
Mortensen, Jørgen, 65
Mortensen, Viggo, 98, 105-106, 122, 127
Moses Maimonides, 151
Muhammad drawings, 96, 109
Musicology, 146-149
Mysterium tremendum, 143, 168

Nardus (Gospel choir), 56
National Baptist Convention, 40
New Age, 4, 68-69, 78
Newbigin, Lesslie, 27, 103
Newsboys, 137, 151
Nida, Eugene, 94
Niebuhr, H. Richard, 44-45
Nielsen, Trine Berg, 52, 75, 165
Nix, W. M., 40
Noiz (Gospel choir), 4, 66, 67-68, 79
Non-firmation, 107
Nørrelykke, Lene Matthiesen, 64, 79, 81
Numinous, 143-144, 146, 149

O Happy Day, 13, 42, 46, 74-75
Ontology, 131, 137
Opstand (Gospel choir), 66
Oslo Gospel Choir, 64
Otto, Rudolph, 143-144, 154

Participant observation, 11, 78
Pathos, 110, 115, 136 (see also ethos-logos-pathos)
Payne, Daniel A., 35
Pentecostalism, 38, 39-40
Perceived attributes of gospel, 57-60
Performance, 159
Persuasion model, 136
Philosophical pluralism (see also pluralism), 124
Pluralism, (see postmodernism)
Pluralism project, 122
Pluralists, 47
Poland, 1
Post-Christian, 73
Postcontextualization (see contextualization)
Postmodern(ism), 9, 10, 16, 34, 46, 111, 114, 121-129, 150
Poststructuralism, 55, 133, 144
Praise and Worship music, 8, 16, 72, 82
Pratt, Ray, 30
Precious Lord, Take My Hand, 41
Prevenient grace, 150, 170
Priestly tradition (Old Testament), 156
Primary Message Systems, 94
Purists, 47

Queen Margrethe, 105

Radwan, Jon, 137-138
Rambo, Lewis R., 136-137
Rational choice theory, 104-105
Reconstruction (post-Civil War), 35

Recontextualization, (see contextualization)
Reformation, 106
Rehearsal (as ritual), 159-161
Re-imaging, 117, 170
Religious "park", 113-115

Revelation and authority, 123
Revitalize (existing congregations), 166-167
Rifkin, Ira, 118
Rifkin, Jeremy, 99-100
Rite of passage, 107-108, 154-158, 168
Ritual process, 153-164
Rogers, Everett, 41-42, 46, 52-75, 131
Rynkiewich, Michael, 118-119

S-shaped curve (see innovation-decision process)
Saints and Sinners (Gospel choir), 63, 66, 68, 70, 71-73, 79, 80
Sandemose, Axel, 99
Sandy church, 171
Saussure, Ferdinand de, 132-133
Scandinavian context, 94
Scandinavian Gospel, 67
Schouten, Ronald, 157-158
Schroeder, Roger, 24-26
Schwarz Lausten, Martin, 105
Schweiker, William, 118
Scratch-ticket Christians, 7, 126
Secondary orality, 34, 46
Secularization, 104, 108, 110-112
Selfhood (see identity formation)
Semiology (in gospel music), 132, 139, 150, 161-163, 167
Separation (see rite of passage)
Set theory, 50
Shakespeare, 96, 126
Sign/signifier/signified (see structuralism)

Sherwood, William H., 39
Slavery, 23, 29, 34
Smallwood, Richard, 42
Smith, James, 150
Snyder, Howard, 119, 121, 132-133, 148
Social construction, 11, 158
Social movement theory, 17, 18
Socialism, 100
Sociological method, 11-12
Song texts, 83-86
Soper, Donald, 169
Sophists, 137
Sound of Gospel, 66
Spencer, Jon Michael, 15, 27, 44-45
Spirituality, 111, 128
Spirituals, 13, 34-38, 67
  Qualities of, 35-36
  And the sublime, 145
Spradley, James P., 11
Stark, Rodney, 103-105, 108, 110-111, 112
Steinvig, Peter, 3, 5, 56-57, 63-64, 66, 70, 71-73
Stiglitz, Joseph, 118
Structuralism, 55, 75, 132-133
Sublime, 139-146, 161, 168, 169
Suffering Servant, 24
Sullivan, Lawrence E., 148
Summer Gospel, 64, 65, 75
Symbol (unconsummated), 147
Symbolic interactionism, 13, 46, 102
Symbols (in gospel music; see Semiology)
Systems theory, 58
Syncretism, 9, 83, 168

Tharpe, Rosetta, 42
Tindley, Charles A., 13, 39
Theomusicology, 15, 27, 161
Toronto Blessing, 157-158
Tribal culture, 96-99, 107

Triune God/Trinity, 21, 22, 169, 171
Turner, Victor, 11, 74, 154-156, 160, 168

Van Gennep, Arnold, 154, 160

Walker, Wyatt T., 30-31, 34, 35, 44
Ward, 151
Wegner, Claes, 64
Wells, Susan, 115
Wesley, Charles, 16
Wessel, Anton, 104

Willibrord, 105
Willimon, William, 108, 136
Wind, Janne, 64
Wonder, Stevie, 79
Worldview (biblical/Christian), 123, 131, 151
   Modern, 123-124, 170

Youth gospel, 69

Zahniser, Mathias, 11, 155, 164
Zeusse, Evan, 164

www.ingramcontent.com/pod-product-compliance
Lightning Source LLC
Chambersburg PA
CBHW020650300426
44112CB00007B/313